FOLLOWING

JESUS

WITHOUT

EMBARRASSING

GOD

FOLLOWING

JESUS

WITHOUT

EMBARRASSING

GOD

Tony Campolo

WORD PUBLISHING
Dallas•London•Vancouver•Melbourne

Unless otherwise indicated, Scripture quotations used in this book
are from the King James Version of the Bible.

Library of Congress Cataloging-in-Publication Data

Campolo, Anthony.
　　Following Jesus without embarrassing God / Tony Campolo.
　　　　p.　cm.
　　Includes bibliographical references.
　　ISBN: 0-8499-4068-0
　　1. Witness-bearing (Christianity)　2. Christian life.　I. Title.
BV4520.C29　　1997
248.4—dc21　　　　　　　　　　　　　　　　　　　97-28505
　　　　　　　　　　　　　　　　　　　　　　　　　　CIP

Printed in the United States of America.
7 8 9 0 1 2 3 4 9 QBP 9 8 7 6 5 4 3 2

To my grandson, Roman Anthony Campolo,
whose imagination and love for stories transports me
from heaviness to the Land of Never Never.

CONTENTS

ACKNOWLEDGMENTS

A book is never created by an author alone. So many others make it possible. In my case, those who enabled me to get this book to you include: Sue Dahlstrom, who not only typed the manuscript, but did a great deal of research for me, and Diana Robertson and Jocelyn Emerson in my office, who helped out whenever asked. A special thanks to Bob and Eve Bolduan who lent me their house in Melbourne, Australia, where a good bit of this book was put together. But as with everything else I have written, the greatest thanks has to go to my wife, Peggy, who edits and corrects the hundreds of mistakes I make during a venture like this one.

When It Comes

to Your Everyday Life

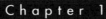

Chapter 1

How to Follow Jesus

without Embarrassing God

In the movie *Oh, God!*, John Denver plays a young man who keeps getting messages from God that he's supposed to relate to the rest of us. In one scene, he goes to hear an evangelistic preacher, who in many ways is a caricature of all the worst things in those of us who take on that role. The John Denver character interrupts the preacher's sermon to tell him that God has a special message *just for him*.

The preacher stops the service. He announces to the audience, "This young man has come with a message from God!"

John Denver looks straight at the preacher and says, "God wants you to shut up because you're embarrassing Him!"

Over the years all of us have said and done things that surely must have embarrassed God. Sometimes we have been pompous. Sometimes we have said things about God that, undoubtedly, have made God shudder. Which of us can deny that, even as we are trying to follow Jesus, we sometimes behave in ways which must make God and Christianity seem ridiculous to those outside the faith.

There is the story of a Baptist preacher who once found himself seated on a train next to Mahatma Gandhi. As they traveled together, the preacher did his best to tell Gandhi about the gospel and to win him over to Christianity. As the trip came to a close, the preacher asked Gandhi if he was ready to accept Jesus as his Savior.

"Jesus!" exclaimed Gandhi with a pretended look of surprise. "I didn't realize you were talking about Jesus. I thought you were talking about some successful oil tycoon from Texas."

I cringed when I heard that story, because I realized that as I try to tell people about Jesus, sometimes I don't do the best job. As I try to help people imagine what Jesus was like, and what He would be like if He were living among us today, I am sure I mess things up so badly that it must be hard for my listeners to get a good idea of what Jesus is all about. Some of the things that I say must embarrass God, because they make God seem ridiculous.

Sören Kierkegaard, one of the most profound critics of the church, once was told by some shocked parishioners that the sanctuary of their church had been used by some teenagers for a dance. Kierkegaard responded, "Using the sanctuary for a dance on Saturday night is not half as bad as using it on Sunday morning to make a fool out of God."

In reality there are times when each of us makes God seem ridiculous. We all do things that make being a Christian seem like the most idiotic thing in the world. And the bad news is that we are likely to go on doing them for the rest of our lives. It all goes with being the kind of people who, as Paul reminds us in 1 Corinthians 13:9–10, preach only a part of the whole truth about God. In our limitations we make mistakes, distort, and present the wonder of God as something stupid.

We should be infinitely thankful that we have a God with so much grace. Otherwise, we would all be struck down for some of the blasphemous pieties we utter. But God *is* gracious and in that graciousness does not condemn us for our foolishness. Instead, God calls us to put away our silly childish ways and move on to a fuller and truer knowledge of the truth. I hope and pray that someday I will be able to apply to myself the words of 1 Corinthians 13:11: "When I was a child, I spake as a child, I understood as a child, I thought as a child: but when I became a man, I put away childish things." This will take a lot of hard work, but such work is the calling of all Christians who would grow out of his or her spiritual immaturity and turn from the ways of the past. It's work that is fraught with danger and even pain, but it's work that no true Christian can avoid.

We read in the letter to the Philippians that we must "work out our salvation with fear and trembling" (Philippians 2:12). What Paul, the premier theologian of Christendom, was telling us in that simple expression was that we must study the life of Jesus and use our imaginations to try and figure out how Jesus would live His life if He were with us here and now. Being a Christian involves embracing Jesus as our ultimate role model (Philippians 2:5).

What would Jesus do if He were living in the flesh as a citizen of our contemporary society? How would Jesus handle the pressures of everyday life? Would He live as a middle-class American, or would He embrace a lifestyle of simplicity, like a Franciscan brother? Would He celebrate all of the medical and scientific discoveries of our modern world, or would Jesus see innovations like cloning as contrary to the will of His Father? Would He look at the rapid pace of life that has come with technological advances in communication and transportation and see it as good, or would He warn His disciples to keep such things out of their lives?

What kind of devotional life would Jesus maintain? Would He attend any of our churches, or would He find our worship so offensive that He would want to restore the church He originally established? How would He answer the kinds of questions that are being posed by both intellectuals and ordinary people in this postmodern world?

Knowing that Jesus came to declare His Father's kingdom on earth, as it is in heaven, what social changes would He try to effect? What causes would He embrace? What methods would He use to bring about social change? And what would Jesus have to say about the political activism being promoted by both evangelical and theologically liberal Christians?

Then, getting down to more personal matters, what would Jesus have to say to us about raising children and holding our families together in a world that seems to be falling apart? In our sensate culture, what would Jesus tell us about sex? And what would be His judgment on the *pop* psychology that governs much of what goes on in our everyday personal relationships?

What Paul is telling us in that simple phrase "work out your salvation with fear and trembling" is that each of us has to figure out the answers to questions like these. To be followers of Christ requires that we imagine what Jesus would think and do in our own given situations. We have to envision how He would handle the challenges that such questions pose for us.

We are not left alone in our quest for answers. We have the Scriptures, and we have the Holy Spirit to guide us in our understanding of what the Bible says (John 14:26). In our struggle to find these answers, we are promised that His Spirit will be a prompting presence in our lives (Romans 8:11–12) providing a constant sense as to whether or not we are on the right track, making the right decisions. "And thine ears shall hear a word behind thee, saying, This is the way, walk ye in it, when ye turn to the right hand, and when ye turn to the left" (Isaiah 30:21).

We are also given the Church, that body of believers that reaches back over two thousand years, to help us. We find in the Church a community of fellow strugglers who join us in our quest for answers. The discoveries and traditions of this body of believers can be a check and balance against our individualistic tendencies to come up with answers that do nothing more than support a lifestyle of culturally created tastes and likings.

God calls us to this struggle because only in and through it can we mature into the kinds of persons God wants us to be. Not to enter into this struggle is to remain spiritually infantile. It is to be deserving of the kind of tongue-lashing that the apostle Paul gave to those immature Christians at Corinth who, like Peter Pan, refused to grow up: "And I, brethren, could not speak unto you as unto spiritual, but as unto carnal, even as unto babes in Christ. I have fed you with milk, and not with meat: for hitherto ye were not able to bear it, neither yet now are ye able" (1 Corinthians 3:1–2).

What follows is one person's attempt to come up with some answers to the question of how to follow Jesus without embarrassing God. There is nothing final or authoritative in these answers. I hope and pray that someday in the future I will look back on what I have written here and shake my head over its superficiality and inadequacy. While I believe that God has begun a good work in me as I struggle for answers, I also believe that God will continue to help me come up with better and better answers until the day of Christ's coming (Philippians 1:6). In this struggle to grow into a person whose lifestyle is Christlike, I hope I will never become satisfied with myself.

What I share with you here is nothing more than where I am right now in my Christian journey. I echo the words of the apostle Paul, who was far beyond where I am in his quest for a Christlike lifestyle, when he wrote, "Brethren, I count not myself to have apprehended: but this one thing I do, forgetting those things which are behind, and reaching forth unto those things which are before, I press toward the mark for the prize of the high calling of God in Christ Jesus" (Philippians 3:13–14). I invite you to join me in this quest for answers, but let me warn you that it will take all you've got to carry through with the challenge. It will take prayer and fasting. It will involve much soul searching. And it will require the regular study of God's Word. "Study to shew thyself approved unto God, a workman that needeth not to be ashamed, rightly dividing the word of truth" (2 Timothy 2:15).

How to Be Rich

and Still Be a Christian

S ome people just have the gift of making money. My friend John
Perkins, a leader in creating economic development programs
for the poor, makes a strong claim that we do not solve the
problems associated with economic inequities by calling for a redistri-
bution of wealth. John says, "Even if we redistributed all the wealth
evenly, within a couple of years the rich will have it all back again."
There is empirical evidence to substantiate John's claim. Following
World War II under the Marshall Plan, every citizen of Germany was
given the equivalent of fifty dollars. In a sense, everybody in Germany
was, as much as possible, reduced to the same level of wealth/poverty.
But within ten years, 90 percent of the wealth of Germany was concentrated in the hands of 5 percent of the population. John Perkins's
point is that being rich is not just *having* money; it's knowing how to
get money. And the rich always know how to do that.

I have another friend who has made a bundle of money in a variety of business enterprises. It seems as though every time he gets a
business up and running profitably, he decides to sell it and retire.
And every time he sells a business, he ends up with a huge profit on
his investment and finds himself wealthier than before. My friend is
trying hard to live out a biblical lifestyle, and he is well aware of what
the Bible says about rich people having a hard time getting into heaven.
He knows that Kingdom people do not often accumulate wealth in

this world. But, as he once said to me, "It's not that simple. It seems as though, no matter what I do, I end up making a lot of money from it."

Recently my friend decided to take a course at a nearby theological seminary. His professor, not knowing anything about my friend, let loose with a tirade about the incongruity of being rich and being Christian at the same time.

My friend could not help but call out in class, "I'm rich! What are you saying about *me*?"

The professor, endeavoring to escape from putting my friend on a guilt trip said, "Oh! I'm not talking about people like you. I'm talking about those *really* rich people who live in mansions out on the Main Line* and have two Jaguars in their garages."

To this my friend responded, "You just described me in detail. I live in a mansion out on the Main Line, and I really do own two Jaguars."

My friend has not gone the way of St. Francis of Assisi, selling what he has and giving it to the poor, but he has tried to use his wealth and talent for making money with some degree of Christian responsibility. For instance, he has spent a good deal of time starting small businesses among the poor in deteriorating neighborhoods in North Philadelphia. And he has put much time, effort, and money into helping an African-American pastor in another run-down urban neighborhood develop a ministry that not only tells the salvation story to the lost, but also provides social services, such as tutoring and day care, for those who need them. Furthermore, my friend points out the truth that, in many instances, it is difficult to give away money without doing a great deal of harm to people.

I have become aware that my friend's insights about giving need to be seriously considered by those who give in response to the needs of the poor, especially in the Third World. In the missionary work I have helped develop in Haiti, I have found that sometimes my own generosity and the sacrificial giving of those who have supported our ministries have had a corrupting influence on those we have tried to help. Pastors of churches often plead with visiting work groups

---

*A very rich suburb outside of Philadelphia

from the United States to give them money so that they can provide food and medical care for their people. In more cases than I can count, Christians touched by the needs that seem omnipresent in Haiti turn over large sums to indigenous pastors without also providing any real checks as to how the money will be used. Often when I ask the leaders of such work groups about the possibility that they might be acting irresponsibly, I get this answer: "If we can't trust fellow Christians, then who can we trust?"

What follows is that some Haitian pastor has more money dumped on him in a single day than he ever imagined he would see in a lifetime. Soon relatives and friends are *hired* to do some so-called ministry. Then it's only a matter of time before more obscene corruption sets in. In one instance, I personally got badly burned. The pastor subverted funds to build a house for himself that, even by U.S. standards, would have to be called palatial. And to top things off, he bought himself a huge television disk receiver so that he could spend his evenings watching American television shows. In the end, his changed lifestyle so alienated him from the people he once served that, during a time of political unrest, they rose up, drove him out of town, and literally tore down his house brick by brick.

A special brand of fraud is made possible by the creating of Haitian orphanages. In several cases I know, there is a great deal of double funding. By that I mean that more than one church picks up the entire bill for running the orphanage without being aware that the person in charge is collecting similar amounts from other churches. In one instance, the building that supposedly housed orphan children was empty except when visitors from supporting churches were scheduled to come. Then scores of children were hired at a few cents each to pretend that they were the ones being helped.

I learned the hard way that orphanages are not the means that Haitians use to care for children who are in need. Instead, the Haitian people tend to bring *unconnected* children to live with individual families, often with detrimental results. In many instances, these children become *Rèstavèks*, which roughly translates as "live-ins." Boys and girls are reduced to lifestyles that are close to slavery. They spend their days doing chores, such as toting water and working in the fields. They get leftovers to eat and are regularly abused.

I tell you all of this because, in order to give to the children in Haiti in ways that make certain that we actually are doing them some good, my friends and I have had to do much more than just write out our checks to some Haitian pastor. We have set up a network of some seventy-five small schools to teach literacy to these *Rèstavèk* children. These schools are carefully surveyed by a staff of missionary young people we recruited from across the United States. Our staff directly pays the teachers and covers the other expenses that go with maintaining these schools. The classes for the *Rèstavèks* are held following their day of hard labor from four in the afternoon until eight at night. The cost of maintaining one of these schools is two hundred dollars per month, which is a mere fraction of what such a program would cost if not carefully supervised.[1]

All of this is simply to say: Giving away money to the poor is not as easy as it seems. If you want to be a responsible steward of wealth, then your giving, whether it be to the poor in a Third World country or to some vagrant who stops you on the street, requires care and a great deal of time.

Perhaps one of the most poignant stories of a rich person's sacrificial giving gone awry is found in the account of the life of the great Russian novelist, Leo Tolstoy. In his attempt to live out the lifestyle he believed that Jesus prescribed, this extremely wealthy man sold his vast farmlands and gave all of the money to the poor. Later he found that those who bought his property exploited the peasants who formerly had worked on his farms. Now, these poor workers were not only underpaid, they were abused in almost every conceivable manner. All of this led Tolstoy to ask himself if following the simple words of Jesus, "Sell whatsoever thou hast, and give to the poor" (Mark 10:21) had not brought about a great evil.

Thoughtful use of wealth is difficult but by no means impossible. Many wealthy Christians are investing in small businesses that create jobs for the poor. Opportunities International is a missionary organization that tries to tap into the resources of wealthy Christians in order to provide capital for economic development in Third World countries. This ministry makes small loans to fledgling entrepreneurs among the poor, which enable them to create cottage industries and micro-businesses. Literally tens of thousands of jobs have been created through the efforts of Opportunities International, and those who have invested in these ventures have had the satisfaction of knowing that they have helped the poor to escape their desperate plight—not just for a day but for a lifetime. Furthermore, these Third World entrepreneurs have a very high payback record on their loans. This means that the money provided by wealthy donors not only keeps on doing good but actually increases.[2]

My own ministries among the poor are strongly supported by wealthy donors. These are good people who believe in what we are doing to help urban youth to graduate from high school and get jobs, even as they are being evangelized. But all of the good examples of how rich people have used their money to undergird the work of God's kingdom cannot be used to evade the question of whether or not these wealthy brothers and sisters are doing what the Lord requires of them. In the end, the question is whether or not they have too much left over after they have finished their giving, which prompts the question, "How much is too much?"

John Wesley, the father of Methodism, was aware of a further problem related to riches—wealth changes the way people think. The wealthy are affected spiritually by their possessions. Wesley saw that wealth often turns people away from God. What particularly troubled Wesley was that becoming a Christian creates virtues that in turn generate wealth. In his journals he wrote this:

> Religion must necessarily produce both industry and frugality, and then cannot but produce riches. We ought not to prevent people from being diligent and frugal; we *must* exhort all Christians to gain all they can, and to save all they can; that is, in effect, to grow rich.[3]

Wesley's answer to preventing Christians from being corrupted by their wealth was this:

There is one way, and there is no other under heaven. If those who gain all they can, and save all they can, will likewise give all they can, then the more they gain, the more they will grow in grace, and the more treasure they will lay up in heaven.[4]

Giving it all away, as Wesley suggests, is not common among rich Christians. But there are many who might call themselves "middle-range Christians." This is a designation that I ascribe to those who recognize that they are by no means living out a radical lifestyle (St. Francis-like), but who take the call to do so seriously. These middle-range Christians do not deny that the Lord has laid claim to their wealth or that they have not fully yielded to that claim. But by taking the call to sacrifice seriously, they are *in process* toward what they believe is expected of them. They acknowledge that they are still on a journey. With Paul they assert: "Brethren, I count not myself to have apprehended: but this one thing I do, forgetting those things which are behind, and reaching forth unto those things which are before, I press toward the mark for the prize of the high calling of God in Christ Jesus" (Philippians 3:13–14).

In the midst of all this discussion about selling and giving all to the poor, it is important to remember that giving to the poor is not what makes people into Christians. The Bible says, "For by grace are ye saved through faith; and that not of yourselves: it is the gift of God: Not of works, lest any man should boast" (Ephesians 2:8–9). It's not what any of us do with our money, but what Jesus did for us on the cross, that is the basis of salvation. Giving is a response to God's gift in Christ. It is a way of expressing gratitude. There is no condemnation for those who are in Christ, whether they are rich or poor (Romans 8:1).

There is a famous story about some would-be Christian philanthropists recorded in the Book of Acts.

But a certain man named Ananias, with Sapphira his wife, sold a possession, And kept back part of the price, his wife also being privy to it, and brought a certain part, and laid it at the apostles' feet. But

Peter said, Ananias, why hath Satan filled thine heart to lie to the Holy Ghost, and to keep back part of the price of the land? Whiles it remained, was it not thine own? and after it was sold, was it not in thine own power? why hast thou conceived this thing in thine heart? thou hast not lied unto men, but unto God. And Ananias hearing these words fell down, and gave up the ghost: and great fear came on all them that heard these things. And the young men arose, wound him up, and carried him out, and buried him. And it was about the space of three hours after, when his wife, not knowing what was done, came in. And Peter answered unto her, Tell me whether ye sold the land for so much? And she said, Yea, for so much. Then Peter said unto her, How is it that ye have agreed together to tempt the Spirit of the Lord? behold, the feet of them which have buried your husband are at the door, and shall carry thee out. Then she fell down straightway at his feet, and yielded up the ghost: and the young men came in, and found her dead, and, carrying her forth, buried her by her husband. (Acts 5:1–10)

In the story, it is important to recognize that punishment to Ananias and Sapphira was not because they failed to give all they had, but because they lied to the Holy Spirit and to the Church. They tried to earn the praise of their fellow Christians by pretending to be supersaints who had given their all to the work of Christ, and this is what got them into deadly trouble. Peter makes it clear that giving everything up in the name of Christ is not required to be a part of the Church. Peter asks, "Whiles it remained, was it not thine own? and after it was sold, was it not in thine own power? why has thou conceived this thing in thine heart? thou has not lied unto men, but unto God" (Acts 5:4).

The rest of us must not turn on the rich and lay such a guilt trip on them that they are tempted to fake a charity that has not been demanded of them. St. Francis, who followed Christ by giving all he possessed to the poor, went out of his way to keep rich people from feeling like second-class Christians. Not only did he refuse to make a big deal out of his own giving, but he made people who had great wealth feel comfortable in his presence. If the rich were to give to the poor in the name of the Lord, Francis wanted it to be because of love and not because of guilt manipulation. He hoped that the rich would give away what they had because they too wanted the joyful freedom he had found in poverty. He had no desire for the rich to be embarrassed into giving; he wanted them to give because giving is fun.

Rich Christians, according to St. Francis, are called to use their wealth in ways that bring them joy, and he is convinced that such joy is best known when the blessings of wealth are shared with others, especially with those who are less fortunate. In this, Francis echoes Christ, who urges us to view His kingdom as a wedding feast to which widows and orphans are invited. His kingdom is a party that is open to the poor, the maimed, the lame, and the blind (Luke 14:12–13). These are the people who, according to ancient Hebrew law, were declared ceremoniously unclean and therefore deserved to be shut out of fellowship with the people of God. But those who, because they are committed to Christ, give of themselves and their wealth to those the world declares as outcasts, come to share a special joy and excitement with those who are unexpectedly invited to parties they never thought they would get to enjoy. This vision of the rich sharing their wealth with the poor at a celebration—a party—is all through the biblical message. In ancient days, the Lord commanded that the tithe be used for just such a purpose:

> And thou shalt bestow that money for whatsoever thy soul lusteth after, for oxen, or for sheep, or for wine, or for strong drink, or for whatsoever thy soul desireth: and thou shalt eat there before the LORD thy God, and thou shalt rejoice, thou, and thine household. And the Levite that is within thy gates; thou shalt not forsake him; for he hath no part nor inheritance with thee. At the end of three years thou shalt bring forth all the tithe of thine increase the same year, and shalt lay it up within thy gates: And the Levite, (because he hath no part nor inheritance with thee,) and the stranger, and the fatherless, and the widow, which are within thy gates, shall come, and shall eat and be satisfied; that the LORD thy God may bless thee in all the work of thine hand which thou doest. (Deuteronomy 14:26–29)

16

Out of all of this, my recommendations to those rich people who acknowledge that the ideal is doing what the rich young ruler failed to do, and what St. Francis did do, are as follows:

1. Do not try to justify wealth. It is not necessary. God saves you by *His* sacrifice—not *yours*.

2. Recognize that the more you give and the more you simplify your own lifestyle, the more freedom you will know and the easier life will be for you.

3. As you enjoy the wealth that you have, be sure to invite others to share the joy of what God has made available to you.

4. Day by day, press toward the goal of being the kind of person that God wants you to be, even as you remember the teachings of our Lord in Luke 6:20–21: "And he lifted up his eyes on his disciples, and said, Blessed be ye poor: for yours is the kingdom of God. Blessed are ye that hunger now: for ye shall be filled. Blessed are ye that weep now: for ye shall laugh."

I know a family that is very wealthy and well on its way toward embracing the principles that have just been laid out. This is a Roman Catholic family that has inherited a vast fortune. These people live just outside a midwestern city and, as you might expect, make their home on a large estate with a number of servants. They also have a host of needy people living with them. Over the years they have made room in their large house for more than a dozen foster children and made sure that these children have had all the social and educational advantages their own children enjoyed. In addition, they always have *unlikely* houseguests. The last time I was there, I met a recovering alcoholic in the process of coming out of the pits of despair. Having lost everything and with no place to go, this man was a guest of the family while he was trying to get his life together. Also, there was a priest who worked as an itinerant evangelist conducting preaching missions in Catholic churches across the country.

The priest made this family's home the place where he could, as he said, "always hang my hat."

If you stayed with them over the course of a week, you would realize that this family has turned their home into a ministry center. They host all kinds of groups that need meeting places, from Alcoholics Anonymous to a recovery group for abused women. All of these meetings go on in the context of gracious hospitality that includes snacks and refreshments, along with constant care by the house servants. The servants themselves are treated well, living very much as members of an extended family.

Each year, when this family sends out its Christmas card, it looks almost like a high school yearbook. It has individualized pictures of everybody who is living with them, including the servants, with an account of what has been going on in each person's life. To say that it is a pleasure to visit with this family is an understatement. It's a party. There is always a good meal, good conversation, and good laughs. There seems to be a constant swirl of activity, and there is certainly an atmosphere of caring.

Once, on the streets of Paris, I ran into the wealthy couple who make all of this possible. They were staying at the Intercontinental Hotel and asked if my wife and I could have dinner with them. My friends mentioned incidentally that they had brought some of their foster children along on the trip, because they found vacations more enjoyable when shared. They told me that they had been to Paris many times, but it was always a new experience for them if they brought along some "young folks" who had never seen it before.

These people have learned to enjoy their wealth in a way that blesses others. They have told me that they recognize that they could and should be doing more to use their wealth to help others, and they are always seriously looking for ways to better follow Christ. They take seriously the inscription on a plaque I saw hanging in their kitchen: "For unto whomsoever much is given, of him shall be much required" (Luke 12:48).

Why is it that those who do more than expected are usually the ones who think they haven't done enough? If you saw the film

Schindler's List, you couldn't help but be moved by the scene when the Jews, who had been rescued from the holocaust by this "righteous Gentile," expressed their gratitude. They told Oskar Schindler how thankful they were for the incredible risks he took and the huge financial expenditures he made to save them from the Nazi gas chambers. At their expressions of gratitude, he broke into tears and said, "I could have done so much more." He pointed to his expensive car and said, "See that automobile? I could have sold it and used the money to save the lives of several others." Over and over he said, "I could have done so much more! I could have done so much more!"

Again I ask, "Why is it that those rich people who have done more than we would expect of them are the ones who are always saying that they should have done more?" Perhaps it's because they are conscious of having to give account to a higher Authority of what has been done with the resources that were placed in their hands. Perhaps it's because their blessings come from One who has done far more for them than merely providing them with the means to "the good life" as defined by America.

People like Oskar Schindler and the family I have just described remind all of us that we have more than we need and must therefore be counted as rich. In response to this acknowledgment, we all must be asking whether or not we have begun to live responsibly with the wealth that God has placed in our hands.

Chapter 3

How to Exhibit a Christian Lifestyle

without Moving into a Commune

God has provided enough to meet everyone's *needs*, but not enough to meet everyone's *wants*. There are demonic forces at work in our society that encourage us to want an endless array of things we don't need. The media, in general, and advertising, in particular, are constantly at work trying to seduce us into lifestyles of conspicuous consumption. Day in and day out they try to lure us into a lifestyle filled with artificially created *needs*. If we succumb to their powers, we find ourselves caught up in endless efforts to get more and more money to buy things we really don't need, simply because we have been conned into believing that we have to have them.

The desperation to secure what is not needed is seen in the streets of urban ghettos where teenage boys are ready to kill, if that's what it takes, to get the $150 Nike™ basketball shoes that they are convinced will enable them to jump like Michael Jordan. It's seen in the disintegrating marriages of young couples, who have no time to nurture their relationships. They are exhausting their time and energies holding down multiple jobs to get extra money to buy things they have been led to believe they cannot live without. It is seen in the needless neglect of children, whose parents believe they best express love by getting the children things that are advertised on TV, even if it means leaving the kids home alone while Mom and Dad are out earning the money to buy them.

The absurdity of all this was clearly exemplified as I talked to a young husband who complained about being so tired and edgy that he was constantly nasty to his wife and irritated with his children. He told me that he knew his behavior was wrong, but he couldn't help it because he was holding down two jobs and not getting enough sleep. The reason he gave for working so hard was that he needed the money to pay off the two new cars he and his wife had. When I asked why the family had *two* new cars, he explained that new cars were absolutely necessary so that he and his wife could have reliable transportation to work. And when I asked him why he thought it was necessary for them both to work, he answered, "How else will we have enough money to pay off the cars?"

Recently, the president of the United States, out on the campaign trail, proudly announced that during his administration over two million new jobs had been created. In response, a disgruntled man in the crowd shouted back, "I know! I've got three of them."

Is it really necessary for us to work as much and as hard as we do? Or have we been conned into believing that this is something we have to do in order to be able to buy all the things we have been taught to want? Do we really believe that we have to stay on the exhausting treadmills we have created for ourselves in order to meet the *needs* of our families? Have we been victimized by the media to think that we can never be happy unless we own those new cars, buy those new jeans, and have that special cruise being advertised?

Jesus told us about a certain sower who went out to sow and how some of his seeds fell upon thorny ground. When the sprouts began to grow, the thorny plants around them choked the new sprouts to death. Jesus went on to explain that His story was to illustrate those situations in which people hear His message and try to live out His calling but find that "the cares of this world" kill off their new commitments to live for God.

Hearken; Behold, there went out a sower to sow: And it came to pass, as he sowed, some fell by the way side, and the fowls of the air came and devoured it up. And some fell on stony ground, where it had not much earth: and immediately it sprang up, because it had no depth of earth: But when the sun was up, it was scorched; and because it had no root, it withered away. And some fell among thorns, and the thorns grew up, and choked it, and it yielded no fruit. And other fell on good ground, and did yield fruit that sprang up and increased; and brought forth, some thirty, and some sixty, and some an hundred. And he said unto them, He that hath ears to hear, let him hear. And when he was alone, they that were about him with the twelve asked of him the parable.

The sower soweth the word. And these are they by the way side, where the word is sown; but when they have heard, Satan cometh immediately, and taketh away the word that was sown in their hearts. And these are they likewise which are sown on stony ground; who, when they have heard the word, immediately receive it with gladness; And have no root in themselves, and so endure but for a time: afterward, when affliction or persecution ariseth for the word's sake, immediately they are offended. And these are they which are sown among thorns; such as hear the word, And the cares of this world, and the deceitfulness of riches, and the lusts of other things entering in, choke the word, and it becometh unfruitful. And these are they which are sown on good ground; such as hear the word, and receive it, and bring forth fruit, some thirtyfold, some sixty, and some an hundred. (Mark 4:3–10, 14–20)

This story makes clear what we all know about having lots of *things*—the maintenance and care they require choke the life out of us. Just taking care of all those things leaves little time for the relationships that we claim are dear to us, and for the spiritual disciplines we know are essential for our souls to survive. The bigger the house, the more time we need to clean it. The bigger the lawn, the more time we need to cut it. The more expensive the car, the more attention we give to keeping it looking and running like new. How many couples eat up their weekends just painting, fixing, and polishing the things they believe are essential to enjoy *the good life* that the media has prescribed for them?

If being human requires freedom, then enslavement to the cares of this world is dehumanizing. If fulfillment is gained through giving ourselves to intimate relationships, then allowing ourselves to be consumed with the care of things, instead of the care of persons, is foolish. If sin is what keeps us from God, then such a lifestyle is sin. Such considerations have led many people to look for ways to simplify their lifestyles. An array of books and television talk shows have dealt with the advantages of doing this. Increasingly, people are finding ways to gear down from the hectic, exhausting fast track that goes with the media-prescribed affluent version of the good life.

A Hebrew prophet once asked, "Wherefore do ye spend money for that which is not bread? and your labour for that which satisfieth not?" (Isaiah 55:2a). And across America people are responding to that question by saying, "We're just not going to do it anymore. No longer will we be duped into wasting our lives in an endless quest for things we don't really need. We are going to simplify our lifestyles so we will have more time for the people in our lives, and so we will have enough time to "stop and smell the roses."

Beyond all the personally enriching benefits that may come from opting for a simpler lifestyle, there is an even more important reason for making this choice. People are realizing that it is sinful to do otherwise. There is something very wrong with some people spending a fortune to satisfy artificially created needs while others, both near and far, are without the basic necessities of life. Some people are troubled by 1 John 3:17–18: "But whoso hath this world's good, and seeth his brother have need, and shutteth up his bowels of compassion from him, how dwelleth the love of God in him? My little children, let us not love in word, neither in tongue; but in deed and in truth." And they answer this challenge by deciding to live more simply so that others can simply live.

I know of a man who was challenged by the simple question, "If Jesus was among us in the flesh today, do you think he would drive a BMW?" He asked himself whether or not, in the face of massive privation in places like Haiti and Nigeria, Jesus would buy a luxury car which primarily functions as a status symbol. As he considered the question of what Jesus would do about buying a car if he had fifty thousand dollars in his hands, this man had to conclude that Jesus would drive something far below a luxury car and use as much of that money as possible to feed some of the hungry kids of the world.

This man sold his BMW and uses the money to support thirty children through Compassion International. By providing twenty-five dollars per month per child, he enables Compassion International to clothe, feed, house, educate, and evangelize these children. Compassion International supports children in many Third World countries, but all of the children being supported by this man are in the Dominican Republic, a nation close enough to the United States for him to visit with relative frequency. If you could talk to him personally about the investment that he is making in the lives of these needy children, he would tell you that it has given him more gratification than anything he had ever known in his former affluent lifestyle. He has cut back not only in terms of his car but in many other areas of his life. He speaks with great joy about the freedom he has gained as he has become independent of the material things he once accumulated in his search for personal fulfillment. This man no longer organizes his life around protecting and maintaining all the expensive things he once considered his most precious possessions. He now knows the peace that comes from laying up "treasures in heaven, where neither moth nor rust doth corrupt, and where thieves do not break through and steal" (Matthew 6:20). His regular visits to the children blessed by his giving are a far greater source of joy than any of the things he once thought he had to have. For him, a simpler lifestyle is truly a richer lifestyle.

This man learned a lesson that was once even more fully realized by a young party boy in the town of Assisi, Italy, over seven hundred years ago. St. Francis, as we now know him, abandoned his upper-middle-class lifestyle and adopted the simple ways of a mendicant monk. He and those who followed him went *all the way* in adopting the lifestyle prescribed by Jesus, who once said, "Therefore I say unto you, Take no thought for your life, what ye shall eat, or what ye shall drink; nor yet for your body, what ye shall put on. Is not the life more than meat, and the body than raiment?" (Matthew 6:25). They never had any money or possessed anything of worth because they believed that to possess things meant that you had to carry weapons for protection and must view every stranger as a potential thief. "Fools for Christ" they were called in derision—a label they gladly embraced as they went from place to place, taking literally the instructions of the Lord as they are recorded in Matthew 10:7–14.

> And as ye go, preach, saying, The kingdom of heaven is at hand. Heal the sick, cleanse the lepers, raise the dead, cast out devils: freely ye have received, freely give. Provide neither gold, nor silver, nor brass in your purses, Nor scrip for your journey, neither two coats, neither shoes, nor yet staves: for the workman is worthy of his meat. And into whatsoever city or town ye shall enter, enquire who in it is worthy; and there abide till ye go thence. And when ye come into an house, salute it. And if the house be worthy, let your peace come upon it: but if it be not worthy, let your peace return to you. And whosoever shall not receive you, nor hear your words, when ye depart out of that house or city, shake off the dust of your feet.

Historians, poets, philosophers, and religious leaders over the centuries, since St. Francis so faithfully and naively lived out the words of Jesus, have been fascinated by his boundless joy and his love for life. They, as do we all, sense that if we could somehow give ourselves to that total abandonment to Christ, then something of the spontaneous ecstasy that pervaded his life might again be experienced.

Sadly, not many in any age are about to follow Christ as St. Francis did. Few are ready to forsake all and take up the cross. Seldom are we willing to deny ourselves (Matthew 16:24) or to sell whatever we have and give the money to the poor (Mark 10:21). But much is to be gained in trying. Something of the joy of Francis can be known even in limited excursions into the lifestyle he once heroically lived out at the end of what has been called The Dark Ages. Insofar as we can taste the gratifications of giving up something of our affluent lifestyles, and embracing the simpler lifestyle that begins to approach the biblical ideal, we can gain a glimpse of the freedom and aliveness that belong to those daring saints who in diverse times have been able to make the leap of faith into owning nothing and living in total dependency on the Lord.

26

When it comes to living more simply, it's crucial that we not make the rules governing our changed lifestyle the basis for a new legalism. When I was a youngster, the Christianity that I knew was filled with an array of rules and regulations that were deemed the basis for judging whether or not people were Christians. We didn't believe that Catholics could be real Christians since real Christians didn't drink wine, and they did. We questioned the spirituality of the youth group at the Presbyterian church down the street, because we didn't believe that real Christians danced, and they did. And we even doubted the spirituality of some of the members of our own Baptist congregation because we were convinced that real Christians didn't go to movies, and they did. Those of us who lived by the rules of our pious little subculture assumed ourselves superior to those lesser folks who didn't abide by rules that we deemed to be the habits of the Christian heart. That holier-than-thou legalism undoubtedly was a barrier to our fellowship with other Christians, and it certainly got in the way of the love that we should have had for each other.

Unfortunately, it is all too easy for those who have embraced a simple lifestyle to make the principles governing their spending into a new, but equally oppressive, legalism. When people start bragging about how simply they are living and deem those who live otherwise to be less than saintly, something good has gone bad. When those who have given up the affluent lifestyle prescribed by the dominant culture get into using their more simple ways as a badge of superior godliness, then the motives behind what they are doing and saying become highly suspect. That is why Jesus carefully admonishes His disciples to deliberately conceal all signs of living sacrificially. The Lord who calls us to simplicity and sacrifice clearly tells us that we must always conceal from others any evidence of what we give up in His name.

Take heed that ye do not your alms before men, to be seen of them: otherwise ye have no reward of your Father which is in heaven. Therefore when thou doest thine alms, do not sound a trumpet before thee, as the hypocrites do in the synagogues and in the streets, that they may have glory of men. Verily I say unto you, They have their reward. But when thou doest alms, let not thy left hand know

27

what thy right hand doeth: That thine alms may be in secret: and thy Father which seeth in secret himself shall reward thee openly.

Moreover when ye fast, be not, as the hypocrites, of a sad countenance: for they disfigure their faces, that they may appear unto men to fast. Verily I say unto you, They have their reward. But thou, when thou fastest, anoint thine head, and wash thy face; That thou appear not unto men to fast, but unto thy Father which is in secret: and thy Father, which seeth in secret, shall reward thee openly. (Matthew 6:1–4; 16–18)

A few years ago my old car wore out and was beyond reasonable repair. I called a friend of mine who had a car dealership and told him to pick out a car for me. I told him that I didn't want to pay more than fifteen hundred dollars, and that I trusted him to do the best he could for me at that price. Three days later, when I had the time to pick up the car my friend had gotten for me, I was in for a surprise. He said, "Tony, I've got a decision for you to make. A man came in here the other day to trade in a great car that's completely loaded. It's not new, but anyone would think it was an eight thousand dollar car. When I told him I was looking for a car for you, he said he'd be willing to let it go for fourteen hundred dollars. I also have another car that looks a bit beat up and is stripped down to the bare essentials. It runs well, but the book price is slightly more than fifteen hundred dollars. So here's what you have to decide: Do you want to live out your simple lifestyle beliefs and buy the cheaper car, or do you want to spend a hundred dollars more so you can *appear* to be living more sacrificially for Jesus?" You can guess what I decided to do.

It is tempting for those who embrace a more simple and frugal way of living as an expression of their Christian commitment to work overtime trying to impress others with their sacrifices for God and the poor. As we endeavor to live out the simple lifestyle, it's essential that we not make a show of it, and it's equally important that we not lay a guilt trip on others who do not choose to live according to the values and rules for spending that we have chosen for ourselves. Having given the warnings, allow me to make some suggestions:

1. *Buy secondhand cars.* It's no secret that the minute you sign the contract for a new car you have lost thousands of dollars. Don't ask me why this happens, but it does. Brand new cars have price tags that are significantly higher than even slightly used cars. If having a late model car is a *must* with you, it might be a good idea to go to a car rental place and buy one of the used vehicles they have for sale. Usually rental car companies sell their cars with less than twenty-five thousand miles on them. What's more, you have the assurance that they have been regularly serviced, and in most cases, the rental company will even make the service records on the car available for you to review. That way you can find out if the car you are considering has ever been in an accident or had any serious problems. I have found these cars to be available for about one-quarter less than the cost of similar models at most car dealerships.

If you can get by with an older car that has an even lower price tag, so much the better. The primary thing to be concerned about when you buy a used car, especially when the purchase is made apart from an authorized dealer, is whether or not you are buying somebody else's trouble. Secondhand cars can "nickel and dime" you into poverty, if you get a lemon. If you are not buying from an authorized dealer, then be sure to take the car to a trusted mechanic for a checkover before you buy. Even if you have to pay a few bucks, it's money well spent.

The second thing that should concern you is safety. With air bags now available, you might not want to consider a car that doesn't have them. Increasing the risk of death in order to save money is probably not good stewardship. But in this day and age, you also have to be concerned about the dangers inherent in breakdowns. I personally would not want my wife driving a car that had a high possibility of breaking down and might leave her stranded in some dangerous place. Frankly, I don't wish that to happen to me either! Switching to a used car is a good way to get out from under big monthly payments, but if the risks to you or your family are too high with the particular used car you are considering, you had better keep looking.

2. *Buy at thrift shops.* This is another way of cutting back on expenses. Recycled clothing for children is almost always a great bargain, but adults can save money here too. Both men's and women's clothing items are available at just a fraction of what they are worth. What's more, you will probably end up better dressed than if you had gone to a regular clothing store and bought your clothes at full retail prices. You *can* dress better for less. Simplicity doesn't mean ugliness. There is no virtue in *looking* poor when you don't have to.

Some years ago, a young couple, Bronwyn and Nick Purcell, came to work with us in our urban ministries. They took up residence in Camden, New Jersey, a city that *Time* magazine has called the worst city in America. This couple runs a silk screen print shop that has been especially created to provide employment for at-risk young people who would otherwise be hanging out on street corners. This small factory makes specialized greeting cards, T-shirts, and posters.[1]

The Purcells make very little money and are *forced* to live simply. But they have proven that, with imagination and some throwaway items, it is possible to create a beautiful home. Nick and Bronwyn have decorated their house with things that other people have discarded, sometimes even rescuing items put out as trash. They have also made good use of both secondhand furniture given to them by people who were cleaning house and inexpensive artistic items from thrift shops. The result of their efforts is such a beautiful home that the major newspaper of the city did a feature story on it in their "Houses and Gardens" Sunday supplement. The newspaper did the story, not because the Purcells had decorated their house for next to nothing, but because the reporters were amazed to find such an incredibly attractive home in the midst of what has to be called an urban slum. If the Kingdom of God is about reclaiming what has been ruined and making it beautiful again, then the Purcells are indeed Kingdom builders. Simplicity in lifestyle does *not* have to mean living without beauty. And living the Christian lifestyle does not mean we have to live without style and grace—it means we live in a style that shows our gratitude for grace.

How to Protect Yourself from

Technology without Becoming Amish

Some years ago I took my Eastern College class in the Sociology of the Family out to Lancaster County, Pennsylvania, for a field trip. I thought it would be highly informative for my students to talk with an Amish bishop so that they might get a handle on an alternative family lifestyle. The Amish are commonly referred to as the Pennsylvania Dutch, although the gentle people whose men wear black broad-brimmed hats and whose women wear bonnets aren't Dutch at all. Actually, they are of German lineage and a break-off from the Mennonites and the mainstream Anabaptist movement. As you may know, the Amish are highly suspect of modern technology and what it might do to their lives.

Amish people reject much of what is associated with our modern way of life. Their dress style, their refusal to allow electricity into their homes, their taboo against owning automobiles, and their other rejections of the things of this world have made them into what has been called "a peculiar people." This is a label that they readily accept.

My students were excited about meeting with a bishop from this counterculture community, but they were not prepared for the logical sense that he made out of the Amish lifestyle or the challenges that he presented in terms of the way the rest of us live.

This old bishop told my students that, contrary to what most people think, the Amish don't see anything wrong with electricity.

As a matter of fact, he said they use it in their barns. It's just that the Amish are not willing to let it into their homes. When he was asked why, he explained with great clarity how electricity destroys the kind of family life that God wants all of us to have.

"Electricity," he explained, "changes the rhythm of life. With electric lights, you don't go to bed when you ought to, and you don't get up when you should. And that's just the beginning. Once you've got electricity, it's not long before you are into all the things that go with electricity. You'll have radios, televisions, stereos, and who knows what else."

When asked what was wrong with all of those things, the bishop quickly answered, "If you have those things, they will take up all of your time, and there's not much left to give to those in your family and to other things that matter. Why do you let your children watch television and listen to the radio? Don't you know that sooner or later what they believe to be right and wrong is going to be controlled more by what they hear and see coming over the air than by anything they hear coming from you? We didn't outright reject these things. We just stood back to see what happened to the families that had them. And when we saw what it did to the likes of your kind, we decided that we would just as soon not have those things happen to us.

"The same goes for automobiles," he told us. "Those machines are good things, if you can keep them under control. We aren't against riding in them. We'll even hire people to drive us places we want to go. It's just that we don't think we ought to own them. Cars make it too easy for people to get away from each other, and that's not good for either the family or the community. People ought to stay home with the people they know and love, instead of wandering off to places where nobody knows who they are."

Then he zeroed in on his primary objection to automobiles by telling us that with cars young people find it too easy "to go off and sin."

When my students considered what most sociologists know—that most young people do most of their early sexual experimenting in parked cars—there was little argument from them. The old bishop had made his point about cars and had more than justified the Amish use of horses and carriages, especially after he made it clear that Amish young people were allowed to court only in *open* carriages so that everybody could see what they were doing.

But the bishop's strongest case was made against telephones. He pointed down to the end of the lane leading up to his farm house and called our attention to a telephone booth that stood there. "I paid the phone company extra to put that phone booth there for my use. Got nothing against phones," he said. "It's just that you shouldn't let those things into your house. If you do, you'll be inviting people to interrupt you whenever they feel like it. You won't be able to get through a meal without it ringing. When you're talking about deep things with your children, it's bound to interrupt. When you're in bed with your wife, you almost can count on it sounding off. You can't even say your prayers without it breaking in. I have that phone down there at the end of my lane for emergencies, but I'm not about to let it become an interrupter of all that I believe is sacred."

My students were silenced. They weren't about to give up living in the modern world and become Amish, but they had been forced to think about how so much of the technology they had accepted into their lives had led to a disruption of their lives, put them on edge, diminished the quality of their families, and lured them into hectic lifestyles that leave them exhausted.

Think about it: Because of electricity, we seldom get a good eight hours of sleep, and it shows. With the coming of television and other electronic media, we have surrendered our children to influences that socialize them into values that often shock us. And with the new forms of transportation and communication that have taken over our ways of living, we are seduced into going places we ought not to go, and listening to a lot of people whom we would do better to ignore.

If we are looking for a simpler, more godly lifestyle, it's a good idea to ask ourselves some serious questions about technology and what it's doing to us. We ought to become more careful to keep what we should control from controlling us. We have to ask ourselves whether or not we have too much technology in our lives.

My son would have said amen to what the bishop said about television. Bart has a bumper sticker on his car that reads, "Kill TV." Furthermore, he practices what he preaches. He doesn't let his kids watch television except on rare occasions, and usually then it's a video that the whole family can watch together. There's a lot that is frightening about what television does to us. My son is aware of that, and he acts accordingly.

First of all, television changes a child's ability to pay attention to anything else for very long. The programmers for television have learned how to keep people interested in what comes across the tube by providing viewers with rapid technological changes. Just consider how quickly visual images on the screen change. The content of the shows need not be very interesting, because as long as people are bombarded with different images in rapid succession, they can be counted on to keep watching.

The advertisements on television excel at this. A good television ad throws image after image on the screen to keep the viewer riveted. There's a young couple dancing, followed by a *hunk* surfing, followed by some with-it guys playing volleyball, followed by some couples having a water fight. It goes on and on. All of this occurs in less than thirty seconds. It's fascinating! You don't have to be interested in the message, because the medium has become the message. The medium of television with its rapid-fire images offers us technical changes at their dazzling best.

The problem is that anything lacking technical changes becomes boring by comparison. What teacher with a blackboard and a piece of chalk can seem exciting after they've seen Sesame Street? Big Bird and Ernie teach children the alphabet with a thousand and one images and with songs and dances for every letter. After a show like that, reading is much too slow to keep kids interested. Television performs a diabolical magic trick that makes real life seem boring. Real life just doesn't offer as many technical changes.

What real father can compare with Bill Cosby in cleverness and wit? And which mother can solve the problems of life, each in the span of a half an hour, as is done by the wise mothers on the sit-coms that are everyday watching fare? It was no surprise when a recent survey revealed that young people, when asked whom they most preferred for a father, chose movie star Burt Reynolds over their real fathers.

In case you don't think that television impacts your kids, just stop and reflect on how MTV, the rock music network, has changed everything our kids think about sex, violence, and the meaning of life. When some colleagues in my field asked one of the top executives of MTV how much influence his network had on teenagers, he answered, "We don't *influence* teenagers! We *own* them!"

I'm not sure what to do about television, but something must be done to break its spell over us. Even our expressions of faith are being molded by television. How many of our contemporary religious programs are simply baptized versions of the *Tonight Show*? I suppose there's nothing wrong with speaking to this generation through methods that are familiar to them, but I wonder what happens to Christian doctrine when everything is reduced to sound bites. And I have to worry about the Christian faith itself being transformed into a media production in our effort to relate to television-nurtured baby boomers and their X-generation children.

Perhaps the best thing we can do is to set time limits on television watching, since the idea of getting rid of the television altogether would probably be rejected. At least with limited viewing time, we and our children would have to carefully choose which programs we would watch. Let's say that you decide that your family will watch television an hour and a half a day. That might seem like a lot, but consider the fact that the average amount of time given to television watching by Americans is five hours per day. With the limited viewing time, there would need to be a family discussion in which each member could lobby for those programs he or she felt should be watched and why. Then I think the family might be on its way to a higher quality lifestyle. At least time would not be wasted on inane channel-surfing done by those who can't make a decision and just continually survey everything that's on. If we are not ready to rid ourselves of television entirely, we should at least try to get it under control.

It is essential for children that what is seen on television be processed by the family immediately. That way parents can have some idea about what the children actually heard and saw and what they thought about it all. Television must be critiqued from a Christian point of view if we are to avoid having our families inundated with a media-created way of life that contradicts the gospel.

I hope I don't sound like a lunatic bent on smashing all machines and getting us back to a pre-industrial way of life. A lot of technology really is a blessing, especially the technology that *protects* us from technology. Consider the answering machine—a bit of technology that has the potential to protect us from one of the tyrannical inventions feared by the Amish bishop—the telephone.

One of my students was asked in a physics class, "What happens when the human body is submerged below the surface of water?" He quickly answered, "The phone rings!"

Indeed it does. And we answer it, telling ourselves that it might be something important, only to find that it's Sears calling to find out whether or not we want to order anything. Adding insult to injury are those mechanized calls which have us answering a call *from* a machine! When Jesus said, "My peace I leave with you," I wonder if He understood what it would be like in houses filled with telephones. We dare not have the contraptions disconnected because, as some women have said of men, "Can't live with them and can't live without them."

Ironically, from the technology of the telephone has come the technology to rescue us from it: the answering machine. Those who think that the only use for these blessed devices is to record messages from those who call when they are not at home miss out on the best contribution the answering machine can make to our lives. Answering machines can be a means for gaining some peace and uninterrupted time for family fellowship. All you have to do is to record the words, "We're not answering the phone right now. Just leave a message along with your phone number." Don't promise that you will call back, because when you listen to your messages, you may have calls you would rather not waste the time, effort, and money to return. That would certainly be true of mechanized recorded advertisements or telemarketing calls you never wanted in the first place.

The answering machine allows you to talk on the phone when *you* want to talk, rather than when the arbitrary callers want to talk to you. Answering machines allow you to choose when you will pay attention to those who call. We must not let the telephone disturb those sacred times we can enjoy with the significant others in our lives.

Most answering machines have some means for listening in on messages even as they're being recorded. This also can be a blessing if you don't want to talk to most people because you're tired or out of sorts, but you do need to be available to some specific people, or you're waiting for an important call. You find out who is calling simply by listening to the message being recorded, and then if you want to talk to whomever is on the phone, you can lift the receiver and break in with the simple words, "I'm so glad to hear it's you."

There's nothing dishonest or non-Christian about any of this. Jesus found ways to be uninterrupted, especially when He wanted to have some quality time with His Father. In our highly technological society, we must find ways to do the same. The answering machine is one invention that can protect what is sacred in our lives.

No, you don't have to join the Amish fellowship or sail off to a deserted island to free yourself and your family from the tyranny of technology. You just have to work on establishing a balanced way of using the technology so that *it* serves *you*, rather than the other way around.

How to Get Ready to Die

without Pretending That It's No Problem

One of the most remarkable sermons I ever heard was delivered by Norman Vincent Peale at the Ocean City Tabernacle in Ocean City, New Jersey. At the age of ninety-two, he stood fully energized before a packed house and declared, "I am going to preach a sermon on a topic I know more about than anyone else here tonight! I am going to preach on the topic, 'Getting Ready to Die.'"

As the venerable dean of American preaching made his claim, there was no one present who was ready to challenge him. Indeed, there must have been many who envied him, because he seemed to possess a confidence in the face of dying that most people wish they had. The old man in the pulpit spoke with authority. It was the authority of one who had come to look death in the face without blinking, had challenged the despair that death can impose on those it comes to claim, and then had won his victory over death. Dr. Peale held that congregation in the palm of his hand. We all recognized that he knew what he was talking about and that what he said could help those of us who had not yet faced the thought of death in a realistic fashion.

Facing death, say both the philosophers and the psychologists, is the most important and difficult task in life. It's no wonder that we want to avoid thinking about it. Yet, dealing with death is something few of us can avoid. Once in a while we hear of someone being surprised by death, and we know that he or she never had to think about it. Usually, when we hear of such cases, we feel a strange kind of envy.

A friend of mine unexpectedly died of an aneurysm. In the prime of her life, she went to bed with her husband. Then, in the middle of the night she woke, got out of bed, and started toward the bathroom. She never made it! After a few steps, she suddenly slumped to the floor and was gone. While we all mourned her death, I sensed a kind of hope among those of us at her funeral that death might come that way for us. "There was no pain!" "She never knew what hit her!" "I hope I go like that!" were some of the comments I heard.

For most of us, death comes in ways that are far more difficult to handle. The anxieties that we experience as death comes inevitably toward us, can sometimes so dampen our appreciation for life that we end up feeling dead long before we actually die. Howard Becker, whom many consider to be the most brilliant modern interpreter of Sigmund Freud, contends that the repression of death in the consciousness is a prerequisite to living a happy life. Becker, in his book *Denial of Death,* argues that when the defense mechanisms we construct to ward off the awareness that we are moving toward death begin to break down, the inevitable result is a sense of *angst* or despair. Becker claims that we participate in an array of socially created illusions designed to hide the reality of the impending end of life as we know it.

Sören Kierkegaard—Danish philosopher and theologian from the nineteenth century—picks up this same theme as he describes our futile efforts to escape from thinking about death. He says that each of us is like one of those smooth stones tossed in play to skip along the surface of a pond. Like the stones, we dance across the surface until we run out of momentum, and then each of us sinks into "100,000 fathoms of nothingness."

Some of us are threatened not only by the pain of leaving this life but also by our fears of what might lie on the other side of the grave. Nowhere in English literature are such fears given more dramatic expression than in Hamlet's famous soliloquy.

To be, or not to be: that is the question:
Whether 'tis nobler in the mind to suffer
The slings and arrows of outrageous fortune,
Or to take arms against a sea of troubles,
And by opposing end them? To die: To sleep;
No more; and by a sleep to say we end
That heart-ache and the thousand natural shocks
That flesh is heir to, 'tis a consummation
Devoutly to be wish'd. To die, to sleep;
To sleep: perchance to dream: ay, there's the rub;
For in that sleep of death what dreams may come
When we have shuffled off this mortal coil,
Must give us pause: there's the respect
That makes calamity of so long life.

We Christians know that there is nothing to fear about death *if we only believe*. We know that Jesus is the resurrection and the life and that whoever believes in Him, though he or she dies, yet shall that person live (John 11:25). But when faced with the reality of death, most of us have a tendency to pray that prayer which a desperate father once prayed to Jesus: "Lord, I believe; help thou my unbelief" (Mark 9:24). Yet Christians *can* work through their sense of dread about death. Our anxieties, honestly faced and taken to God in prayer, can be vanquished by a holy confidence that makes us capable of facing death with our fears under control.

No one I know was more able to do this than my own father-in-law, Reverend Robert Davidson, who died in the eighty-eighth year of his life. Dad was one of the more saintly men I have known. He was the faithful pastor of four Baptist churches and gained the allegiance of each congregation because he truly cared for them. He loved Jesus, and he loved the people Jesus had given him to serve. He loved the Bible, and he loved to pray.

In his later years, Dad gradually lost touch with reality. Or at least he lost touch with the reality that the rest of us live in. He became detached and reticent. But even in his disengagement from the people

41

around him, he showed us a Christ-like character. The hardening of his arteries and all the loss of memory that malady brings could not take away his almost ethereal smile that seemed to say, in the words of his favorite hymn, "It is well with my soul." More and more Dad slipped away from us, and at family gatherings he would simply sit silently at the dinner table, apparently unable to participate or take in the talk of the family. But still he would wear the smile that to me seemed to be evidence of his peace with God.

One Saturday my wife came home from visiting her parents, visibly upset. She wondered how much longer her mother would be able to care for her dad at home. His mind and body were failing fast. Peggy was still troubled as she went to bed that night. Very early the next morning, Peggy received a call from her mother with the good news that Dad would not be going into any kind of healthcare facility because he had gone home to his heavenly Father. Peggy's peace was complete when her mother related the circumstances of Dad's death.

They, too, had had a troubled night, she said. Dad had been unable to get comfortable and had not slept at all. Mother had prayed, "If only he could get a few hours' sleep." Then, at about 4:30 on Sunday morning, Dad had suddenly begun to recite in a strong voice these verses of Scripture from 1 Corinthians: "O death, where is thy sting? O grave, where is thy victory? The sting of death is sin; and the strength of sin is the law. But thanks be to God, which giveth us the victory through our Lord Jesus Christ" (1 Corinthians 15:55–57).

My mother-in-law is not sure whether Dad was preaching to an unseen congregation, comforting her, or reassuring himself, but she *is* sure he knew he was dying, and that he was ready to go. He recited the passage three times in all, each time with greater assurance than before. Then he slipped peacefully away to his heavenly Father.

Dad's dying, like his living, was ample evidence that death need not have debilitating power over us. In his dying hour, my father-in-law gave testimony that death does not have to be the final word about life.[1] But how do people like Norman Vincent Peale and my father-in-law get to that point wherein they are ready to die as true Christians are expected to die? How do they learn to resign themselves to dying, yet remain fully alive as victors over fear and anxiety? Nobody can answer that question for sure, but as a pastor who has been with a number of people as they worked through the reality of their own mortality, I want to share a few things that I have learned from those who were able to gain peace, and even joy, in the face of death.

DENIAL

When first confronted with the knowledge that the end of life is at hand, our first reaction, as we might expect, is *denial*. All of us cling to the absurd thought that it is *other* people who die. We make the idea of our own death unreal. On an intellectual level, everybody knows that he or she is going to die. But it is still difficult to embrace the idea subjectively. To *feel* the reality of one's mortality is far different from merely thinking about it as an inevitable fact of life. It's one thing to affirm with your mind that you are part of the human race, every member of which eventually dies, but quite another to face up to that subjective awareness that makes you reluctant to go to sleep at night because, as you put your head on the pillow, you hear a voice out of nowhere whispering in your heart and mind, "You are one day closer, and there aren't many days left." It takes a while before we can deal emotionally with the reality of our own temporality and inwardly acknowledge that, for us *personally*, time is running out. It is so difficult that most people do everything they can to avoid it and become preoccupied with other things. But sooner or later all of the distractions break down, no matter how interesting they might seem to be for a while. As Kierkegaard once said, "There comes that moment when even Beethoven is not enough!"

BARGAINING

Sooner or later, the defense mechanism that keeps us from accepting the fact that death is closing in fails. We come to realize that death is real and there is no escape from that reality. This is a hard, depressing truth, but if we wait long enough, it drives away all of our denials. We then move into the next stage, which is *bargaining*. We tell God that, if He will just deliver us from death, we will be different, and we promise to do some incredible acts of service for God and God's kingdom. We begin a long litany of imploring petitions, usually beginning with the words, "If only you spare me, I promise that . . . " This bargaining with God is all part of the dying process. But in most cases, it doesn't work, and we realize that God is probably not going to cut us a special deal that will temporarily save us from death. Then we are ready to accept the inevitable.

ACCEPTANCE

Acceptance, and the peace it brings, comes as a welcome relief from the painful inner struggles that accompany denial and bargaining. But for Christians, coming to this final stage of acceptance is not simply a matter of making some necessary psychological adjustments on the way to the grave. Instead, it is a process through which we are led by the Lord Himself. In the Twenty-third Psalm, we are given the promise that, though we walk through the valley of the shadow of death, He will be with us every step of the way. In our passage from this earthly life into God's loving hands, God provides comfort and strength. These, too, are promised in the Twenty-third Psalm.

The comfort and help that God gives come in a variety of ways, but probably most important in the face of death is the assurance of God's *radical grace*. In the face of death each of us, like the apostle Paul, becomes convinced that he or she is the worst sinner in the world. Certainly Paul had this sense about himself when he reflected on his character. Most of us will probably come to the same conclusion about ourselves that Paul did. Regardless of any religion we might have had, or any good works we may have done, our just due is condemnation from God and all that goes with it. But if we take time to really get into the Bible, we will hear the message that God loves us anyway. If we can stop putting our trust in how good we might have been and living in fear over how sinful we really are, we can know peace because of the *good news* that Jesus did everything necessary to guarantee us heaven. Grace, that word that appears over and over again in the New Testament, means that we will receive what we never earned and don't deserve. The Scripture that drives home that truth better than any other I know is Ephesians 2:8–9: "For by grace are ye saved through faith; and that not of yourselves; it is the gift of God; Not of works, lest any man should boast."

Many people think that God, like the Statue of Justice, has a scale of some sort and that, on the Day of Judgment, God will balance out all the good that we have done against all the sins in our lives. The ways in which movies and TV portray Judgment Day certainly reinforce this kind of thinking. People who get caught up in that *stuff* are led to believe that God will let us through the pearly gates only if the good that we have done outweighs the evil.

Well, it doesn't work like that! Sin is more like poison. It only takes one little drop to kill you. And the Bible says that everybody has taken more than enough of this poison to warrant the eternal spiritual death we call hell. The Bible says, "For all have sinned, and come short of the glory of God" (Romans 3:23). That puts every man, woman, and child in deep trouble. Nobody has what it takes, according to the Bible, to escape the wrath that is his or her due. That's the bad news. Every single person who has ever lived (but One) has inherited the traits of Adam, the founder of the human race, which include an inborn tendency to sin and a record of living out that tendency. However, over and against the bad news is the *good news!* And here it is:

> For if by one man's offence death reigned by one; much more they who receive abundance of grace and of the gift of righteousness shall reign in life by one, Jesus Christ. Therefore, as by the offence of one judgment came upon all men to condemnation; even so by the righteousness of one the free gift came upon all men unto justification of life. (Romans 5:17–18)

In case you didn't get it, the Bible tells us that we had nothing to do with becoming the spiritually messed up people we are. It's part of being in that long line of *Homo sapiens* that traces its lineage all the way back to the biblical couple that got humanity going. The flip side of what the Bible is telling us is that we have nothing to do with becoming acceptable to God! What needed to be done was done for us on the cross by Jesus.

Please don't ask me to explain how all of this works, but this is what you've got to believe: When Jesus died on the cross, all the sin in your life was absorbed into His personhood, and you are freed of sin and its consequences because of that! You don't deserve what He did for you and, in all probability, you haven't shown much gratitude for what He did since you found out about it. But it's a done deal! The Bible says, "For he hath made him to be sin for us, who knew no sin; that we might be made the righteousness of God in him" (2 Corinthians 5:21).

We need to stop and reflect on all of this in the face of death. *Objectively,* we ought to just keep telling ourselves over and over again, "I don't have anything to worry about. Jesus took care of everything that would have made me unacceptable to God and barred me from eternal life." As the Bible says, "There is therefore now no condemnation to them which are in Christ Jesus, who walk not after the flesh, but after the Spirit" (Romans 8:1).

Subjectively, you ought to be allowing Jesus, who is an invisible presence resting on every inch of your skin, to penetrate your mind, heart, and soul. When you face death, Jesus will be there, waiting for you, longing for you to shut out the world and yield to the invasion of His Spirit. As you do that, you will sense His loving Spirit flowing into you, even as the depressing fears that come with dying are driven out. "There is no fear in love; but perfect love casteth out fear: because fear hath torment. He that feareth is not made perfect in love" (1 John 4:18).

You need to take time to think about what Jesus did *for* you on the cross, but you also must take time to let His Spirit do something *to* you now. You must go off by yourself. Shut the door of your room (Matthew 6:6). Sit still and ask God to help you feel Jesus penetrating your psyche. In the words of that old gospel hymn, you must "take time to be holy." Let Jesus happen to you in the stillness! In all of this, His Spirit will work on your state of consciousness and give you the assurance you long for in the face of death. "The Spirit itself beareth witness with our spirit, that we are the children of God: And if children, then heirs; heirs of God, and joint-heirs with Christ; if so be that we suffer with him, that we may be also glorified together" (Romans 8:16–17).

There is something else that has to be settled in the face of death if you are going to be able to die with what the saints have called "the peace that passeth understanding." You have to be freed from the burden of guilt that goes with remembering how you have hurt others. Even if you are able to sense a freedom from guilt and an assurance that you really are a child of God bound for glory, you cannot help but be deeply troubled by all the anguish and pain your sins have brought into the lives of others.

Perhaps you're a woman who, in loneliness and neglect, found affection in the arms of a man other than your husband, and you believe your sin has had ruinous effects not only on your husband, but in the lives of your children.

Or maybe you're a man who left your wife and children to go off with another woman, and you know that the wounds you inflicted on them are still open and have meant a lifetime of suffering for them.

You may fear death because you have lived a lie. You got where you are because people don't know the real story about you, and you fear that in the next life those you deceived will learn the truth.

Samuel Taylor Coleridge, in *The Rhyme of the Ancient Mariner*, declared that "a deed done in time is irrevocable." He told us that once an evil thing is done, its effects cannot be undone, and that the guilt that comes with the evil goes on forever. *Coleridge was wrong!*

There are two reasons to reject the despair defined by Coleridge. The first is the good news that God can undo the consequences of the evil that we have done. That is the meaning of the often abused verse, Romans 8:28: "And we know that all things work together for good to them that love God, to them who are the called according to his purpose."

This verse does *not* tell us that God causes everything that happens. He certainly is not the author of the sins we commit (James 1:14). What Romans 8:28 does mean is that in the *midst* of all the good and evil that goes on in our lives and in the lives of those with whom we are involved, God is at work figuring out how to make things good for those who trust Him with their lives.

Thousands of years ago there was a young man named Joseph (Genesis 37) whose brothers did him dirty in a horrible way. At first, they threw him into a deep pit and planned to leave him to die. But when they saw a caravan passing by on its way to Egypt, they figured they could make some money by selling off their brother to the leaders of the caravan to be a slave. The woes of Joseph are well known to those who know the Bible, but so are the triumphs of Joseph. Against seemingly insurmountable odds, Joseph overcame his adversities while in Egypt and rose to be the king's prime minister.

Years later, Joseph's brothers came to Egypt because a famine had brought them to the verge of starvation. They had heard of the wise prime minister of the country who had made sure that ample food supplies were stored in the king's granaries to meet just such an emergency. And so they came to ask the prime minister to share some food with their family, not knowing that the wise and spectacular prime minister was none other than the brother they had wronged.

After some painful theatrics, Joseph revealed his identity to his brothers. They shuddered at the thought of what Joseph would do to them, but Joseph comforted his brothers with some words that offer hope to all of us who repent of our evil: "But as for you, ye thought evil against me; but God meant it unto good, to bring to pass, as it is this day, to save much people alive" (Genesis 50:20).

Leslie Weatherhead, in a brilliant little essay entitled *The Will of God*, helps to put what I am trying to say here in a most logical form. He contends that, first of all, there is *God's intentional will*. Weatherhead means that before the world began God meant for there to be no evil in the world at all. He wanted goodness to reign and love, joy, and peace to be evident everywhere and in everything. But we foolish people rejected what God planned for us. We came up with our own plans for life, and they were disastrous.

The good news is that God didn't give up on us, even though He had every right to, because that was what we deserved. Instead, God established what Weatherhead called the *circumstantial will of God,* meaning that God goes to work in the midst of the messes we create. God devises a plan to take the evil actions and the troublesome circumstances we have generated and weaves them into an outcome that works out for good for all involved. I'm not sure about the details of how all this works, but by faith I leave the world I help mess up in God's hands. I have to believe that God not only can undo the consequences of the evil for which I am responsible, but that He can turn the evil into accomplishing some good. The death and resurrection of Christ is all the evidence I need to believe that He can. After all, were there ever such evil plans and actions as those which were carried out against our Lord on that tragic Friday when they nailed Him to the cross? Yet God took the evil of Judas, the high priests of the Temple, Herod, Pilate, and that bloodthirsty mob and turned it into the greatest blessing of all time. There is just no telling what God can do when He takes the evil that we commit and uses it to do good.

Weatherhead completes his essay by telling us about the *ultimate will of God* and the end of history when evil will be finally and absolutely defeated. His will shall be done on earth as it is in heaven. The miraculous reality is that God will ultimately make everything new (Revelation 21:5) and right.

Finally, as we face death we should find comfort in the declaration that God, by His grace, forgives and delivers us from all that would bar us from the joys of heaven. He not only undoes the consequences of the evil that has marked our lives, but God also *forgets* that we ever sinned in the first place (Isaiah 43:25). Because of God's work in our lives, on that great day when we are presented to the Father, we will be introduced as faultless. The Book of Jude affirms this truth: "Now unto him that is able to keep you from falling, and to present you faultless before the presence of his glory with exceeding joy" (Jude 24). I can just imagine Jesus saying, "Father! I want you to meet my friend

Tony . . . the perfect one!" And that is just what God will do for everyone who trusts in God on the other side of the great divide.

In light of all this good news about how those who understand and live out the gospel can face the last enemy, we can more fully understand why Jesus said what He did, in what many consider to be the most comforting passage of Scripture in the face of death:

> Let not your heart be troubled: ye believe in God, believe also in me. In my Father's house are many mansions: if it were not so, I would have told you. I go to prepare a place for you. And if I go and prepare a place for you, I will come again, and receive you unto myself; that where I am, there ye may be also. And whither I go ye know, and the way ye know. (John 14:1–4)

PART TWO

When It Comes

to Spiritual Growth

How to Talk about Prayer without

Saying Things That Make God Look Bad

I do it every morning, but I don't have it figured out yet. The more I'm blessed by it, the less I understand just what it is. The more God fails to give me what I desperately beg for, the more assurance I have that God understands me, suffers with me, and will carry me through. Of course, I'm talking about my prayer life.

It never made sense to me to believe that I had to tell God in prayer what I was sure God already knew. For instance, I cannot imagine when I pray, "Dear God, Sister Mary is sick and in the hospital," that God is up there in heaven saying, "Whoa! I did not know that! Which hospital?" The God of the Bible "knows what we need before we even ask" (Matthew 6:8).

Nevertheless, I regularly spend time telling God what God already knows. I do it not only because the Bible tells me to do it (Philippians 4:6), but because I am driven to it, especially in times of desperation. I do it because prayer stabilizes me in times of trouble, comforts me when I hurt, encourages me when I am about to go a-wobbling, and keeps me alive when I think I'm going to die. When my cynical friends chide me and say, "You use prayer as a crutch, Campolo, because you don't feel strong enough to face up to what your life is all about," I can only answer, "Of course!" Those who believe that they are self-sufficient are, on the one hand, people who don't think they need prayer, and on the other hand, people who are most deluded. To these cynics I can only say, "Your time will come. And when it does, the good news is that God will be there waiting and willing to carry you through the valley of the shadow of death." But before I go into all the good things that prayer *is* about, I want to cite a few things that prayer is not.

Prayer has gotten a bad name in many quarters because so many people make prayer into something selfish and stupid. For far too many of us, prayer is not far removed from being what it was for my boy when he was just seven years old. One night, just before going to bed, Bart came into the living room and said, "I'm going to bed. I'm going to be praying. Anybody want anything?"

First of all, prayer is not *magic.* Bronislav Malinowski, the great British anthropologist who studied various forms of religion crossculturally, differentiated magic from prayer in an almost classical manner. Magic, he contended, is an attempt to control supernatural powers so that people get what *they* want. Prayer, on the other hand, is a process wherein people spiritually *surrender* so that they might become instruments through whom the supernatural powers can do *their* work.

Malinowski nailed it! And as I thought about his clear differentiation between magic and prayer, I wondered how much of my own praying and the praying of most of the people in the church is not really prayer at all, but magic.

When we reduce prayer to magic, we trivialize God. A lady I know told me that her washing machine would not start one day, so she prayed, and God healed her washing machine. I don't want to join the army of cynics out there, but I do have some questions to ask about a God Who heals washing machines but doesn't give healing to a godly single mother I know who only wants to be cured from cancer so that her three small children will not be left alone in the world. Do we have a God who responds to a pious-talking lady who doesn't want to spend a few bucks on a repair person for her washing machine, but ignores the desperate pleas of a loving mother on behalf of her children?

In the case of that dying mother, somebody out there will probably put on one of those tight-lipped religious smiles and say, "Well, she probably didn't use the right words. Did she end her prayers with, 'In Jesus' name'? Because if she didn't, that's why her prayers weren't answered." It is that kind of *stuff* that gives God a bad name. Can you imagine God saying to that poor mother on Judgment Day, "I wanted to save your life, and your children would not have had to be placed in foster homes, but you didn't end your prayers with the right words." Such a god is far too small to be the God we find in the Bible and who was revealed in Jesus Christ.

When Jesus told us that, if we prayed in His name, He would give us what we asked for (John 14:13), He certainly was talking about something far deeper than the reciting of a religious formula. That kind of thing would reduce prayer to cheap magic. Instead, our Lord was telling us that, if our prayers are to be effective, we must grow into people who are so like Jesus that our prayers will be an expression of His concerns and love.

In the ancient world, a person's name had a deep significance that has been lost in our modern world. To those who lived in the ancient world in which Jesus lived, a person's name was meant to embody everything that the person was about. A name expressed a person's essential character and tapped into the spiritual core of the person's identity. So when Jesus told His disciples to pray in His name, He was telling them that if they would yield to His transforming power in their lives and let His mind be in them (Philippians 2:5), then their prayers would be like His. Such prayers are answered.

Several years ago, I was asked to lead a training seminar at a federal penitentiary. There was a group of men serving life sentences who had become Christians under the care of the prison chaplain, and they were anxious to learn how to share their faith with their fellow con-victs. This training seminar was designed to help them to that end. In the time that I spent with them, I heard an array of heartbreaking stories. One man had raped and murdered the sixteen-year-old girl who had lived next door to his home. His wife and children never wanted to see him again, in spite of the fact that he had repented and become a Christian.

Another man had a mother dying of cancer and longed to be at her bedside. Still another of the inmates talked about how his wife had taken up with another man while he had been locked up for the last dozen years. The painful stories went on and on.

At the end of that training seminar, there was a worship service designed to serve as a kind of graduation exercise. The special music for the service was provided by an effervescent young woman from a local church who just seemed to be overflowing with joy. However, before she did what she had been invited to do, she announced, "Before I sing, there are just a few words that I want to share with you. On my way over here, I was driving my new car. I was right behind a big truck that was carrying a load of stones. And a stone fell off of the truck. It hit the cement highway and bounced up and hit my windshield. That stone put a nick in my windshield. When I got out of my car, I was feeling so bad. So I went over to the side of the car, put my finger on the nick, and prayed, 'God! You know how unhappy this nick on my windshield is making me. Please heal it!' And would you believe that when I lifted my finger the windshield was healed!"

With one voice the twenty men sitting there on folded chairs shouted back, "No!"

I suppose that one of the advantages of being in prison for life is that you don't have to play social games. I mean, what more can they do to you? As I listened to all of those men, it was hard for me to keep a straight face. I have to admit that I got some pleasure out of their answer. What they did not need to hear was talk about some God who would heal windshields but would not do a thing in response to the urgent needs of their own lives. That young woman had reduced prayer to magic, and those men would have none of it. *Good for them*, I thought to myself.

The so-called *prosperity theologies* that I often hear articulated on Christian radio and Christian television networks try to sell this kind of magic in the name of authentic prayer. And, to add insult to injury, some of these prosperity preachers have the audacity to suggest that their listeners' prayers will be answered if they will just send in some money to keep *them* on the air. The Book of Acts has some strong words for those who would commercialize the work of the Holy Spirit.

And when Simon saw that through laying on of the apostles' hands the Holy Ghost was given, he offered them money, Saying, Give me also this power, that on whomsoever I lay hands, he may receive the Holy Ghost. But Peter said unto him, Thy money perish with thee, because thou hast thought that the gift of God may be purchased with money. Thou hast neither part nor lot in this matter: for thy heart is not right in the sight of God. (Acts 8:18–21)

The second thing that prayer is not, is that it is not something that works if you are extra good or extra spiritual. Some people seem to think that there are some spiritual giants out there and that when *they* pray, their prayers get answered. Following this kind of logic, the rest of us who don't get our prayers answered are deemed just not good enough to deserve God's help. The truth is that none of us deserves anything from God. The Bible says that there is none righteous, no, not one! (Romans 3:10). Even those who seem to be superspiritual have a righteousness that the Bible calls "filthy rags" (Isaiah 64:6). The good news of the gospel is that God loves us anyway. By grace, God reaches out to all of us, regardless of our shortcomings.

I am in no way arguing with the apostle James, who said that the prayers of someone who is faithful "availeth much" (James 5:16). I am just convinced that "the faithful" to which James is referring are those who lovingly live out the gospel and are ready to accept whatever happens with a peace that passes understanding (Philippians 4:7). The faithful are those who take no credit for what comes from prayer. *And most important, what their prayers availeth often has little to do with what we, in our shortsightedness, call answered prayer.*

I really get ticked off with those holier-than-thou people, who suggest that they get answers to prayer because they are more spiritual than others. For those arrogant members of the God Squad to suggest to that single mother dying of cancer that, if only she were as "wonderful" as they were, then healing would be automatic, sickened me. The end result was that these Joblike "comforters" only added guilt to the suffering of this dying mother who faced leaving her small children alone in the world.

Just recently I heard a man give a testimony about how he and all the men in his battle unit prayed just before they landed on the beaches of Normandy on D-Day. "God answered *our* prayers," he said, with an air of superiority. The overall suggestion was that those poor guys that got blown away by enemy fire just didn't pray right, or else they weren't on God's list of favorite people. It's no wonder God has such a bad name. It's no wonder that so many people don't believe in God, when those who go by God's name make God so unbelievable.

The Bible says, "Blessed are the poor in spirit" (Matthew 5:3). The poor in spirit, the Scripture claims, are the ones who *really* belong to the Kingdom of God. It is for those who acknowledge the things of the spirit (i.e., faith, spiritual depth, etc.) that the Kingdom of God is available. Those name-it-and-claim-it prosperity theology folks do not understand God's kingdom as well as those who know that they are losers when it comes to being properly spiritual. With prayer, as with everything else in our relationship with God, it is grace that provides the conditions for what we receive from the Lord. Grace is unmerited favor. It is getting what we don't deserve. It is the amazing gift from God (Ephesians 2:8).

Third, prayer is not something you can understand. It follows no logic. You cannot systematically predict how it will work. As Jesus said, "The wind bloweth where it listeth, and thou hearest the sound thereof, but canst not tell whence it cometh, and whither it goeth: so is every one that is born of the Spirit" (John 3:8).

Mother Teresa once said, "When I see God, He's got a lot of explaining to do!" It seems to many of us that God does not respond to those pleas that we think deserve grace and healing, yet sometimes performs miracles for those who, from our point of view, do not deserve any compensation from God, let alone a miracle. Another time, Mother Teresa said, "God, you would have a lot more friends if you treated the few that you do have a little better."

Like Mother Teresa, I can't figure out why God answers prayer for some people and does not for others, especially when those who don't get the desirable answers seem to be the most deserving. There is just no rhyme or reason, so far as I can figure out, as to *how* God chooses those for whom to perform miracles. Perhaps the best I can do is to believe that *sometimes* miracles are performed through prayer when they are absolutely essential to save a person's faith.

When I was a boy of thirteen, things got very tough for my family. I tried to be a good kid and help out the family in every way possible. While going to junior high school, I held down a couple of jobs at the same time. One of those jobs involved making deliveries on a bicycle for a neighborhood pharmacy. I had finished my deliveries one cold, rainy night. It was nearly midnight, and I was about five miles from home when the front tire of my bicycle blew out. I had worked so hard making deliveries to earn a few extra dollars to help my mother pay our bills. I had done everything I knew how to do to be a good boy, and I was worn out and tired beyond anyone's imagination. So when the tire blew out, I just sat down on the curb of the street and cried. I remember saying, "God! Everybody thinks you are good and kind. But if you really were good and kind, this would not be happening. I would not be out here stranded on this cold miserable night. You would help me."

I don't know how long I sat out there, but I eventually got up and began to push my disabled bike in the direction of home. With every step I cried, even as the driving rain soaked through my thin jacket, making me more and more cold and miserable. It was, I suppose, a testing of the faith of an exhausted and downhearted thirteen-year-old boy.

After going less than a block, I came upon a gasoline station that was closed. I have no idea why I did what I did then, because it made no sense at all. I went over to the air pump at the service station and tried to inflate the blown-out tire. First of all, the air pumps at service stations are turned off after hours. And second, even if by some miracle air had come out the nozzle of that airhose, there was no way that the blown-out tire could hold it. It turned out that I was wrong on both scores. Air *did* come out of that airhose, and the blown-out tire miraculously inflated. I jumped on my bike and pedaled home as quickly as I could.

When I got home, I lifted the bike onto our front porch and locked it. Then, as I was about to put the key into the lock on the front door of my house, I heard it. There was a sudden strong hissing sound, and in just a few seconds all the air in the blown-out tire was gone. It was as though God had understood my desperation and my doubts on that cold and rainy night and had recognized that the faith of a thirteen-year-old boy was at stake. Perhaps that miracle was the only thing that could have saved an exhausted, sad teenager from being lost to the Kingdom of God.

First Corinthians 10:13 reads, "There hath no temptation taken you but such as is common to man: but God is faithful, who will not suffer you to be tempted above that ye are able; but will with the temptation also make a way to escape, that ye may be able to bear it" (1 Corinthians 10:13). It just might be that miracles are what happen when faith is not strong enough to carry us through. Certainly, a miracle was needed to keep a boy who was trying to be good, and for whom things had become more than he could bear, from throwing up his hands and giving up on the whole Jesus thing. I just don't know. I have wondered if prayer, rather than being a reward for the faithful, might not be a means of saving those of us with little faith.

Having outlined some of the things prayer is *not*, it is important that I lay out what I, as a Christian, believe prayer really *is*. At the top of the list is the fact that *prayer changes people*. It is a proven reality that, even if prayer doesn't change *things*, it certainly does change those who pray. When circumstances seem to overwhelm us, praying can be the means for strengthening our faltering souls and enabling us to endure. How many times have you heard someone say, after having gone through a time of tragedy and loss, "I don't think I would have been able to make it without prayer." And when we ask, "What did prayer actually change?" we are told that it really didn't change anything, but rather provided a strengthening of the spirit that made it possible to endure the storm. Through prayer, we are able to establish a spiritual foundation that enables us to endure when the rains fall and the winds blow (Matthew 7:24–27).

Prayer also gives us the strength to accept that which is our lot in life, even when it seems that we are being called to endure the darts and arrows of outrageous fortune. Certainly, Jesus found that to be true for Him in the Garden of Gethsemane. In those torturous hours leading up to the crucifixion, He knew the horrors that were waiting for Him. He knew that, in just a little while, He would not only have to go through excruciating physical pain, but "He who knew no sin, would have to *become* sin for us all." Jesus knew that on the cross He would have to connect with every person in the past, the present, and the future and absorb out of them all the filth and corruption in their lives. He, who knew no sin and who was repulsed by sin, knew that on the cross He would have to *become* sin for our sakes. Our Lord would literally have to become every rapist, murderer, child molester, liar, blasphemer, and lustful adulterer of all time and history. The prospect undoubtedly sent chills and shudders through His body. The whole thing must have seemed more than He could bear. Yet, in the garden of prayer Jesus found it possible to accept His lot and say, "Not my will, but thine, be done" (Luke 22:42). In that agonizing time in Gethsemane, our Lord was able to struggle through the specter that lay before Him and emerge with the peace that passes all understanding.

It is in prayer that many of us find the ability to resign ourselves to the pain we must endure in this life. A friend of mine once struggled for days in the face of the painful reality that his daughter had been raped and strangled to death. He didn't know how he could go on living. Then one night in total spiritual, physical, and psychological exhaustion, he lay on his bed and cried, "Oh God, I just give up!" It was then that an indescribable peace overwhelmed him, and he thought he heard God say, "I've been waiting for you to say that!" In the resignation of the spirit in the context of prayer, there comes a soft still voice that speaks with groanings that cannot be uttered and says, "Peace, be still."

Beyond the peace, there is an even greater thing that comes through prayer—assurance. In prayer we gain the confidence that, in the midst of all that is happening, God is at work bringing about a good that we can never anticipate (Romans 8:28). If we feel God-forsaken (and there will be such times), prayer will drive away that despair. In prayer we experience the indescribable assurance of the Holy Spirit that all will be well. I love the verse that reads, "For ye have not received the spirit of bondage again to fear; but ye have received the Spirit of adoption, whereby we cry, Abba, Father. The Spirit itself beareth witness with our spirit, that we are the children of God" (Romans 8:15–16). But the best news of all comes from the same eighth chapter of Romans— the promise and confidence that all things *will* work together for an incomprehensible good. It's a promise that we know will be realized, because the Holy Spirit—that crucial third member of the Trinity— prays to the heavenly Father on our behalf, thus overcoming our own limitations in prayer.

> Likewise the Spirit also helpeth our infirmities: for we know not what we should pray for as we ought: but the Spirit itself maketh intercession for us with groanings which cannot be uttered. And he that searcheth the hearts knoweth what is the mind of the Spirit, because he maketh intercession for the saints according to the will of God. And we know that all things work together for good to them that love God, to them who are the called according to his purpose. (Romans 8:26–28)

Our prayers are immature. When we pray, our incredibly limited understanding and our shallow spirituality keep us from praying as we should. But we need not fret, because the Bible tells us that the Holy Spirit is always there lifting up the prayers that we *ought* to have prayed to the heavenly Father but were not able to pray. The Holy Spirit actually prays for us!

When I was seven years old, I wanted to be a cowboy. I had seen a Hop-Along Cassidy movie and was so impressed by Hop-Along's heroics that I was sure I wanted to be just like him. I asked my father if he would help me to become a cowboy, and he smiled and said, "Let's wait and see." I'm glad my father didn't give me what I thought I wanted at the age of seven. Suppose that I, at the age of seventeen, had asked my father about going to college and he had said, "College! You can't go to college! When you were seven, you said you wanted to be a cowboy. I went ahead and bought you a ranch in Texas with fifty head of cattle!"

I would have said, "How could you? Being a cowboy was the request of a kid who really didn't even know what life was all about."

Fortunately, because my father didn't give me what I, in my immaturity, had thought I wanted, he was later able to give me what I really needed. So it is when we pray to our Father. According to Romans 8:26, when we are finished praying, we will have prayed all wrong. But no sweat! When *we* finish praying, the Holy Spirit prays the prayer that we *should* have prayed and *would* have prayed, if only we were spiritually mature. It is as though, at the end of my prayer, the Holy Spirit turns to the Father and says, "Father, I know it was a stupid prayer that Tony prayed. *This* is the prayer that he should have prayed," and then goes on to pray on my behalf.

If that isn't comforting, I don't know what is. Even if I don't have some itinerant faith healer or some super-Christian praying for me, I do have an intercessor—the Holy Spirit. And with the Holy Spirit praying for me, I really do know that all things will work together for good (Romans 8:28).

How to Have a Devotional Life

without Becoming a Monk

If there's anything that Roman Catholics can teach Protestants, it is how to do devotions. They're experts at it. For more than a thousand years, Roman Catholics have had monks who wanted nothing more than to experience Christ, even as Paul did when he wrote, "That I may know him, and the power of his resurrection, and the fellowship of his sufferings, being made conformable unto his death" (Philippians 3:10).

The whole purpose of a devotional life is to grow into what Christ wants us to be. This means to be so much into Him, and to have Him so much into us, that we are transformed into the likeness of Christ. That is what the ancient monks were all about, and in the process, they endeavored to follow the paths to spirituality established by Christ Himself.

The Benedictine monks discovered the instrument for their devotional life in the Book of Psalms. Like Jesus, they learned to *pray* the Psalms, not just read them. And in the Psalms they found the words to express groanings too deep for their own mere words to express.

Jesus always resorted to the Psalms, especially when ordinary words would not do. It's not surprising to discover that, in the midst of His final prayers from the cross, Jesus prayed from the Psalms. Most biblical scholars are convinced that when He uttered the words, "My God, my God, why hast thou forsaken me?" He was not crying out in despair, nor was He declaring that His Father had forsaken Him, even as He took upon Himself the sins of the world. The truth is when Jesus hung on Calvary's tree, "God was *in* Christ, reconciling the world unto Himself" (2 Corinthians 5:19). At that crucial hour on the cross, Jesus was praying the Twenty-second Psalm. At a time before numbers were used to designate psalms, the first lines of psalms were used for that purpose. In citing the words, "My God, my God, why hast thou forsaken me?" Jesus let us all know the psalm He was praying. The significance of that Twenty-second Psalm in relationship to Jesus' death and resurrection is all too obvious, even to the casual reader. Here are some of the verses of Psalm Twenty-two:

> My God, my God, why hast thou forsaken me? why art thou so far from helping me, and from the words of my roaring? O my God, I cry in the daytime, but thou hearest not; and in the night season, and am not silent. But thou art holy, O thou that inhabitest the praises of Israel. Our fathers trusted in thee: they trusted, and thou didst deliver them. They cried unto thee, and were delivered: they trusted in thee, and were not confounded. But I am a worm, and no man; a reproach of men, and despised of the people. All they that see me laugh me to scorn: they shoot out the lip, they shake the head, saying, He trusted on the LORD that he would deliver him: let him deliver him, seeing he delighted in him.
>
> I am poured out like water, and all my bones are out of joint: my heart is like wax; it is melted in the midst of my bowels. My strength is dried up like a potsherd; and my tongue cleaveth to my jaws; and thou hast brought me into the dust of death. For dogs have compassed me: the assembly of the wicked have inclosed me: they pierced my hands and my feet. I may tell all my bones: they look and stare upon me. They part my garments among them, and cast lots upon my vesture. (Psalm 22:1–8, 14–18)

Not only does this psalm give specifics about what happened on that incredible day of our atonement (such as making direct reference to the Roman soldiers who cast lots for Jesus' robe, and to those who mocked Him), but more importantly, this psalm ends on a note of triumph. Despair is turned into victory in this psalm. And in praying this psalm, Jesus anticipated His own victory over the grave and the good news that we have been living with for almost two thousand years.

> For this corruptible must put on incorruption, and this mortal must put on immortality. So when this corruptible shall have put on incorruption, and this mortal shall have put on immortality, then shall be brought to pass the saying that is written, Death is swallowed up in victory. O death, where is they sting? O grave, where is thy victory? (1 Corinthians 15:53–55)

Jesus used Psalms as a prayer book. It is in following the example of our Lord that the Benedictine monks made praying the psalms a part of their spiritual discipline. What they learned was that Psalms covers the whole spectrum of human emotions and concerns and can give expressions to the deepest longings of the heart. That is why you should consider using Psalms in your personal devotional life. Whether you're looking for words to express that sense of ecstasy that accompanies those times when you are caught up in gratitude with the rest of God's creation (Psalm 148) or you are looking for ways to cry out to God to relieve depression (Psalms 42 and 43), you will find the help you need in this precious book.

For Jesus, Psalms was not the only biblical instrument and guide for His devotional life. It may have been from Isaiah that He learned of the need for quietude and stillness. "For thus saith the Lord God, the Holy One of Israel; In returning and rest shall ye be saved; in quietness and in confidence shall be your strength" (Isaiah 30:15).

We know that Jesus got up early in the morning, while it was still dark, and went off by Himself to have personal communion with His Father (Luke 6:12). Jesus practiced what He preached. Even as He told us that we should allow time to be alone with God, shutting out the world, so to speak, in order to give God a chance to mold us into what God wants us to be, Jesus did the same. I believe that what Jesus wants to happen to us in such early morning stillness is given expression in the prayerful hymn, "Spirit of the Living God, Fall Fresh on Me."

> Spirit of the Living God, Fall fresh on me.
> Spirit of the Living God, Fall fresh on me.
> Melt me, mold me, fill me, use me.
> Spirit of the Living God, Fall fresh on me.

Nowhere is the purpose of Jesus' quiet time better described than in the account of His praying in Gethsemane just prior to His crucifixion. This was a time when He must have experienced intensive inner turmoil. He, who knew no sin, had grown into the awareness that on the following day He would Himself become sin (1 Corinthians 5:21). He must have been painfully repulsed by what He knew was going to happen to Him at Calvary. Jesus knew that on the cross He would not only have to accept the punishment for humanity's sins; He knew that he would actually have to *become* what we are in our deepest hours of darkness. Oh, the agony that Jesus, the Sinless One, must have endured in the garden overlooking Jerusalem as He realized the full enormity of what was about to happen to Him. It is no wonder that beads of blood seeped like sweat through the pores on His forehead as He prayed on that horrendous night (Luke 22:44). The pressure was such that He struggled with the thought of backing away from the ordeal. The old hymn writer said it well when he wrote, "None of the ransomed ever knew, how deep were the waters crossed."

What kept Jesus on the course that had been set for Him from before the beginning of time was what happened to Him in the quietude of His time in Gethsemane. For Him, this time of stillness was a time of yielding and being prepared by His Father for the struggle with those awesome and ugly forces of darkness that were already closing in on Him. As His time of quiet yieldedness came to an end, Jesus was able to say, with ultimate resignation, "Not as I will, but as thou wilt" (Matthew 26:39).

As Jesus moved to leave the garden, He came upon His disciples sound asleep, and there was a painful sadness in His voice as He asked them, "Could ye not watch with me for one hour?" (Matthew 26:40). His sadness may have been for them as well as for Himself. They, too, were destined to endure temptation and trial in the hours that followed but, unlike Jesus, they were not prepared. For them, what might have been a time for spiritual regeneration had become another hour of sleeping. Jesus knew that, without a time for the renewal of their hearts and souls, they would not be ready for what was awaiting them. On the day that followed, Peter, who had vowed that under no circumstances would He ever betray His Lord, would do exactly that when questioned by a teenaged girl as he warmed himself by a fire. James and John, who had asked if they could share Jesus' power when He came into His kingdom by sitting on His right hand and on His left, would be nowhere to be found when He stood before Pilate and needed witnesses. Jesus was pained by the awareness of how unequipped and doomed to failure His dear friends were, because they had not taken the time to become yielded in stillness to the empowering that comes to those who wait patiently for the Lord.

Once Mother Teresa was asked, "When you pray, what do you say to God?"

She answered, "I don't say anything; I listen!"

Intrigued, the inquirer asked, "When you pray, what does God say to you?"

Mother Teresa's answer was, "He doesn't say anything. He listens!"

It is in such listening that we hear the soft still voice that, paradoxically, says nothing. But the stillness in such times of prayer moves more powerfully than an earthquake, a hurricane, or a raging forest fire. It has been said that the soul is like an atom, but more powerful than an atom bomb. If the soul can root itself in stillness for just a little while, the laser power of God's spirit will penetrate the electrons that keep warding it off, split the nucleus, and release the kind of power that can stagger our imaginations. For this to happen, in mind and heart, we must retire to "a secret place" where in quietude He can penetrate our personhood.

The Benedictine monks have allowed Jesus to teach them to pray. From the Benedictines we Protestants can not only learn much about prayer, we can also learn how to imitate Jesus and to use the Scriptures as a devotional book. We rationalistic theological types are all too prone to view the Scriptures only as a textbook from which to gain theological insights. But the devotional experts in the Benedictine monasteries have learned to read the Bible more like we would read a love letter. As they read Scriptures, they not only learn theological truth, but they also feel the emotions and experience the power that comes from the poetry of the words. As they read the Holy Writ, they are able to feel something coming to them from over and under and around the words. They know that there are such ineffable dimensions of spirituality in Scripture that those who *know* cannot *say*, and that those who *say* do not *know*. There is something that comes from meditating on Scripture that penetrates the psyche and permeates the soul in such a way that no tongue or pen can explain it.

Perhaps the most common mistake we are prone to make in our devotional reading of Scripture is to read it as though it were a textbook. There is a place for the scholarly examination of the Bible, but in times of personal devotion, the Bible becomes much more than a basic theological treatise for rabbis and seminary professors.

Sören Kierkegaard once said that reading the Bible is like coming to a street corner and waiting for the traffic to pass before crossing the street. And while you are waiting, you overhear the conversation of the two women in front of you. They are oblivious to your presence, but as they talk, you realize that the conversation is about you. And what they say reveals to you things you never suspected about yourself.

When I read the Bible in the power of the Holy Spirit, it's just like that. Though it was not written *to* me, I sense that it was written *for* me. I don't hear just what the Bible says to people in places long ago and far away. Rather, I feel as though I am *overhearing* messages that were meant just for me. In my *devotional* reading of Scripture, as distinct from my times of *study*, I feel my soul being opened up to glimpses of Truth that are incredibly personal.

I have always admired those who, in a given year, can read through the entire Bible. There is no doubt in my mind that this is a good way to get to know *the Book*. But I'm not sure it's the best way to get to know the Author. Rather than reading the Bible from cover to cover, perhaps it would be better to read through those parts of the Bible which are easiest to grasp and, because of their simplicity, most likely to nourish the life of a spiritual novice.

For me, the Gospel of Mark was a good place to begin. I think it is best for Christians to start with the story of Jesus, and Mark tells that story in its clearest form. Without doubt, it is the most uncomplicated of the Gospels and the easiest to understand. For instance, it has none of the complex and, to the uninitiated, seemingly convoluted profundities of the opening chapter of John. I could never figure out why some evangelists give new converts copies of the Gospel of John, instead of copies of the Gospel of Mark. It seems a little much to expect new Christians to start off with words like John's initial verses:

> In the beginning was the Word, and the Word was with God, and the Word was God. The same was in the beginning with God. All things were made by him; and without him was not any thing made that was made. In him was life; and the life was the light of men. And the light shineth in the darkness; and the darkness comprehendeth it not. (John 1:1–5)

Mark has a simpler way of telling the story. It has even been suggested that Mark wrote this Gospel specifically *for* new converts. There are those who say that Paul took Mark along on his first missionary journey simply to provide basic teaching for the new converts gained through his evangelism. Mark may have been the first minister of Christian education in history. There are some scholars who think that the early Christians may have been expected to memorize what is now the Gospel of Mark. Regardless of the historical evidence that may exist for this suggestion, allow me to suggest that Mark's Gospel is a good place for Christians to start their Bible reading as each one ventures forth on his or her spiritual journey.

It is best to read Mark *slowly*. Don't set goals for yourself like reading a chapter a day. Read until something strikes you in a special way. That will happen! We have the promise of Jesus on this. He told us before He ascended into heaven that He would send the Holy Spirit to be our teacher, and that the Spirit would lead us into all truth (John 14:26).

I am convinced that when I read the Scriptures the Holy Spirit is at work in my heart and mind, helping me to sense what God wants to share with me through what I read. It is the work of the Holy Spirit that makes the messages of Scripture so very personal to me. The Spirit is the great teacher who applies what I read to my daily experiences and needs. That is why I always try to read the Bible *after* my time of quietude with God. I believe that it's in the stillness that the Spirit prepares me for a personal word from the Word of God. And I am convinced that what has proven true for me will prove true for you too.

When you finish with Mark, you don't necessarily have to move on to another book of the Bible. Why not read Mark again? And then, perhaps, still another time. Become so familiar with the Book of Mark that the stories he tells are like family to you, and verses from the book become firmly etched in your mind. Know the book so well that throughout the day you can recall its words and reflect on its messages to you. It's when you know Scripture in this way that it will be available for recall and help, both in times of trouble and in times of quiet reflection. Eventually, you will move on to another part of the Bible, but don't do it until Mark has become a trusted friend.

The next book you might consider is the Epistle of James. For me, this has been an instruction guide that has proved most practical. In living out the Christian life, James's book gives me what I need when the rubber hits the road. The Epistle of James talks about how we ought to talk to one another and what we ought to say. It covers the dark side of our humanity, handling subjects like anger and greed. James challenges us to live out our faith in practical service to others. For our faith to be worth anything, it has to translate into feeding the hungry and speaking out for the oppressed, and that is a primary emphasis of this little letter. James, more than any other book, calls us to walk the walk of Christ, and tells us how necessary this is if we are going to make any claims to having Him as a presence in our lives.

If I were scheduling your Bible reading, I would next get you into Galatians. A Christian needs a personal theology, and Paul gives to the Church its richest source of theological truth (excepting, of course, the words of Jesus Himself). But theology, too, has to be made personal. So go through the same discipline and practice that I suggested for reading the Gospel of Mark. Let the Holy Spirit teach you. When it comes to reading Galatians, you might do well to carry on some study of this book *alongside* your devotional reading. Don't let the former replace the latter. But knowing the issues and concerns of Paul, and knowing something of how the verses of Galatians have been interpreted by the great thinkers of the Church, can prepare you to read the book with more understanding. Let me emphasize again, however, that what scholars can teach us is not to be compared with what the Holy Spirit can teach us, if we come prayerfully prepared to hear the Spirit as we read this epistle.

I have said so much about what we can learn from the Benedictine monks that you might be wondering why I don't just become one. That is because I believe that I, like most of us, have not been called to the vocation of the cloister. Protestants, like me, as the sociologist Max Weber once said, want to turn the whole world into a monastery. By that, he meant that with us there is little differentiation between the sacred and the secular. Spirituality, we Protestants believe, must be lived out in the everyday world. Therefore, we look to our devotional lives not as a realm that is separate from the real world of the marketplace, but rather as preparation to live in that real world. We want to have a good devotional life because we want to be more Christlike when we enter the highways and byways of life. We need a solid devotional life, because we want to become people whose lights so shine before others that they will experience in our time together something of the Jesus who has filled our lives in private.

Sometimes I am asked why I put such an emphasis on doing my devotions in the early morning. My students, who seem to make a great virtue out of spontaneity, ask me if I am being a bit rigid when I say devotions should always be in the morning. To them and to you I give the same response that I learned from a long-departed saint, "Why tune up your instrument at the end of the concert?"

The story is told of a student at a seminary who arrived at morning prayers too late to share in the service. As he rushed up the steps to the chapel, he ran into one of the professors coming down the steps. He exclaimed, "I suppose I missed the service!"

"Oh no!" answered his professor. "You missed the prayer time. The service is just about to begin."

That old professor had it right. Prayer time is not a time for escape *from* the world. Instead, it is a time to prepare for engagement *with* the world. I have nothing against monasteries, but for me, my devotional meditations are times to get ready to live and do ministry in the larger world beyond them. I want to follow Jesus into the real world He came to save and not embarrass God by hiding from it in the name of devotion.

How to Look Forward to Jesus' Return

without Becoming a Date-Setter

Someone asked Pope John what he would say to the Church today if he knew that the Second Coming of Christ was going to happen tomorrow.

With a wry smile and a twinkle in his eyes, the pope answered, "Look busy!"

Of course he was being facetious. But the question remains as to how we should live in light of the biblical declaration that, at any moment, a trumpet may sound and our Lord may return to bring this epoch of human history to an end. Almost two thousand years have passed since Jesus told His disciples to look for His return, and there is a temptation to join that chorus of skeptics who contend that those who yearn with hope for His return are guilty of wishful thinking and unwilling to face reality.

The great missionary Albert Schweitzer, in his classic essay *The Quest for the Historical Jesus,* suggests that, even though Jesus really believed what He was saying when He urged the apostles to expect His return in glory in the near future, He was somewhat deluded. Others argue that when Jesus promised He was coming back soon, He was not talking about a physical return in which He would set up a new social order. Instead, He was talking about a *spiritual* return in which He would be in us and among us, nurturing us and directing our lives. C. H. Dodd has given primary expression to this particular interpretation of the Second Coming, which he describes as "realized eschatology."

Most Christians, however, are more in tune with Billy Graham, who constantly tells his audiences that they should live in the expectancy of Christ's physical return to earth, after which He will set up His rule on earth, even as it presently exists in heaven. This is certainly the traditional belief of many Christians. It is regularly articulated in Sunday morning worship services around the world as believers recite the Apostle's Creed and say that the Jesus who ascended into heaven "will come again to judge the quick and the dead."

Whenever we start talking about the Second Coming of Christ, we can count on some *date-setters* popping up to give us their brilliant interpretation of how current events fulfill biblical prophecies, and then telling us that they have figured out exactly when, in the next little while, we should expect Jesus to return. In a used-book store, I recently came across a book by such a date-setter. It was entitled, *Why Jesus Will Return in 1974*. I sometimes say facetiously that when Jesus was asked about when we should expect His return, He said, "I don't know, you'll have to ask some American evangelist." There is some justification for my jesting, since Jesus Himself said, "But of that day and that hour knoweth no man, no, not the angels which are in heaven, neither the Son, but the Father. Take ye heed, watch and pray: for ye know not when the time is" (Mark 13:32–33).

On those grounds alone it seems right to be skeptical about those would-be prophets of the future who claim to know more than Jesus knew about all of this. Remember that Jesus said, "And then if any man shall say to you, Lo, here is Christ; or, lo, he is there; believe him not: For false Christs and false prophets shall rise, and shall shew signs and wonders, to seduce, if it were possible, even the elect. But take heed: behold, I have foretold you all things" (Mark 14:21–23). Those who object to this line of thinking point out that there are contemporary events specifically referred to in Scripture which point to the imminent return of Christ. However, they would do well to consider that Jesus told Christians in the first century that everything that had to be fulfilled prior to His return would be fulfilled before their generation would die. "Verily I say unto you, that this generation shall not pass, till all these things be done" (Mark 13:30).

That is why those in the early church were filled with wild anticipation as John, the disciple who lived the longest, grew older and older. Church historians tell us that many were convinced that Christ's return would occur before John died.

> Peter seeing him saith to Jesus, Lord, and what shall this man do? Jesus saith unto him, If I will that he tarry till I come, what is that to thee? follow thou me. Then went this saying abroad among the brethren, that that disciple should not die: yet Jesus said not unto him, He shall not die; but, If I will that he tarry till I come, what is that to thee? (John 21:22–23)

Jesus never said that He would return before John's death. Yet speculation, without support from the Lord or the Bible, has always been rampant among the date-setters for the Second Coming.

What particularly intrigues me is the way that those who want us to believe that they have the return of Jesus all figured out often cite the terrible things going on in our world as evidence that His coming is at hand. I can almost hear them mumbling, "Hallelujah" and "Thank you, Jesus" as they hear news of such things as rising crime rates, the increased incidence of sexual promiscuity, and the persecution of Christians in far-off countries. According to the way they think, all these deplorable happenings are empirical evidence that the end is near. Their theology suggests that things have to get so incredibly bad that Jesus will *have* to come back to put an end to all such evil. Thus, for them, the bad news is good news, because it is a sign that His kingdom is at hand.

When I was a young seminary student, I was invited to preach at a small rural church in New Jersey. After the service, a dear elderly woman invited me to join her for Sunday dinner. Being a poor student whose breakfast had consisted of Twinkees and a cup of coffee, I gladly accepted. She took me to her car—a brand-new Chrysler sedan—and drove me to her home. As we rode along in luxurious comfort, she started to talk about the Second Coming. I can still vividly remember her saying, "That was a good sermon you preached. Just the kind we need to hear in these last days."

When I asked her why she thought we were living in the last days, she quickly alluded to how we Christians were having to suffer. "It's all in the Book," she told me. "In the last days Christians will have to endure suffering and persecution."

I had a hard time figuring out how she related all of that to the two of us riding along in her luxurious, air-conditioned Chrysler.

When we got to her house, she sat me down in a special leather lounging chair which, at the press of a button, started to vibrate and give me a massage. She turned on her color television so I could watch my Philadelphia Eagles play their Sunday afternoon game while she went into the kitchen to get a wonderful chicken dinner ready to serve. As I sat there comfortably vibrating, watching my favorite team, and smelling the chicken that was being prepared, she continued with her litany about how she knew the Lord was about to return because of all the suffering that we were having to endure in these last days. I tried to keep a straight face through all of this, but inside I was thinking, *If this is the suffering of the last days, bring it on! Bring it on!*

As I look to the Scriptures to get some instruction about what to expect as the end of history (as we know it) draws near, I find particularly helpful one of the parables of Jesus:

> Another parable put he forth unto them, saying, The kingdom of heaven is likened unto a man which sowed good seed in his field: But while men slept, his enemy came and sowed tares among the wheat, and went his way. But when the blade was sprung up, and brought forth fruit, then appeared the tares also. So the servants of the householder came and said unto him, Sir, didst not thou sow good seed in thy field? from whence then hath it tares? He said unto them, An enemy hath done this. The servants said unto him, Wilt thou then that we go and gather them up? But he said, Nay; lest while ye gather up the tares, ye root up also the wheat with them. Let both grow together until the harvest: and in the time of harvest I will say to the

reapers, Gather ye together first the tares, and bind them in bundles to burn them: but gather the wheat into my barn. (Matthew 13:24–30)

In this parable, I believe that Jesus uses the wheat to mean the kingdom of God and lets us know that it has been growing toward fruition throughout human history. The tares stand for the kingdom of evil and all that goes with it, so evident all around us. Like the kingdom of God, the kingdom of evil is growing and flourishing as time moves us inexorably forward. Jesus lets us know that *both* kingdoms expand as history unfolds.

This parable suggests that the optimists who think that as God's kingdom grows the evil of this world will simply fade away had better think again. The pessimists, like the dear woman who invited me to dinner, are reminded by this parable that the people of God will not crawl out of history as a beaten-down and battered Body of believers, but as a triumphant Church waving its flags. There is a balance here. We social activists ought to have an optimism about what we can achieve in this world, even as we are also aware that the work of the Evil One will be healthy and strong, regardless of how hard we work to bring down his kingdom. This parable gives grounds for hope and keeps us from the defeatist pessimism that would have us believe that no progress is possible for those of us who work to change the world into what we believe God wants it to be.

All of this makes a strong case for my belief that, as we wait for the Lord's return, we should be committed to doing kingdom ministries. We should be at work feeding the hungry, building houses for the homeless, struggling to end wars and wipe out diseases. We ought to be striving to eliminate racism, sexism, homophobia, militarism, and economic oppression. But as we live out our calling in such efforts, we are warned that we cannot complete the job. What God achieves through our efforts prior to His Son's return must be viewed in the context of a world in which the evils of the demonic are everywhere, expanding in scope and terror. But as we move forward in our activism, we know that our labors are not in vain (1 Thessalonians 3:5) because the Bible tells us that "He who hath begun a good work in you will perform it until the day of Jesus Christ" (Philippians 1:6). On that day we will be made into all that we should be (all evil eliminated from our personalities). On that day the kingdoms of this world will be delivered from the works of the Evil One and transformed fully into the kingdom of our God. In this way, the promise of His return is grounds for us to attempt great things for God, and to expect great things from God.

On an even more personal level, it is also essential that we develop a balanced attitude toward the Second Coming. Reinhold Niebuhr, perhaps the foremost of the recent Christian philosophers of history, once said that Christians should live as though Christ might return within the day. And we ought to plan as though He might not return within our lifetime. That is excellent advice. Living in the belief that our time is limited because His return is imminent creates an urgency about life. We realize that our opportunities to do the good that we have been called to do are limited. Are there people whom we should visit? Are there family members to whom we should be reconciled? Are there neighbors with whom we ought to be sharing the gospel story? Let us get on with fulfilling these responsibilities today, because we may not have tomorrow.

There was a woman in one of the churches I pastored who, it seemed to me, was always picking on me. She seemed sure that her young pastor was unable to do anything just the way it should be done. One day she lectured me about the way I did funerals. She let me know, in no uncertain terms, that I had better make the gospel exceedingly clear in my funeral sermons, because she had friends and relatives who would be at her funeral who might never hear the gospel if they did not hear it at her funeral. I didn't mean to be offensive as I blurted out, "Mrs. Jones, don't blame *me* for that."

We all have responsibilities to carry out God's call to witness and to serve. And we had better get on with responding to that call right away. Whether it be death or the sound of the trumpet that heralds His coming, there *will* be an end to the time that we have available to address these urgent concerns.

I am perplexed by those who are forever voicing their hope that the Second Coming might occur right away. The biblical expression "Maranatha!" is a plea that His coming might come quickly. Personally, I have always been of the mind-set of those who hope that He does not come back for quite a while. I have loved ones who have not yet responded to the message of the gospel, and I want more time to reach them. There are many things that I have left undone, which I know I ought to have done; I want more time to make up for my past failures. Realizing that today might be the last day prior to His coming generates a sense of urgency within me. I have serious responsibilities and I *need* more time to do those things I ought to do.

The other emphasis made by Niebuhr is also of crucial importance. We must not use the possibility that Jesus may return any moment as an excuse for failing to do careful planning for the future, or not fulfilling the responsibilities that go with long-term commitments. The apostle Paul has some strong words for those who make excuses for not engaging in life's responsibilities by claiming that there is no point to it since the Lord will be returning any day now. It seems that there were those in the early church who saw no reason to take jobs and work since Christ's return was close at hand. These lazy people didn't plan their futures or do those things that would have shown concern about the ongoing Church, a future society, or the next generation. Paul says:

> For even when we were with you, this we commanded you, that if any would not work, neither should he eat. For we hear that there are some which walk among you disorderly, working not at all, but are busybodies. Now them that are such we command and exhort by our Lord Jesus Christ, that with quietness they work, and eat their own bread. (2 Thessalonians 3:10–12)

Every once in a while, a student of mine here at Eastern College comes into my office to tell me that he or she is dropping out of school because there is no point in preparing for the future since Jesus will be returning soon. For such a student, the words of Rienhold Niebuhr should be very meaningful. We all must address those concerns that are immediately at hand in terms of witnessing and serving. But at the same time, we should be taking those steps which will make it possible to live out a well-planned life of service for years to come. It is possible to do both, and Christians are called to do both in the face of all that we do not know about Christ's Second Coming.

How to Be Involved with Your Church

without Letting It Eat You Up

Some years ago when I was pastoring a church in suburban Phila-delphia, I received a note from a pastor in Georgia with the good news that one of his most faithful families was moving into my community. Since the members of this family were all solid Baptists, my pastor friend was sure that they would all join my church and greatly strengthen the ministries of my congregation. He told me that in his church in Georgia, the mother and father both had been loyal church members. The father had served on the Board of Deacons and had been the chairperson of a building committee that had just completed a new Christian education building at the cost of seven million dollars. The mother had served as an officer in the women's missionary society, as well as heading up the church nursery.

The children of this family had all been active members of the youth programs of the church and always could be counted on for support of special programs. Whether it was a carwash to raise money for a mission trip or a youth visitation evangelism program, the kids of this family had always been actively involved.

You can imagine the enthusiasm with which I rushed over to make a visit on this special family with the express purpose of inviting them to become a part of our church. My pastor friend in Georgia had kindly sent me their address and encouraged me to get right over there and *get them* before any of the other ministers in the neighborhood invited them into their churches. I was all excited over the prospects of what these outstanding Christians could do for us. Ours was a new congregation that needed a lot of help, and I wanted these good people to know that there was a warm welcome at the Upper Merion Baptist Church. I wanted them to know that we could really *use* them. (When you stop to think about it, the idea of *using* people doesn't have a very Christian ring to it.)

I have a vivid memory of what happened when I made that visit. I rang the doorbell, and when the father answered, I said, "Mr. Holly? I'm Tony Campolo, the pastor of Upper Merion Baptist Church. I understand you're Baptist, and I stopped by to invite you to be a part of our church. May I come in and talk to you about it?"

The look on his face was one of shock and fear. "How did you find us?" was his response.

"The pastor of your church in Georgia wrote and told me that you were moving into our community and that I should do my best to get you involved in the ministries of our church," I answered.

"Dear Lord!" he exclaimed. "Is there no escape? Is there no way we can have some peace and time to ourselves? Will there always be somebody out there waiting to *get us* and swallow us up into a hundred and one church programs?"

This man went on to explain how their church in Georgia had just about destroyed his family. Everyone in his family had been so involved in the activities of that church that they hardly ever saw each other. Every night of the week at least some of them had been involved in something going on at First Baptist. This busy schedule had not only kept them from maintaining any sense of togetherness; it also had left them all exhausted.

"This is a family that has been burned out by the church," he said. "We've all had enough, already. When my company had a job opportunity a thousand miles away, I took it, primarily to escape from that church down there. And now I find that they've traced my whereabouts and sent you to get me involved in the same kind of rat race again. Well, thanks! But no thanks."

I never got inside the house to make my planned visit. My protestations that our church would be different didn't have any convincing effect on that man. He politely, but firmly, ended the discussion and closed the door.

Undoubtedly, this is an extreme case. But all too often churches do hand out this same kind of treatment to their most loyal members. It is so easy to use guilt manipulation on sincere people and make them believe that if they give less than their all to the work of the Church, they are being unfaithful to Christ and not participating in His Great Commission (Matthew 28:19–20).

Christians are certainly called to be part of the Body of Christ (1 Corinthians 12), but at the same time they must defend themselves against the hyperactivism that too often goes with being a part of organized religion in America. It is to this end that I want to make some simple but crucial suggestions.

Before you can figure out the time and energy that you should invest in a church, you have to figure out what your own life is about. In short, you have to draw up a personal mission statement. Only if you know what you want to do with your life will you be able to figure out what kind of church you should join. Obviously, your church should be a body of believers that will affirm your personal life mission, and it should itself have a mission statement which is in harmony with your own commitments in life. Few things can be more frustrating than to be part of a church which is at odds with your own values and mission in life. If you are in such a situation, you will probably end up being a contentious person who will make everybody, including yourself, very unhappy.

Drawing up a personal mission statement isn't all that hard. Stephen P. Covey, in his book *Seven Habits of Highly Effective People*,[1] gives some helpful directions for doing this. What Covey suggests is that you imagine your own funeral. Imagine that your corpse is lying in an open casket and that all the important people in your life are on hand for the occasion. As they are seated, waiting for the funeral service to begin, they talk about you. Your spouse and children are present. Your business associates are there, as are your neighbors. Those who are your fellow church members are in attendance, along with the many friends you have made over the years.

Now, imagine that you, as an invisible spirit, are allowed to move among all of these significant others in your life and to listen to their conversations. What do you hope they are saying about you? What things do you hope they will remember about you? What is it that you hope they will view as the significant achievements of your life? What do you want your children to say about you as a parent? What kind of marriage partner do you want your spouse to say you were? How will those who knew you well define your Christian walk?

Covey suggests that you write these things down and then list them in the order of priority that you want them to have in your life. Carefully figure out how much time you must give to each of these concerns in order to have them realized. Covey even suggests that you have this prioritized list printed out in an attractive manner, framed, and hung in a place where you can regularly see it and be reminded of what your life is supposed to be about.

Figuring out what you want to accomplish in life, and the ways in which the Church can be a means for helping you achieve your goals, is a prerequisite to any kind of sane and effective management of your church involvement. Ask if your church has a clearly defined mission statement. All too often you will find that the people of a given congregation have never gotten together to figure out just what God is calling them to do and be, given the social situations in which they find themselves. Only if a church has established a clear sense of mission can you easily figure out if that church has commitments that fit in with where you want to go in your Christian life. In my own case, my personal mission in life is very much in harmony with what my church is about.

Mt. Carmel Baptist Church in Philadelphia used to be in a middle-class neighborhood with intact families caught up in the American dream. It is now in a very different kind of setting. The neighborhood has changed, and the church is now situated in the context of high levels of unemployment, drugs, street crime, children born out of wedlock, deteriorating housing, and families living on welfare. Of necessity, the mission of our church has had to change. Fortunately, we have had the kind of leadership that has helped us redefine our mission in the face of the challenges that are at our doorstep. Today our church is committed to meeting the needs of the poor and helping troubled teenagers find their way into positive, constructive lifestyles. And my own personal mission statement is very much in harmony with the mission of my church. I really want it to be said of me when I hang up my sneakers at the end of life that "Tony Campolo lived his life for the poor in the name of Christ, especially for poor children and teenagers." What my church is about, and what I am about, are very much on the same wavelength. I don't feel that we are in any way at cross-purposes.

The degree to which your *primary* mission in life is in harmony with what your church is committed to being and doing is of crucial importance in determining how much of yourself you should give to the ministries of your church. If, as a case in point, you see that your primary responsibility at a given time in your life is to rear children to become strong and healthy Christians, this should very much determine the kind of church to which you should belong. Don't be afraid to change churches, if the one you presently belong to is not effectively assisting and undergirding you in your mission. If your church doesn't see its mission as being primarily the nurturing of children and building of strong families, then you ought to realize that such a church is not going to do for you what you need it to do, if you are to live out your sense of calling and mission in life.

There are still other factors that you should consider before you determine how much of yourself you are going to give to ministry through your church (and constantly remember that the church is only one avenue through which you can live out your personal mission in life). You must also take a good look at how effectively your church *lives out* its declared mission. Is it efficient in the use of people's time and money, so that there are good results from what its members invest? Does it get things done, or is it so much into holding meetings to *talk* about doing things that it leaves little time and energy for actually getting ministry done? There has to be a bottom line for evaluating the effectiveness of a church. Granted, the bottom line for the church is vastly different than that prescribed for a business, but there still has to be a bottom line. You have to ask yourself if you will get a good enough *bang* for your investment of time and dollars to warrant what you will give to your church. And you have to weigh the answer to that question against whether or not you would achieve more good for God's kingdom through intensive involvement in some other church or, in some cases, through a parachurch organization.

The nineteenth-century Danish theologian, Sören Kierkegaard, tells a make-believe story about some people preparing a deep sea diver to make a dive. In the story, great attention is given to the expensive diving suit and helmet that had been purchased to undertake the task. Also, huge air pumps are secured so that the diver will have ample air to breathe once under the water. Scores of assistants scurry around attending to the hundred and one details that would go with putting a diver a mile down into the deep. The story goes on to describe the extensive training that the diver has had to undergo in order to prepare for this dive.

After all of these elaborate preparations, expenses, and efforts, the story comes to a ludicrous ending when we learn that all of this hoopla is simply to enable the diver to get into a bathtub and pull out the plug. Kierkegaard told this story to take a poke at the Church. From his point of view, the Church was an organization that produced very little considering all the money and human resources it consumed.

Certainly this is not a valid judgment of all churches but, unfortunately, it is a judgment that holds true for far too many of them. That's why it's a good idea to make sure that the church you choose will not dissipate your investments of time and money without giving you a sense that what you put into it reaped great benefits for the realization of your life mission. Make sure your church won't consume you with "busy" work. Too often churches can burn you out with committee meetings, wherein the people talk things to death without turning the talk into action. It has been said that God so loved the world that God didn't send a committee.

Once you choose a church, be proactive. Don't just wait around hoping that somebody will discover you, your talents, and your interests. Don't wait for somebody to ask you to participate in the particular ministry activity that you believe fits your mission statement.

Instead, go to the pastor or some other appropriate church leader, and let it be known that you would like to serve and exactly what you would like to do. Tell about your personal mission statement and how you want to live it out in the life of that church.

I know of a young man who had considerable skills and interest in youth ministry, but he never told the people in his new church that he very much wanted to be an advisor for the youth group. His former church was on the other side of the country, and word had not gotten to his new church about how effective he had been in relating to young people and how much experience he had in programming youth meetings. This particular young man spent a year doing little else for his church but painting the walls of the church basement with his Sunday school class and serving tables for church suppers. It's not that there is anything wrong with such activities, it's just that this particular church very much needed help with its youth program and was denied the opportunity to gain the services of a young man who could have met a real need. After more than a year of personal frustration, the young man left the church. Both he and the church had failed to take advantage of what would have been a perfect match between a gifted person and a ministry need. When the pastor of the church later found out about the young man's capability and desire to do youth work, he asked him why he had failed to let anybody in the church know of his ability and desire to do youth work. The young man's answer was, "I didn't want to toot my own horn. And besides, I wanted to show that I wasn't above servant ministry."

Humility is a good thing. But in this case, false humility had sad results. It is not good stewardship to conceal your gifts in the name of humility. This falls into the category of "hiding your light under a bushel." Jesus said, "Let your light so shine before men, that they may see your good works, and glorify your father which is in heaven" (Matthew 5:16).

SOME BASIC RULES TO KEEP YOU TURNED ON TO SERVICE

Now comes some important advice that is seldom followed: Define, and let it be known, how much time you will be giving weekly to any specific ministry you commit to doing. Also, give clear notice as to the number of months you are willing to serve in that ministry.

If you fail to define how much time you will give each week, the result may be a great deal of disappointment all the way around. Church leaders may end up disappointed in you because they feel that they didn't get what they expected. On the other hand, if you failed to communicate to them from the beginning how much of a weekly time investment you were willing to make, you will probably sense their disappointment in you and end up feeling unappreciated.

Perhaps the most successful volunteer program in the country is the Girl Scouts of America. The ability of the Girl Scouts to recruit people for leadership roles and to provide them with gratifying service experiences has become legendary. I learned from a group of key organizational advisors of the Girl Scout movement some of the principles that guide what they do and how they do it. Let me share them with you:

1. *Volunteer workers need a clear job definition.* Every volunteer should know exactly what will be required of him or her. Specific descriptions must be provided as to exactly *what* the volunteer will be expected to do each week, *how* it should be done, and the desired results.

2. *Each volunteer must know what help and resources are available.* When volunteers are left on their own and don't know where to turn for advice, they can easily be driven to give up because of a sense of inadequacy.

3. *The length of time that the volunteer is expected to serve should be carefully spelled out.* If the volunteer knows the specific date that his or her responsibilities will be completed, there will be a dramatic increase in the probability that he or she will *tough it out* during the difficult times. Volunteers are more willing to stay the course in what they are doing when they can see an end in sight.

Churches too often fail to address any of these concerns, and inexperienced volunteers for the ministries of the church are unlikely to ask for clarification on such matters. Churches are particularly reluctant to address the matter of a time limit on a particular service rendered. If somebody accepts the challenge of teaching a Sunday school class or leading a youth group, the church seldom sets any limits on his or her term of service. Hence, the unwary volunteer usually hangs on until the poor soul either burns out or dies. My own wife once told me that one reason she was glad she was having a baby was that it would give her a way to stop teaching her Sunday school class for a while. In most churches, if somebody takes on a job, it is assumed that this faithful servant will just keep on doing what needs to be done until death do that person and the job part.

What is sad about all of this is that even those people who do church work effectively too often give up their tasks with a sense of failure. Instead of ending a term of service with a feeling of accomplishment and *with all the flags waving,* they find themselves worn out and desperate to get out of what they've been doing. Too often people stay on in leadership roles long after they have lost enthusiasm for what they are doing, simply because they don't know how to get out of their responsibilities without feeling like losers. Consequently, the ministry suffers while these worn-out workers hang on until they reach the point at which they hate what they're doing so much they just quit and never want to get involved in church work again.

If a definite expiration date for a given service commitment is known by all concerned, everything works better. If a person knows exactly when he or she can leave the assigned task without anybody referring to him or her as a quitter, that is an encouragement to stay with it until the term of service ends. If, at that time, he or she wishes to enlist for another go at that particular ministry, it is usually easy to arrange, but under this system, the individual doesn't feel as though he or she is stuck with a given church job forever.

As you get involved in the work of the church, why not adopt these guidelines and urge the leaders of your church to consider them for every ministry opportunity that requires volunteers. If you can pull this off, you will be very much in control of your personal participation in the work of the church, and it will be less likely to get to you.

Furthermore, you will be helping your church to secure effective and happy service from those who volunteer to serve in ministry.

Another benefit derived from defining in advance the length of any term of service is that this enables the church to move people out of leadership and ministry roles when they prove to be ineffective. *Firing* people from volunteer ministry positions never works. Such action nearly always leaves an individual with hurt and bitter feelings and can even cause a church split. If there are set times for expiration of terms of service, ineffectual leaders can be moved out of what they are doing and encouraged into other ministries that are more suited for them. There is a task for everyone in the church, but not everyone in the church can do every task.

Most of all, protect your family from the tendency of all active church members to run off in a dozen different directions, totally overinvolved in church activities. Those churches that have something going every night of the week can be dangerous. The kids are out two nights for this. Dad is out a different night for that, and Mom doesn't know whether she's coming or going with all the demands made on her. It *is* possible for a church to be bad news for family solidarity. Churches that are supposed to be instruments of God for building family unity can destroy a family by getting its members so overcommitted that they have no time left to be committed to each other.

An important task of the Church is to bless and build us up emotionally and spiritually. If, instead, we find that our involvement with the Church is hurting us, then it's time to raise some questions. The Church belongs to you and me. We *are* the Church. We must demand of the Church what Christ created it to do. We must make it into a body of believers that nurtures each of its members into the fullness of the stature of Christ. Only then will the Church be empowered to live out Christ's mission in the world.

How to Figure Out the Will of God

without Hearing Voices from Heaven

When I was on the speaking circuit for youth retreats, I could count on it happening every Saturday night. There would be a campfire service. Thirty to forty kids would gather around, sing gospel choruses, and give testimonies. Generally after fifty verses of "Kumbaya, My Lord," a youth leader would give a somber talk on discipleship, and then the kids would really get into a decision-making mode. There would be "weeping and gnashing of teeth," and then the commitment time would follow.

You can poke fun at these campfire meetings and call them sentimental orgies or whatever, but the truth of the matter is that life-changing things happen at these times. Informal research will bear out the truth of what I say. While making small talk with groups of ministers and missionaries that I meet from time to time, I often spring the question, "When and where did you commit your life to Christ?" I wish I had kept track of all the times that the answer was, "I made my decision at a youth retreat," or, "I gave myself to Christ at a campfire service." These emotionally charged campfire meetings can really do a job on kids. When they finish wiping away all the sentimental tears, there are, more times than one might suspect, some significant decisions made that have lasting consequences.

If you ever have been through one of these campfire mountaintop experiences, you can almost predict that the youth leader will end his or her inspirational talk by asking, "How many of you are ready to commit yourselves to Christ—all the way? How many of you are willing to lay it all on the line for the Lord? How many of you are willing to say tonight that you'll go wherever He wants you to go, and that you'll do what He wants you to do? How many of you are willing to step forward and boldly declare before everyone here that you will endeavor to do God's will for the rest of your life?"

You've got to be impressed with the responses that follow. Kids step forward and, with undeniable sincerity, make it known that they are willing, ready, and able to carry out the will of God. Emotionally they are into this *commitment thing* 100 percent. But afterward there is an element of ambiguity that creeps in, because they face a great deal of difficulty trying to figure out just what it all means and what is involved. They are *willing* with all of their hearts to do God's will, but in most instances, they haven't a clue as to what that specifically means in their lives. And when they ask their youth leaders or the pastors of their home churches about how they might discover God's will for their lives, they usually get evasive responses like, "Pray about it and the Lord will show you!" or "Be patient and wait! In due time it will all become clear."

The *waiting* response is often a *wasting* response. I've talked to too many young people on Christian college campuses and at summer Bible conferences who are doing little or nothing in the way of Christian service, because they are still waiting for the *great revelation* as to exactly what it is that the Lord wants them to do. (At least that's what they claim is the reason for their inactivity.) To be frank about my reactions to their claims, I often have the sense that, whether consciously or subconsciously, these young people are simply copping out. But by giving the *waiting* bit, they can make themselves appear to be spiritual while getting out of any obligations to take advantage of the opportunities presently available to them for serving Jesus. Jesus has already told them, via Scripture, to go into all the world and preach the gospel (Mark 16:15). I don't know what further marching orders they need. It seems to me that if they would be faithful in the *little* opportunities that are everywhere at hand, then they would be led to the *bigger* things that God wills for them to do with their lives (Matthew 25:21). I find that those who are waiting for the *great revelation from on high* before they attempt to do anything for God seldom accomplish much for the kingdom. On the other hand, people who are into redeeming the time (Ephesians 5:16) by getting on with whatever good for God they can do in the present end up being persons in whom we see great evidence of God's guiding hand.

Eastern College, where I teach, offers a well-developed Christian service program. Every student is encouraged to get involved in some kind of outreach to the many needy people who live in the greater Philadelphia area. There are opportunities to tutor disadvantaged urban kids in a variety of afterschool programs, to get involved in prison ministries, or to work with youth groups doing everything from Bible studies to sports programs. Nevertheless, I regularly encounter Christian students at Eastern who are not involved in any kind of ministry whatsoever because they "just don't feel led" to do so.

When I hear that kind of talk, I am reminded of the story of Jonathan recorded in 1 Samuel 13–14. We all know that David was a great warrior for the people of Israel, but not too many realize that Jonathan, the son of King Saul and David's best friend, was a heroic warrior in his own right. This particular episode in Jonathan's life comes at a time when the Philistines have gained the upper hand over the people of Israel, succeeding for the most part in disarming them. The Israelites have only two swords left. One belongs to the king, and the other is in the hands of his son, Jonathan. To add insult to injury, the Philistines are humiliating the people of Israel by taking up positions on a plateau from which they are "trash talking" the Israelites, keeping up a constant barrage of insults. In all probability, the Philistines are calling out the kinds of taunting barbs that street gangs have made all too common today, declaring loud and clear that they think the children of Israel are nothing but a bunch of "chickens."

The reactions of the Israelites are twofold. We read in the Scriptures that most of the soldiers do nothing. They are gathered, along with King Saul, around the high priest of Israel, who is wearing his *ephod*.

(According to the Old Testament scholars, the *ephod* was a special garment worn by the high priest of Israel that supposedly aided him when he was called upon to figure out God's will for the people.)

Can't you just see these guys gathered around "a pomegranate tree," as it says in Scripture, claiming that the only reason they haven't yet gone up onto the plateau to take on those Philistines is that they haven't yet gotten a definite "go ahead" from the Lord? Jonathan reacts quite differently. This brave warrior tells his swordbearer to join him in an assault on those loud mouths up on the plateau. Jonathan's swordbearer is understandably reluctant for just the two of them to take on that whole arrogant mob of Philistines, and he looks for some pious *out* by asking whether or not it's God's will for them to attack.

Jonathan's response is classic. He tells his swordbearer, "Let's go for it!" Then with a funny kind of Spock pragmatism, Jonathan says that if they prevail over the Philistines they will have all the evidence they need that they are in the will of God. Furthermore, he points out, if it's not the will of God, then they'll know, because they'll probably get killed.

The rest of the story is history. Those two brave guys climb up onto the plateau, go after the Philistines, and blow them away. The rest of the army is still down there under that pomegranate tree waiting for a definite sign from God. While they are "waiting for His leading," they hear a big commotion from up on the plateau, and they start asking what's going on. When they find that Jonathan and his swordbearer are missing, they figure out that the noise must be the two of them routing the Philistines. Suddenly, the soldiers get brave and charge up onto the plateau to join the battle and participate in a great victory.

I often use this story with young people because it helps me to make the point that there is something wonderful about those people who know what needs to be done, figure that with God's help they can do it, and then just *go for it*. I tell young men and women quite simply that, if they see a need and realize that they can meet that need without taking anything away from fulfilling godly obligations to which they are already committed, they should step up and go for it. "Unless there is something better at hand that you are already doing for God," I tell them, "do what you see that needs to be done for God."

Whenever I hear of a Christian copping out of some undertaking for God in order to wait to learn God's will for his or her life, I have to ask, "Where in the Bible does it tell you that God will reveal the divine plan for your whole life? It seems to me that it's just the opposite. The Bible lets us know that God leads us one step at a time." Then I go on to explain that this is the way God keeps us in a constructive and spiritually edifying state of dependency.

"There are two ways I could tell you how to get to my house," I tell them. "I could draw you a map, and you could use the map to figure out how to get to my house on your own. You might or might not get there, depending on how good a mapmaker I am and how good you are at reading maps. But better than giving you a map would be if I got in the car with you and guided you all the way. If I showed you every road to take and every turn to make as we rode along, you would get to my house without any trouble."

I then go on to explain that God directs our lives by being a constant guiding presence, rather than by giving us directions to follow by ourselves. We are not given a road map for the rest of our lives, because that would enable us to chart life's course without leaning on the Lord. Rather, as it says in John 16:13, Jesus sends the Holy Spirit to us with the promise that the Spirit will be a guiding presence in our lives.

For those who maintain a close relationship with Christ through a daily surrender to the Holy Spirit, there comes a sense of *oughtness*. I know this may seem a bit subjective at first, but as I will try to explain, there are ways of overcoming pure subjectivity and having the assurance that what you feel really *is* "His Spirit bearing witness with your spirit" (Romans 8:14–16). Many who nurture a right relationship with God through a consistent devotional life give testimony to the fact that they feel a sense of *oughtness* and affirmation when they are doing the will of God. Contrariwise, they claim to have an inner awareness of when they are *not* in the will of God. There are a couple of safeguards in all of this to protect us from confusing God's actual will with what we *feel* is God's will. These two safeguards are Scripture and Christian fellowship with close friends.

It's a foregone conclusion that God doesn't lead us in ways that run contrary to the clear teachings of Scripture, even though I once heard of a prominent preacher who told his congregation that he felt "led of the Lord" to leave his wife. He claimed that God was telling him to marry another woman in the church, because his wife was not interested in "the things of God." We can rightly conclude that such a "leading" is absurd when we read what the Bible has to say about marriage in general, and what it specifically says about those who are married to "unbelievers" (1 Corinthians 7). Of course, when it comes to interpreting Scripture, inevitably the question will be asked as to whether we are merely being subjective rather than discerning God's will for us. "After all," the cynic is prone to ask, "how do you know you're not reading into the Scriptures your own personal biases? Perhaps you are simply finding in Scripture that which confirms what you already believe."

In response to this disturbing question, I appeal first to Church tradition. I believe that in the process of interpreting what the Bible means, appealing to Church tradition can save us from errors of subjectivism. I know that this sounds a bit Roman Catholic for a Baptist like me, but Church tradition is one safeguard that can keep us from reading our own meanings into Scripture. The Bible has been around for a long time, and over the last two thousand years, deeply committed Christians have been at work figuring out what the Bible means. Over the centuries, from the reflections of these Christians, a consensus has emerged about most biblical teachings, and that consensus must be taken seriously. Most evangelical theologians would agree that the consensus of praying Christians down through the ages should be considered as the leading of the Holy Spirit. It is more than arrogant to claim that one's personal interpretation of Scripture should take precedence over such an historic, unified understanding of biblical teachings. Every one of us is expected to stand accountable to that great crowd of witnesses who, down through the history of the Church, has defined the basic meanings of Scriptures. Private interpretations of the Bible that stand in opposition to the way Scriptures have been traditionally understood represent what has rightfully been called The Protestant Heresy.

The second means for helping us to figure out the will of God is through membership in a support group of fellow Christians who share our faith and commitments. I constantly urge Christians to form such support groups. The Bible tells us that whenever two or three such fellow Christians are gathered together in God's name, the Spirit is in the midst of them (Matthew 18:20). Such a promise assures us that when Christian partners who love each other in the Lord come together regularly in a support group to seek God's leading, there will be a special sense of God's presence among them. When an individual has a support group like this, his or her concerns can be heard out, prayed about, and weighed. Over against the personal feelings of the individual will stand the collective wisdom of the group as to what is God's will for that person in a particular situation or time.

In my own life, when I had decisions to make wherein I desperately wanted to discern the will of God, I have followed this scenario, and I can personally testify that, for me, the results have been more than satisfactory.

In your quest to discover God's will, you should never be discouraged by the fact that you have not sought God's direction in the past. I regularly meet people who claim that it is too late for them to do God's will because, at an earlier time, when they should have followed God's leading, they failed to seek and yield to God's will.

I recently had a man in his sixties tell me that he wished he had heard the challenge to be a missionary forty years earlier. He explained that he could see now that God had wanted him to be a missionary back there and then. But he believed that, since he had not been in tune with God at that point in his life, he now had no choice but to acknowledge sadly that living out the life of service which God had planned for him was forever lost.

Hogwash! I am absolutely convinced that, at any point in life, a person can yield to Christ as Lord. I am also convinced that, at that point of surrender, God will enter into a new relationship with the person to construct a whole new plan for his or her life. I believe God takes whatever has happened in a person's life up to that point and says, "Let's see what we can do with the things in your past. I am the

God who can use even your tragedies and failures as the basis for ministry to others. Let Me take what you are, break you, and remold the components of your life in such a way that your flaws and failures become the clay from which a special instrument of My will is molded. I am the God who makes all things new (Revelation 21:5). I am the God who can achieve glorious things through the weaknesses and shortcomings of your life (2 Corinthians 12:9). I am the God for whom miracles are never impossible and the words 'too late' do not exist, as long as there is life."

The apostle Paul was not in the will of God as he sought to achieve salvation through good works. Yet who can deny that when he surrendered to Jesus, God took the scholarly achievements of Paul and used them as part of a new design for his life? And who can deny that Paul's prideful days of trying to earn his salvation through the study of the *Torah* were later to be used dramatically and effectively for reaching people with the gospel? God has a way of taking past life experiences— Paul's, yours, or mine—and finding ways to use them to accomplish for the kingdom things beyond what any of us could hope or think.

The great evangelist Billy Sunday was very much into the ways of the world before his conversion. But once he gave his life to Christ, God took his *earthy* experiences and used them to create Sunday's ability to relate to those whose past sins had made them feel unredeemable.

And who will deny that former gang members like Nicky Cruz and Tom Skinner were led to use experiences in their pre-Christian lives as launching pads for ministries to inner-city young people? Because of where they had been and what they had done when they were out of the will of God, they were able to relate to, understand, and witness to tough teenagers later on when they *were* in the will of God.

All of this is simply to say that, if you yield to God in the here and now, through the Holy Spirit a new plan will be constructed for the rest of your life. Regardless of how much time or how little time you have left in this world, God can make your life count for the kingdom. God's will for you will be determined, moment by moment, as you yield to the Holy Spirit and seek to be and do as the Spirit leads from this day onward. No wonder they call the message of God to us "good news."

PART THREE

When It Comes

to Thinking Through

What You Believe

How to Be a Theologian

without Being an Intellectual Snob

Recently, I was talking to a friend of mine about a tragedy on the campus of Pennsylvania State University. A psychologically disturbed young woman killed a lovely, bright coed who was preparing to graduate. She also wounded three other students. The deranged killer came to the campus one morning, sat down on a grassy knoll, read a newspaper for half an hour or so, unwrapped a cloth covering that was concealing a rifle, and proceeded to fire the gun at students she chose indiscriminately.

My friend's comment about all of this was, "I'm no theologian, but I'm sure that God must have had a purpose in all of this. I'm positive it all must be part of His great plan."

My response was, "You're wrong on both scores! First, you *are* a theologian. And secondly, I really don't believe that what happened at Penn State was in any way willed by God."

Everybody is a theologian. Some of us are good at developing a theology; others of us are not so good at it. Some of us go about the task of putting together a theology in a deliberate and careful fashion, while others of us come up with theologies that are confusing, because we pick up our ideas about God and about life in an unthinking, helter-skelter, slipshod manner. But whether our theologies are sophisticated and systematic, or incoherent and overly simplistic, we all have them.

Our theologies are nothing more than our attempts to express what we believe about what is ultimately important to us in life. On the surface, there is much about life that seems absurd, and each of us forms a theology in an attempt to create meaning out of that absurdity. We put our theologies together from what people have told us, from what we have read in the Bible, and from our reflections upon the experiences of our own lives.

Our theologies are important because they have a decisive effect on the way we handle the difficult events and circumstances in our lives. They determine how we deal with painful realities, such as a baby born with severe birth defects. They provide us with guidelines for living our lives. In the end, our theologies give us some comfort and meaning when we face our own inevitable "crossing of the bar" as our lives draw to an end.

Bad theologies can have devastating effects on people. When I was a young pastor, I visited a man who had stopped coming to church after his eight-year-old son had gone through an excruciating death from leukemia. I tried to tell him that he shouldn't give up believing in God because his precious son had been taken from him. I will never forget his reply. "Tony," he said, "you really don't understand me at all. I haven't stopped coming to church because I don't *believe* in God. I've stopped coming because I *hate* God."

This good and caring man had been victimized by a bad theology that made God the author of evil. Somewhere along the way, he had picked up the idea that God causes everything that happens and, therefore, is responsible for everything that happens. This brokenhearted father saw a God who would make an innocent eight-year-old boy go through indescribable agony as part of His "great plan," and he hated that God. He never considered the idea that there might be forces other than God at work in the world. He ignored what the Bible has to say about Satan and the fact that we live in a world that is fallen because of the disobedience of our first parents. His theology didn't allow room for the possibility that dark and evil forces sometimes have their way in this world, too often making the innocent their target.

I did my best to give this hurting man another theology. I tried to help him to see a loving God who is hard at work trying to undo the effects of the evil that so constantly impinges on our lives. I did my best to convince him that those who blame God for tragedies are wrong. I told him that those who had suggested that some sin in his own life had led God to punish him with his dear son's suffering were wrong, and that such persons dishonored God with their theologies. I tried to explain that such people are like Job's comforters, whose superficial explanations about why suffering had befallen that righteous man only made matters worse (Job, chapters 4, 8, 11). But try as I did, and in spite of the many people who prayed for him, this tortured soul never recovered from his bad theology, nor returned to the Church.

Theologies dramatically impact the ways we decide on some of the most crucial issues of our times. They guide us in everything from our beliefs about abortions to our ideas about what America should be doing about the needs of Third World countries. In the end, theologies determine how we view ourselves as well as the others around us. Bad theologies gave legitimization to those churches who supported Adolf Hitler, while good theologies can lead people to become like Mother Teresa.

Unfortunately, there are professional theologians who all too often lead us to wrongly conclude that theology is some esoteric discipline. Listening to them, one can easily conclude that creating a theology means spending a great deal of time and energy to come up with answers to questions that nobody seems to be asking. In reality, this is exactly what good theology is *not!* Good theology is about answering those pressing questions that are of ultimate concern in our everyday lives. Furthermore, good theologies are not necessarily complicated theories full of big words. Consider the fact that our Lord, the greatest theologian of all time, set His theology in simple, easy-to-understand stories that through the ages have yielded for all of humanity their profound truths.

THEOLOGY SHOULD BE AS SIMPLE AS POSSIBLE

Someone has described an imaginary scene in which the obtuse theologian, Paul Tillich, meets Jesus on the final day of our Lord's earthly life.

Jesus asks Tillich that crucial question that was asked of Peter at Cesarea Phillippi: "Whom do men say that I am?" Tillich answers, "Thou are the ontological ground of all being, the teleological basis for the categorical imperative of the transcendental unity of apperception!"

And Jesus asks, *"What?"*

The first requirement of any good theology is that you have to be able to understand it. We need simple answers to questions like these:

- What happens to me when I die?
- Why was I created?
- What do I do when tragedy strikes?
- How do I get rid of guilt?
- How can I learn to forgive?
- How can I learn to love?
- Am I worth being loved?

If we can't understand the answers to these crucial questions, the answers won't do us any good. That is why some inquiring men in ancient Israel once came to Jesus and pled with Him, "Tell us plainly."

The good news is that whether or not we can understand and express ultimate truths does not determine our salvation. Our relationship with God is not determined by how smart we are, but by how much we yield ourselves to Him in love. That means that someone whom the world considers stupid, but who is yielded to God in love, can have a better handle on the truth than the most brilliant member of the intelligentsia who is leaning on his or her own philosophical reflections. This is what Paul meant when he wrote in 1 Corinthians 118–28:

> For the preaching of the cross is to them that perish foolishness; but unto us which are saved it is the power of God. For it is written, I will destroy the wisdom of the wise, and will bring to nothing the understanding of the prudent, Where is the wise? where is the scribe? where is the disputer of this world? hath not God made foolish the wisdom of this world? For after that in the wisdom of God the world by wisdom knew not God, it pleased God by the foolishness of

preaching to save them that believe. For the Jews require a sign, and the Greeks seek after wisdom: But we preach Christ crucified, unto the Jews a stumbling block, and unto the Greeks foolishness; But unto them which are called, both Jews and Greeks, Christ the power of God, and the wisdom of God. Because the foolishness of God is wiser than men; and the weakness of God is stronger than men. For ye see your calling, brethren, how that not many wise men after the flesh, not many mighty, not many noble, are called: But God hath chosen the foolish things of the world to confound the wise; and God hath chosen the weak things of the world to confound the things which are mighty; And base things of the world, and things which are despised, hath God chosen, yea, and things which are not, to bring to nought things that are.

The spiritual revivals now sweeping through Latin America are evidence of this Pauline message. They began when small groups of Christians, meeting in what have come to be called "base communities," studied Scripture with no other teacher than the Holy Spirit. In their unsophisticated reflections, they came up with theological answers to the questions of their everyday lives that left professional theologians in a state of amazement. True theology is more the result of revelation from the Spirit teaching the reader what the Bible is saying about the problems and questions of our everyday lives, than it is the result of scholarship, as this world knows it. Even the most simple of us can develop a good theology. Jesus made this promise to His disciples almost two thousand years ago, and it still applies today: "But the Comforter, which is the Holy Ghost, whom the Father will send in my name, he shall teach you all things, and bring all things to your remembrance, whatsoever I have said unto you" (John 14:26).

THEOLOGY MUST BE BIBLICAL

As you do your theological thinking, keep it biblical. When people say that they believe in the authority of Scripture, like those in the

New Testament church at Berea, they will test out all theological ideas to see whether or not they can be harmonized with what the Bible teaches (Acts 7:11). It is not unfair to ask a person who presents a new doctrine or belief how it can be supported by Scripture. It never ceases to amaze me how few people have taken the time to study the Bible well enough to be able to support their beliefs and convictions with particular passages of Scripture. A primary reason Billy Graham preaches with such effectiveness is because he punctuates every doctrine that he articulates with the simple statement, "The Bible says. . . !"

The Bible says this about itself: "All scripture is given by inspiration of God, and is profitable for doctrine, for reproof, for correction, for instruction in righteousness"(2 Timothy 3:16). That passage declares the Bible to be the ultimate source of theology. All human-made theologies must answer to the infallible theology given to us in Scripture under the guidance and inspiration of the Holy Spirit. I believe that when the authors of the biblical texts sat down to write those books that we now define as the *canon*—the only books that should be considered holy scripture—God's Spirit was with them in a way unlike anything any other author in history has ever experienced. When we say that these writers were *inspired* by the Holy Spirit, we are saying that something miraculous was happening to them as they wrote. Shakespeare was inspired, as were Plato, Homer, Milton, Bunyon, and a host of other great literary figures and philosophers. But none of them ever had the kind of inspiration the writers of Scripture had when they wrote the books of the Bible.

When the authors of Scripture gave themselves over to the task of penning their works, God was uniquely guiding them, whether they knew it or not. What they wrote about what we should believe about God, humanity, history, and eternity was protected from any possibility of human error. When these writers wrote out the principles and defined the values prescribing and undergirding our personal and social ethical decisions, they did so in such a way that what they wrote would be universally applicable. What they wrote about right and wrong applied not only to what was happening there and then, within their cultures, but to *all* people, in all times, and in all situations.

THEOLOGY MUST BE CONTEXTUAL BUT NOT RELATIVIST

It's popular in some circles to claim that we should be cultural relativists and not try to make all the teachings of Scripture rule us in modern times. Going along with this suggestion is the idea that what was right or wrong when these ancient men wrote cannot be the norms for right and wrong in our modern society, because social conditions are vastly different nowadays. This may appear to be an enlightened way to think. But it is against just such an idea that the Bible asserts its unique claim to being inspired by the Holy Spirit. As scandalous as it may appear to the critics, those of us who view Scripture as divinely inspired are declaring loudly and clearly that the truths of the Bible apply to all peoples throughout human history. In fact, it's more than a claim. Over the centuries these writings have withstood the tests of time. Around the world, as the gospel has been spread to other cultures, it has demonstrated its unique capacity to set forth eternal truths that meet the needs of the peoples in those cultures.

Those who would attack this high view of the inspiration of Scripture are likely to point out that there are many things the Bible calls us to do that we, for the most part, ignore. For instance, the New Testament says that women ought never to cut their hair and that the wearing of rings (jewelry) ought not to be allowed (1 Timothy 2:9). Yet both have become common practices in the context of even the most conservative evangelical churches. Our critics hold up such examples as evidence that we don't really believe what we say about the Bible, and that in the end we are really *closet* cultural relativists.

What these critics don't understand is that there is a big difference between being cultural relativists and being what we call *contextualists*. Over the past century, modern missionaries have developed careful techniques for preaching the *principles* that lie at the base of biblical perspectives on social customs, in order to maximize their effectiveness as guiding principles for the indigenous peoples. Customs may vary, but principles remain the same.

For instance, when Paul wrote to one early church and told women not to cut their hair, it was not because there was some divine ordinance that made short hair for women a sin. Instead, it was because cut hair in that context was a way in which a woman sent out a message that she was available for sex. Paul, in giving this directive, was making a point that is universally binding—none of us, male or female, should dress or behave in any manner that signals to those around us that we are morally loose people. Thus, the principle declared in this scriptural passage must be *contextualized* to define what practices in a given society would communicate the same sexual meanings that cut hair or rings communicated in the ancient Hellenistic world.

CHECKS AGAINST DISTORTIONS

There is one more important thing that must be kept in mind when using Scripture as the touchstone against which to test a personal theology: The Bible can easily be distorted by the individual who reads it. Social backgrounds, political beliefs, individual hang-ups, and a variety of other subjective factors may all combine to lead a person to *read into* Scripture meanings that really aren't there. If there are no checks against this sort of thing, each of us may invent our own version of what the Bible says, regardless of how inspired the original writers might have been. Fortunately, there are ways to keep this from happening. There are checks!

Church Tradition. The Bible has been around for centuries, and down through the years, godly church people have struggled to interpret its meaning within the context of their own respective social situations. As we study what those departed saints had to say about the Bible, we often find that they speak with an amazingly singular voice. When this happens, we have to take what is said seriously and question our individual right to stand against this *church tradition.* Any individual theologies we might develop that contradict church tradition must be held as suspect. As a case in point, when the founder of the Jehovah's Witness religion comes up with biblical ideas that have been considered and consistently rejected by Christians down through the ages, we have to ask if it's not arrogant for him to suggest that he's right and nineteen hundred years of Christian thinking is wrong.

As we run "the race which is laid before us," we must be mindful that we do so surrounded by a "great cloud of witnesses" (Hebrews 8:12). In light of this fact, we must not impetuously allow ourselves to dream up personal interpretations of Scripture without patient regard to what has been said by those who have gone before us. There is a community of believers who down through the ages have interpreted the sacred narrative of Christianity, and they must not be ignored.

Support Groups. Since the time when Jesus chose Peter, James, and John to be His closest spiritual partners, His followers have found that establishing support groups has been an essential means of gaining the inner strength and sense of direction that they need in everyday life. But these groups have another important function when they keep us as individuals from developing beliefs and convictions that are at odds with what orthodox Christianity is all about.

Over the years, I have been a part of such a group that does its best to meet each week just to talk, exchange ideas about our faith, and pray. As I read the Bible day by day, I use it to guide me in developing theological answers to the questions of my life, and then I bring these answers to my support group and run them by my friends. They hear me out and let me know if they think I'm off base in what I am thinking, or if they think I'm on track with what Jesus would have me believe and do.

This may, at first, seem like a somewhat inconsequential means of checking subjective distortions of the gospel, but I believe it is supported by Scripture. Jesus made the promise that wherever two or three are gathered together in His name He would be in the midst of them (Matthew 18:20). This promise gives assurance that the Holy Sprit, who guides us to all truth (John 14:26), is especially at work whenever a small group gets together to seek His will and experience the shared ecstasy that can be a part of such times of fellowship in the

Spirit. A small support group can take on powerful significance in all aspects of the spiritual formation of its members. If personal interpretations of Scripture move you away from the essential message of the gospel, your support group can be a correcting influence.

THEOLOGY MUST BE HONEST

Finally, a personal theology must be honest. To the questions of life, it must offer answers which ring true within the innermost recesses of your heart, mind, and soul.

A little boy was once asked if he understood what it meant to have faith. His answer was, "Faith is believing what you know isn't true."

Faith cannot be like that. A theology that will work for you is a theology that is authentic. It isn't a set of worked-over phrases and worn-out platitudes that you picked up from the folk religions of others. Rather, it is a set of responses to life's crucial questions that you have worked out for yourself with fear and trembling (Philippians 2:12). If it isn't real for you personally, it will not survive the tests that all of us must face along life's way.

A woman in my church had picked up a commonly accepted version of what many people have called "the prosperity theology." Her theology included a too commonly accepted belief that, if she lived a good life, God would bless her and her family and "give her the desires of her heart." She had picked up interpretations of Psalm 37:4 from some televangelists, who had persuaded her that if she sent money to support their ministries as acts of faith, then God would reward her and her family with wealth, health, and success. She had been told that she was one of The King's Kids and that the King always gives His kids the riches of His kingdom.

This woman mouthed her theology in a way that made her intolerably pious. When others had misfortunes or financial setbacks, she let it be known that, if they had just been as faithful a Christian as she had been, things would have gone as well for them as they had for her. She gave testimonies about how the Lord had really blessed *her*, with all the emphasis and implications that such a declaration might have for

112

those who had not had life turn out so well for them. She was one of those women who sprinkled every other sentence with some mention of how the Lord was always giving her so much, and how God had been so extra good to her. As she talked about God and threw around phrases like, "Jehovah jirah!" it came across as a form of profanity. I hate profanity, but I have to admit that I prefer the street variety to the kind that drips from people's lips in the form of vain un-thought-out repetitious phrases meant to impress others with their own spiritual virtues.

Then one day it all came crashing down. One of her children was swallowed up by drugs and ended up supporting her habit as a prostitute. Her son came down with a high fever that rendered him brain damaged. In the midst of these horrendous troubles, her husband drifted away, and one day she found herself divorced and trying to live on small alimony checks. Her superficial prosperity theology did not allow for things like this to happen, and when they did, not only did her theology fall apart, but so did she.

As she sat crying in the pastor's study one lonely afternoon, she exclaimed, "God isn't supposed to let things like this happen!"

Our pastor took her hands, held them in his, looked her squarely in the eyes, and asked, "Did you honestly and truly believe in that prosperity theology of yours and the God that goes with it?"

After a long poignant pause, she looked away and slowly and quietly whispered, "Not really, I suppose." And with that simple statement, she began her comeback to emotional and spiritual wholeness. She had begun the process of separating what she honestly did believe from those paraded pieties that she had never really admitted to herself did not resonate with the Spirit of Truth. Never before had she allowed that soft still voice to contradict the superficial prosperity theology she had mouthed for so long and with such ease.

Your theology must be honest. If you haven't come up with answers to some of life's crucial questions, don't sweat it. Give it time. And even if you never do come up with the answers, it's better to say "I just don't know" than to mouth words that lack the ring of authentic truth. Plagiarism is bad enough when it's done by school kids trying to write term papers, but it can spell painful disaster for those who do it when putting together their theologies for life.

When Jesus was on trial, Pilate asked Him if He were really the King of the Jews. Jesus asked him, "sayest thou this thing of thyself, or did others tell it thee of me?" (John 18:34). Two thousand years later, the same Jesus confronts you. As you formulate conclusions about who He is and what He means in your struggles with life's haunting inquiries, He asks the same question, "Do you say this of yourself, or did another tell you?" Are you honest about what you say, or is your theology simply an array of half-truths you have picked up from others?

How to Think about God without Being

Brainwashed by Modern Philosophies

The scholars responsible for social commentary tell us that we are moving into a postmodern era. What they mean is that, in the years that lie ahead of us, science will no longer be king, nor will it be able to claim that its methodologies for evidence are the only criteria for truth. More and more, our modern society will come to believe that there are different kinds of truth, and that perhaps the most important of them don't readily lend themselves to the judgments of reason and empirical investigation.

We are learning anew what was affirmed long ago by the seventeenth century genius Blaise Pascal when he said, "The heart has reasons which reason can never know." This is because, in the coming era, our understanding of truth will no longer be limited to that one-dimensional thinking, which precludes any claim for serious consideration of transrational religious experience.

The explanations for the passing of modernity, with its allegiance to reason and empirical science, are varied. Perhaps the best explanation is simply that reason and science have failed us. They have failed to answer the most important questions of our lives. They have not solved our most pressing problems, and therefore, we have sent both science and reason to the back of the class.

The social philosopher Jeremy Rifkin offers us a scenario for the demise of modernity that I find very interesting. Rifkin argues that we are giving up on science because it has failed to provide us with a cure for cancer, just as the medieval people lost confidence in the Church when it failed to deliver them from the bubonic plagues.

In medieval times, the Church held sway over society; all ideas and discoveries had to pass religious tests before they were accepted by the general public. What the Church declared as unacceptable was squeezed out of the halls of academia. But the Church lost its absolute hold over the people of Europe, largely in response to the bubonic plagues. When the plagues hit Europe, people turned to the Church for help. The Church readily made promises that, if people would just rely on their faith, do homage to their religious institutions, and make offerings to God, they would be spared. The people heeded the advice of their clerics. They made *novenas*. They went on pilgrimages. They sacrificed their worldly goods in accord with the directives of their spiritual leaders. But the plagues hit them anyway.

When the horrors of the plagues eventually passed away, the Church's authority was left greatly diminished. The Church *seemed* to have survived the onslaught but, in reality, came out of the ordeal deeply wounded. It still elicited reverence, but people began to look elsewhere for answers to questions and solutions to their problems. That opened the door for reason and science, and the Renaissance and the Age of Reason were at hand.

Science today has become too haughty. Humble science has become *Scientism*. It has taken on a religious character and, in its own way, has become a religion. The devotees of science too often have made it the basis for determining, in absolute terms, what is true and what is false. That which does not yield to its methods of investigation is discarded as meaningless superstition or as having only aesthetic value.

This reign of reason and science as the ultimate arbiter of truth has been seriously challenged of late by another plague: cancer. This new plague seems everywhere evident among us. One out of three of us will be touched by it, and there seems to be a high likelihood that things will only get worse in the short run, if indeed they ever do get better. In the face of the threat of cancer, we called on science to help us. We were told by our research scientists that, if we just threw enough money their way, they would find a cure for the scourge. They led us to believe that, if we believed in them and did our obeisance, then they would find the cause of cancer and deliver us from this dreaded disease.

Not only did we hear them out, but for more than half of a century we gave them the best that we had. Yet, while there have been many advances and a lot of new treatments found, the gurus of the scientific world have yet to utter the words we long to hear: "We've found a cure for cancer!"

And when faced with the limitations of science, people increasingly turn elsewhere for help. There are many who are convinced that one of the main reasons for the incredible growth of Pentecostalism in America is that, now that the "experts" have declared that they have no cure for cancer, people are searching for some good news from faith healers.

As science has failed, panic-stricken people have turned, not only to the kinds of cures that they believe will come from faith in the work of the Holy Spirit, but also to New Age cures. Everything from tapping into the magical powers of crystals to the techniques of transcendental meditation are being tried. In desperation, they are looking outside the realms of reason and science.

Whatever the causes may be, science *has* lost its hammerlock on the public consciousness. There is a growing awareness that there may be another kind of truth that lies outside the canons of the logical empiricism that has long dominated our thinking. Talk about miracles is no longer laughed out of the courts of sophisticated discussion. The evidences of public acceptance of the miraculous are all around us. A television series on angels is a blockbuster on the Nielsen rating scale. Pollsters make it clear that religious skepticism is increasingly beating a hasty retreat. Those who run for public office know that it helps their public images if they declare themselves to be people of faith. Teen Challenge——a Pentecostal-based ministry to teenage drug addicts—has a cure rate that is more than triple that of any other treatment system presently in place, and its workers readily talk about casting out demons as part of the therapy they offer. It is easy to find people with Ph.D. degrees who unashamedly talk about living in the context of *spiritual warfare,* wherein they claim to be struggling against "the principalities and powers" of Satan. More of us than not believe in miracles that defy any kind of scientific explanation. To those scientific rationalists who claim that such things don't fit into their world-view, or *Weltanschauung* (as they call it), there is an increasingly common response that God is greater than their Weltanschauung. Many of us hold fast to the biblical claim that God is able to do abundantly more than any of us, with all of our scientific categories, could ever hope or think.

It is interesting to note that the demise of this postmodern era was anticipated by none other than the prince of atheism, Frederick Nietzsche. This philosopher, who called himself The Anti-Christ and coined the phrase "God is dead," was strong in his belief that rational approaches to understanding reality were bankrupt. The cold rationalisms, so common in the schools of the Hegelian thought that dominated German thinking in the nineteenth century, were, to Nietzsche, merely the reflections of those who lacked the passion to truly embrace life and taste its pleasures and pains. Nietzsche referred to these philosophers as being *Apollonian* in their approach to reality. And for him, Apollonian thinking was the deadly rational reflection on life of those who had lost the emotional capacity to live it. The Apollonian way of life, according to Nietzsche, was that which was advocated by Socrates and Plato, and then later adopted by Christian theologians. It was, in Nietzsche's opinion, an approach to life that would have us believe that truth can fit into the categories of logic.

Over and against the Apollonian way of life, Nietzsche held out what he claimed was a glorious alternative—the Dionysian way of life. The Dionysian, according to Nietzsche, was the lifestyle embraced by the ancient Greeks, before Socrates or Plato ever showed their faces in history. It was the way of life depicted by the poets and dramatists who wrote the Greek tragedies. It was the Greece of Sophocles and Homer (rather than the Greece of Plato and Socrates) that Nietzsche embraced. For him, our humanity is to be affirmed in passionate living rather than in emotionless reflection. Nietzsche found what he was looking for in the intensive hates and loves described by the pre-Socratic authors of Greek tragedies.

In my attempt to give you some idea as to what Nietzsche was getting at, consider with me a scene from the movie *Star Trek V, The Final Frontier.* (Philosophical gems have been gleaned from stranger places!)

In this film, the spaceship *Enterprise* is taken over by some invaders led by a Vulcan, who turns out to be Spock's half-brother. (You would think that, as often as the spaceship *Enterprise* has been taken over by aliens, they would put in some kind of alarm system!) As Spock confronts his half-brother Sybok, a conversation ensues which will shed some light on our discussion of postmodernism. Spock's half-brother reminds him of their childhood days and how they were the two brightest and best in their school. He goes on to remind Spock of the parting of their ways as each chose a different route to seek truth and the meaning to life. Sybok reminds his half-brother that Spock chose the way of reason, while he, himself, chose to find truth through his emotions.

Indeed, anyone who has ever watched the *Star Trek* series on television or viewed any of the *Star Trek* movies is well aware of Spock's absolute rationality. He seems to be the embodiment of what Nietzsche called the Apollonian approach to life as he calmly and tonelessly utters such statements as, "Captain, unless my calculations are mistaken, which is highly unlikely, in fourteen minutes and thirty-two seconds the spaceship *Enterprise* and all of its occupants will be atomized."

Captain Kirk goes ballistic and shouts, "Is that all you can say, Spock? We're all going to die, and all you can do is to tell us the facts without any feelings?"

Spock coolly answers, "I fail to see how emotions can in any way alter the equation."

In words that stand in stark contrast to the deadly emotionless thinking of Spock, Sybok declares, "Has it ever occurred to you, Spock, that truth cannot be approached by reason? Have you ever considered that you might have to *feel* your way there with love?"

Now there's a statement that deserves our reflections! Doesn't it get at the message that the apostle Paul endeavored to communicate when he wrote 1 Corinthians 1:25–29?

> Because the foolishness of God is wiser than men; and the weakness of God is stronger than men. For ye see your calling, brethren, how that not many wise men after the flesh, not many mighty, not many noble, are called: But God hath chosen the foolish things of the world to confound the wise; and God hath chosen the weak things of the world to confound the things which are mighty; And base things of the world, and things which are despised, hath God chosen, yea, and things which are not, to bring to nought things that are: That no flesh should glorify in his presence.

If rational thinking revealed the truths about spiritual things and brought us close to God, then the intellectually elite would be able to be better Christians than those whom the world calls *stupid*. In reality, we often find that it is those people who are labeled stupid by the world who seem to have a handle on real truth; often they are the ones who know God best. Knowledge of God is not so much determined by how deeply we can *think*, as it is determined by how deeply we can *love*. This means that a common laborer with an IQ of ninety who loves God passionately may know more about God than those scholars who are caught up in sophisticated theologies but lack that passionate love for God. This is difficult for intellectuals to swallow, because it strikes a death blow to their pride and reminds them that ultimately all their brilliance is no substitute for a heart on fire for God.

Nietzsche would not have lauded the unsophisticated Christian as I have done, but I do believe that he would have appreciated the intensive irrational bursts of passion and the zeal of such simple Christians. What Nietzsche reacted against most in the Christianity of his day, especially in the Christianity expressed by his Lutheran pastor father, was its fervorless worship, its insipid rationalized theology, and its bourgeois ethics. I often wonder if Nietzsche thought God was dead primarily because the Christianity with which he was familiar was so dead.

There are those who argue that Nietzsche was anti-intellectual in his rebellion against the Hegelian rationalism that dominated the culture in which he lived. I suppose that there is some validity to that accusation. In the final analysis, Nietzsche believed that the essence of our humanity lies not in our rational abilities but in our capacity to *feel* passionately with a range of emotions that transcend anything that it is possible for animals to experience.

Bill Gates, of computer fame, at one time stated that there is only a quantitative difference between a computer and a human being. Gates argued that it is only a matter of time before we will produce computers capable of the whole range of human experiences and emotions. It was against such "antihuman" thinking that Nietzsche was rebelling when he located the essence of our humanity in our ability to experience the agonies and ecstasies that go with living life with passionate awareness.

This kind of postmodern thinking should not frighten Christians, even though I have heard a host of sermons decrying postmodernism. On the one hand, there are those who worry that, in this rebellion against the concrete kind of thinking that went with the rationalistic theologies of the last century, we will be left with little more than subjective beliefs that rest solely upon emotions. But, on the other hand, this new approach to viewing reality may simply be a facing up to the *ways* in which we do theology, and it may expose some of our false claims of being absolutely objective.

Whenever students at the secular university where I used to teach asked me how I, as an educated man, could believe the Bible, I would simply assert, "Because I decided to!" That would always take them back a step or two. Then I would ask them, "Why *don't* you believe the Bible? Isn't it really because you have decided not to?"

In the end, I would argue, we all make our commitments to what we believe because of the irrational forces at work in each of our lives, and then *after* we do that, we construct some kind of rational substructure to support our irrationally grounded convictions. In short, we are all ideologists who construct rational arguments to support the beliefs that we already hold for reasons that transcend reason itself. Consider the fact that I, like most Christians, contend that faith is something I have as a gift of grace. I don't take credit for being a believer, because I'm convinced that I would never have come to faith in Christ had it not been for the Holy Spirit prompting me and leading me to Him. Indeed, I know that on that final day when I stand at the seat of judgment, I will not be able to take credit for being a believer, for He will say to me then, as He said to His disciples long ago, "Ye have not chosen me, but I have chosen you, and ordained you" (John 15:16).

To sum up what I have been saying, it was and is the work of the Holy Spirit, rather than my own rational and scientific thinking, that led me to faith in Christ. My faith is a gift of God. It is not some *work* that I did and in which I can boast. Paul once said, "In the end, I am saved only by His grace."

The truth is that, having become a Christian, I now go back and create arguments to intellectually validate my faith commitment. But, if I'm honest, I have to admit that my commitment came about because of promptings that were transrational. Those who are atheists do the same thing in reverse. Don't they, for reasons that are hardly rational and scientific, decide against God and then seek rational and scientific arguments to support their *a priori* convictions? Aren't they people who have their own convictions about what is true and false, and then go around looking for arguments to validate what they assert to be reality?

Anthony Flew, one of the premier logical positivist philosophers of this past century, constructed a make-believe story in which two men walking through a forest come to a clearing. The *believer* contends that there has been a gardener there, and he points to all the flowers to validate his claim. The *nonbeliever,* though, contends that there has been no gardener, and he points to all the weeds to validate his claim. The point of the story is that each of the men collected solid evidence to support his claim. But in analyzing what happened, we have to conclude that the evidence each man collected was chosen to support what he already believed before any evidence was even considered. The story clearly shows what is problematic for those who think that truth can be established on logical or empirical grounds. There is something beyond the empirical data that makes us into believers or nonbelievers in the gospel story, and that *something* is known in the heart before it is ever sustained by rational/scientific arguments of the mind.

When I was a kid, my Calvinistic pastor told me that I should never trust my emotions when it came to establishing the grounds for my Christian faith. He said that the important thing was that I had to believe what the Bible told me about salvation. But I wanted more than a passage of Scripture to assure me of my salvation. I wanted to *feel* God in the depths of my being. I am increasingly convinced that nothing less than *feeling* an explosive ecstasy of the Spirit within can give me the kind of assurance that satisfies my craving for spiritual certainty. This inward convincing feeling is exactly what is promised in Scripture as we read this: "For ye have not received the spirit of bondage again to fear; but ye have received the Spirit of adoption, whereby we cry, Abba, Father. The Spirit itself beareth witness with our spirit, that we are the children of God" (Romans 8:15–16).

It is this inner certainty that differentiates Charles Wesley from John Calvin. The former was postmodern, long before we talked about postmodernity, the latter was modern and had an epistemology that, in every way, belonged to the world of systematic logic and science. (What is more rational that Calvin's *Institutes?*) It is Wesley, rather than Calvin, who belongs to the *Zeitgeist* (the spirit) of our times.

From this present-day tirade against modernity, one can easily conclude that reasonable thinking and scientific proofs have little value. That is not the case. It is just that, in the emerging consciousness of postmodernism, reason and science have to assume a new humility. They must accept the role of *undergirding* convictions, rather than *determining* them. Reason and science must be called upon to support our convictions, and even allowed to call our convictions into question, when they don't make any sense in rational and scientific terms. It is just that reason and science no longer can be the basis for establishing what is true or false.

Personally, I like things better this way. When science and reason determined truth, we Christians were caught up in a constant struggle to achieve accommodation with the modern mind. Just when we got into some kind of a comfortable arrangement with what the scientists and the philosophers of the modern world were saying, so that we were not impossibly at odds with them, they would come up with new scientific discoveries and new rational categories of thinking. Then we would have to go through a painful period of reassessment and readjustment to bring our faith into harmony with their new thinking. Well, that day is coming to an end as we enter into this era of postmodernism. Scientific truth and human reason have been relativized and no longer have a corner on truth. Their new role is to help us to evaluate and substantiate what we believe. They are no longer the *source* of truth. Instead, they are called upon to help us make sense out of what we believe and to enable us to critique and develop what we believe into a theology and guide for everyday living. This is what Peter was telling us to do with reason and science when he wrote this: "But sanctify the Lord God in your hearts: and be ready always to give an answer to every man that asketh you a reason of the hope that is in you with meekness and fear" (1 Peter 3:15).

Many years ago our church youth group used to sing the old gospel song, "He Lives." The closing lines of that hymn are:

> You ask me how I know He lives?
> He lives—within my heart.

Strange as it may sound to rationalistic Calvinists, those lines will have more and more acceptance as people trust less and less in the pseudo claims to objective truth that have long held sway with those who trust in reason and science. In the emerging postmodern mindset, what is felt in the depths of our being will more and more be taken seriously.

There is the acknowledged danger that religious faith may be reduced to pure subjectivity, as was the case with the great nineteenth century theologian Frederick Schleiermacher. But on the other hand, it just may be that in the *Zeitgeist* of postmodernity, we will find authentic New Testament ground for faith. To that end, we may have to give new consideration to Paul Tillich, who found the essence of faith to be the *depth* awareness that one has touched "the ground of all being." The apostle Paul talked about faith in very postmodern terms when he said, "Now faith is the substance of things hoped for, the evidence of things not seen" (Hebrews 11:1).

Faith, for Paul, was not built on reason or science, but on truth that is not yet part of the world as we know it scientifically. Paul knew what we in the modern world have just begun to learn. Our acceptance, by faith, of this biblical truth set forth by Paul is our best guide into the kind of thinking that characterizes the postmodern world into which we are moving.

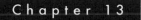

Chapter 13

How to Hold on to That Old-Time Religion without Letting Go of the Post-Modern World

I n 1966, Randy Johnson, a nephew of President Lyndon B. Johnson, was the quarterback for Oklahoma State University. By the experts' judgment, he proved to be a mediocre quarterback for a mediocre team. But mediocre or not, quarterbacks and teams at Oklahoma State could be lifted to legendary greatness if they could just beat their arch rival, the University of Oklahoma, at their annual meeting at the end of the season.

This particular year had not been a happy one for Randy or his team, and there seemed to be little hope for redemption as the clock was running out in their game with the University of Oklahoma. Oklahoma State was behind by six points. Rain was pouring down, but the mud-covered suits didn't look half as bad as the battered, despairing faces of the State players.

As a gesture of goodwill, the Oklahoma State coach put in all the seniors for the last play of the game so they could end their college football careers on the playing field. He told Randy, the despairing quarterback, to call whatever play he wanted, since they were almost eighty yards from the goal line and had *zilch* chance of scoring.

The team huddled, and to the surprise of his teammates, Randy called play 13. It was a trick play that had never been used before in a game. It had never been used for good reason—it had never worked in practice.

Well, the impossible happened! Play 13 worked! Oklahoma State scored! Randy Johnson's team won the game by one point. The fans went wild. As they carried Randy, the hero of the game, off the field, his coach called out to him, "Why in the world did you ever call play 13?"

Randy answered, "Well, we were in the huddle, and I looked over and saw old Harry with tears running down his cheeks. It was his last college game and we were losing. And I saw that big 8 on his chest. Then I looked over and saw Ralph. And tears were running down his cheeks too. And I saw that big 7 on his jersey. So, in honor of those two heartbroken seniors, I added 8 and 7 together and called play 13!"

"But, Randy," the coach shouted back, "8 and 7 don't add up to 13!"

Randy reflected for a moment and answered with a smirk, "You're right coach! And if I had been as smart as you are, we would have lost the game!"

I love that story because it reminds me that the correct answers are not always the right answers. Certainly, when it comes to matters of faith, sometimes reason and cleverness don't count for very much. Sometimes the right answers are answers that "just don't add up." Sometimes the neat, rational approach to things just won't lead us to the answers we need in the struggles of life.

AN INTRODUCTION TO POSTMODERN THINKING

If Jesus were to suddenly appear in the flesh on the campus of an Ivy League university, there is no way that He would back off from the intellectual challenges He would meet there. Jesus would seize opportunities to dialogue with modern-day professors in academia, even as He did with the rabbis in the Temple of Jerusalem two thousand years ago. He would not only deal with the questions posed by those steeped in the ways of modern intellectualism, He would also be prepared to take on the challenges that go with postmodernism, the most recent mind-set to invade college and university campuses. But what is postmodernism? We cannot answer the question as to how Jesus would respond to it unless we get some rudimentary feel for what postmodernism is all about.

Intellectuals on the Continent have long recognized that reason and science can lead us to only one kind of knowledge. They contend that there is another kind of truth that cannot be apprehended by reason and science alone. These European thinkers have given names to each of these two categories of knowledge and have determined the academic disciplines that fall into each of them. Those disciplines that rely on science and reason are called the *Naturwissenschaften* disciplines, and those that depend on intuition and revelation are referred to as the *Geistenwissenschaften* disciplines. It is in this latter kind of knowledge and truth that European intellectuals are now seeking answers to the problems posed by religion and philosophy.

I have always thought that their clear division of the two categories of knowledge saved the European thinkers from a lot of confusion. They realized that when it comes to trying to understand (*verstehen*) what is at the heart of religion and faith, reason and science can provide very little help. They have recognized that understanding the ultimate questions about life and death requires a different kind of thinking and reflecting than that in which rationalists engage. They are beyond those who cannot accept anything that transcends the empiricism of test-tube research. It is no wonder that existentialism— that approach to life's ultimate issues which rebels against a reasonable and scientific approach to things—came out of Europe, or that its seminal thinkers lived on the other side of the Atlantic. The pragmatism of Americans makes it difficult for them to buy into any kind of thinking that gives more credibility to feelings and faith than to cold hard facts.

I suppose the European approach to things is in my Italian blood, and for that reason, I have not been particularly impressed by the attacks on Christian beliefs from those who argue that Christianity just doesn't fit into the categories and framework of modern science. While some of my evangelical colleagues have worked overtime in the field of creationism, I have been concerned with other things.

I have never given much ground to those who intellectualize their approach to religious truth. Like Randy Johnson, I feel like saying to them that, if we were all as smart as they claim to be, we would end up losing in the game of life. This is not to say that reason and science do not have a crucial role to play in the life and practice of Christians. Quite the opposite! Reason and science can help us to make sense out of our lives once we have established our identities through faith. It is in what God reveals to us in the Word and through that still small voice that rumbles in the depths of our being that we find the ultimate basis for Christian truth. The Bible itself admonishes us to have a "reason for the faith that lies within us," but that faith is not *established* by reason.

One of the best uses of reason and science is to help us to understand the limits of reason and science. These days, it's not only Christians who are using reason and science to these ends. There is a growing awareness among the rationalists and the scientists themselves that ultimate truth is something they just can't get at by using their empirical methodologies. These worldly thinkers increasingly are humbled by the fact that there is a reality—an ultimate reality—that eludes them. And in their rational and scientific efforts to grasp that reality, they are like blind men in a dark room looking for a black cat that isn't there.

Let me try to define what is meant by postmodern thinking. When we talk about postmodernity, we are talking about an emerging consciousness that allows for the mystical and miraculous that is beyond and *other* than the rational and scientific. We are talking about a way of viewing reality that humbly admits that we can't trust the empirical realities that are explored by our five senses to give us the final word about what truth is.

This section of the book is designed for those who want to understand these new currents of thought that are flowing through the halls of academia. Maybe you're a college student, and you want some hints as to how to go about talking about your faith with the brighter students at your school. Maybe you have a son or daughter who has come home from the university with a style of thinking that you find difficult to understand, even though you want to understand very much. Then, perhaps, what follows will help. I have attempted to put into simple form some of the ways in which postmodernists think and to explain *why* they think in these ways. I have tried to show how postmodernism has opened up room for us to talk about the gospel, as well as to point out the pitfalls it poses for Christian thinking. If what follows does not always seem reasonable or logical, please remember that postmodernism itself is hardly understandable if one approaches it with reason and logic alone. However, trying to grasp something about this new way of looking at life is crucial if we are to be able to speak about Christ to people in the twenty-first century. Postmodern thinking will be very much a part of their mind-set, and only if we have a feel for it will we be able to relate the gospel to them in ways that will meet their needs.

This description of postmodernism is, of necessity, extremely limited, because the movement that goes by that name encompasses so many different things that it does not lend itself to one simple definition. It really is much easier to say what postmodernism is *not* than to say what it *is*. But as you will see in what follows, we can definitely agree that postmodernism is not a continuation of the ways in which intellectuals since the Age of Enlightenment have been trained to think. Instead, it's a way of thinking that leaves room for the mystical. It invites us to be open to spiritual realities which previously had been precluded from serious consideration by those who called themselves "modern thinkers." It is a style of thinking that is both exciting and dangerous.

Those who enter the domain of postmodernism ought to do so with great care. But enter it we must. Entering this strange domain is a forced option for Christians who would preach the gospel to the increasing number of people who live there. Postmodernism is not a way of thinking that is reserved only for an academic elite. Instead, it is a way of thinking that is permeating all sectors of society, from the simple to the sophisticated. It is a mind-set that is likely to be encountered in the man and woman on the street. It can be found in storefront Pentecostal churches. It subtly evidences itself in the mass media. It is only given the name postmodernism by those who are looking for labels to designate it for analysis. For the rest of society, it is an emerging way of thinking about our taken-for-granted world.

WHERE IT ALL STARTED

The beginning of modernity was René Descartes's famous dictum, "I think, therefore I am." In contrast, both the baby boomers and the X-Generation say, "I *feel*, therefore I am." *I can only think w/ feeling*

If there is any hunger in the souls of people at the end of the twentieth century, it is for a life marked by passion. They want to be passionately alive, passionately aware, passionately in love with nature, and passionately in love with their significant others. They are a people who are well aware of the deadening effects that modernity has had on people all around them. They see it on the deadpan faces of those watching television. They sense it in children at Disneyland, who have lost their sense of wonder. They experience it in their sex lives as what were once acts of passion are reduced to mechanized operations that try to mimic what they have viewed in R-rated movies.

The lack of passion in their world is also revealed to these late-twentieth-century men and women in the evening news. As the results of murder trials are announced, they too often hear commentators say, ". . . and when the verdict was announced, *the defendant showed no emotion*." They have learned how to be indifferent to the televised images of the agonizing deaths of people in the Third World. It is easy for them to be desensitized to it all when these images of horror are usually followed by an announcer saying, "Don't go away! We'll be right back with sports results after a word from our sponsors."

People have learned how to minimize the impact of broken marriages by achieving a detachment from reality that is so deep that, in the end, they feel nothing. Too often the children of these broken marriages develop an emotional numbness that makes them incapable of passionate love or committed relationships. Words like *estrangement*, *separateness*, and *alienation* become descriptions of what they know in their relationships with nature, with each other, and even with their own essential selves.

There are those who say that it all began with a scientific approach to nature. Something has been lost for those of us who were reared to look *objectively* at the sun, moon and stars, trees and flowers, mountains and rivers, the fish of the sea, the birds of the air, and the animals that struggle to share this planet with us. St. Francis, who preached to birds and called the sun and the moon "brother and sister," would be called crazy by most people if he lived among us today. Sadly, we don't have to ask what this world would say about Someone of whom it was rumored that "the wind and the waves obeyed Him" when He spoke. Such things don't fit into our modern categories of what is real and, therefore, we would not accept such tales.

We reject any sense of spiritual wonder in favor of an empirical approach to life. We see the moon only as a cold celestial body 250,000 miles away, spinning on its axis once every 28 days with a specific gravity one-third that of the earth. I remember my children commenting one night on the beauty of the moon as it hung like a silver dish in the crisp stillness of a cloudless winter night, and my mother saying in response, "You should have seen it before they walked all over it." It was a funny response and yet, in its humor, there was valid commentary on life today. Something mystical has been lost as nature is explored scientifically, instead of being revered as something mysterious and awesome.

What fascinates me is that, while the rest of us seem to live in a universe disenchanted by a scientism that reduces everything to quantifiable atoms, the astronauts—those icons of modernity—seem to be finding something out there that generates within them a rebirth of awe. To everyone's surprise when they return from space, they often do so with a sense of the spiritual. It is as though they have pushed their way to the frontiers of rational thinking and empirical science and have encountered there what the scholar Rudolf Ott has emphatically called the *mysterium tremendum.*

The astronauts, who in so many ways are the humanity of the future, seem to be telling us that, in the future, there will be a rebirth of wonder and a rediscovery of emotion in our responses to nature. "The Earth from space," they told us, "does not appear as a piece of rock mostly covered with water, but instead seems to be a living organism." Time and time again, as astronauts first glimpse the view from the portholes of their spaceships, they have gasped and seemed to grasp something of what we are increasingly calling a postmodern consciousness.

What these men and women have reported to us about what has happened to them out there in space has stirred the hope in many of us that science has a limited perspective on reality, and that there is something more to our universe than that which can be understood with scientific formulas. Astronauts tell us that there is something so magnificently beautiful about our world that rational language cannot give expression to it. These space travelers seem to have experienced what the Bible calls "groanings that cannot be uttered"—feelings so deep that there are no words that can make them part of our world of databases and computers.

These astronauts are to be envied because they have gone "where no one has ever gone before," but the rest of us have to languish in a world that has reduced all of nature to *things* with which we cannot empathize. It is not surprising, therefore, that we who live in this modern world seldom have any passionate responses to nature or enjoy a sense of nature feeding our souls. For the most part, we are cut off and alone in a universe that seems to have grown cold in the hands of scientific reductionists. We are a people who were created to sense a spiritual rapport with nature, but science has taught us to look at nature with a detached objectivity that is devoid of such spiritual blessings.

In the end, we are strangers and aliens in a strange and distant land. We hide behind a veneer of sophistication that we call modernity, and yet we hunger to once again become like little children. We long to be like people of another era for whom the miraculous was everywhere.

That things are changing is obvious. But in this postmodern era, we are coming to know that part of being spiritual in the biblical sense is being alive to the sacramental quality of nature. We know that spiritual awareness assures us that *something* of God comes to us through nature. While we know that God is *totally other* than nature, there is *something* that can be emotionally tasted in nature that makes God very real to us.

In the ancient Celtic myths, there was talk about "the thin places" in the universe. To these people of long ago, there was a sense that the generally thick wall that separates us from the world of the spirit has some thin places in it. They claimed that when we touch these thin places, we can feel something mysterious and wonderful on the other side. The citizens of the postmodern world believe in these "thin places." If we have no room for them in our Christianity, we should not be surprised if people go elsewhere to search for someone or something who will affirm what they intuitively sense is true. We should not be surprised if people stray away from churches that all too often demystify the world in which we live, as though there is nothing spiritual in nature. Their quest for wonder will not be denied, and if they do not find what they are looking for with us, then we set them up for the proselytizing efforts of the cults and covens of the New Age Movement.

Even more important to postmodern people than sensing something spiritual coming through nature is their hope of gaining a feeling of oneness with other people. There is a sense on their part that it is in personal intimacy with others that we gain and sustain our humanity. Postmodern people know that being cut off from fellowship and intimacy diminishes who and what we are. Our humanity is maintained though interaction with other human beings.

The communists of North Korea knew this all too well and used it as a means for what has come to be called *brainwashing*. During the war we had with them, they would take their prisoners and put them into solitary confinement, denying them any kind of contact with others. These communists were well aware that in such social isolation their prisoners' humanity would be so diminished that their original identity would evaporate. Once that happened, their jailers would then resocialize the prisoners with an alternative consciousness that supported communism and despised American democratic capitalism.

Our humanness is a thin veneer covering an animal nature that we have learned to repress. In William Golding's famous and controversial novel, *Lord of the Flies*, this theme is played out in dramatic fashion.

A group of English choirboys are marooned on an island in the middle of the Pacific. Having no adult supervision, they are forced to fend for themselves. As the story unfolds, these boys gradually lose any semblance of civilization and revert to primitive behavior. Before they are rescued, they verge on cannibalism, and we get a sense that, given enough time, any vestiges of their humanness would disappear.

The Bible calls the dark side of our personhood "the flesh," and the Scriptures warn us that the flesh is always waiting to express itself should the forces that maintain our humanness be removed or even diminished.

Interaction with other human beings is essential for the development of any semblance of what we call humanness. But all of us are looking for relationships in our lives that are more than that, more than just pleasant sociability. In this postmodern era, more than ever we are looking for a passionate intimacy that can take the deadness of our souls away. We have always known that those social scientists who described us as nothing more than sophisticated versions of Pavlovian dogs, programmed by systems of stimulus and response, had missed the mark. We have also known that those Freudian psychologists, who defined us as "pleasure machines looking for partners with whom we could diminish our libido tensions," didn't have a clue about what really makes us human. We have always known the truth that we are creatures who have an insatiable and noble hunger for a humanizing love, ultimately expressed in sacrificial giving one to another. This is not simply a Christian assertion. Erich Fromm, the neo-Freudian and Marxist psychotherapist, once one of Freud's protégés, makes this same kind of claim in his classic book, *The Art of Loving*. Fromm says:

> The awareness of human separation, without reunion by love—is the source of shame. It is at the same time the source of guilt and anxiety. The deepest need of man, then, is the need to overcome his separateness, to leave the prison of his aloneness.[1]

It is sin that keeps us from such loving intimacy. According to Fromm, it is best to define sin as that alienating force that not only cuts us off from God, but also cuts us off from one another. This is true for a multiplicity of reasons, not the least of which is the truth that sin is anything that destroys or prevents love. God is not just a transcendental unmoved mover in the sky. God is love. "Beloved, let us love one another: for love is of God; and every one that loveth is born of God, and knoweth God. He that loveth not knoweth not God; for God is love" (1 John 4:7–8).

In love we find God, and in God we find love. God is the energizing power that flows between persons who are experiencing His love for each other. That's why the Scripture says that those who are experiencing real love are experiencing God, whether they realize it or not (1 John 4:16). Lust craves expression with our bodies, but love involves the total engagement between people and, strange as this might seem to some, may not involve touching at all.

In reality, some of the deepest expressions of love between persons can be made with just the eyes. Have you ever sat face to face with another person and locked into the other's eyes with love? Have you ever focused the energy of God into another person, using the eyes as the entrances to his or her soul? Jesus once said, "The light of the body is the eye: if therefore thine eye be single, thy whole body shall be full of light" (Matthew 6:22). I am convinced that Jesus was telling us that the eyes are windows to the soul and that we can look into the ground of another person's inner sanctum through that person's eyes.

Do you wonder what it would be like to have Jesus look into your eyes? Do you ever reflect on how He might peer into your soul and pour His love into you, fixing His eyes on yours? What would flow into you as He connected with the innermost recesses of your being? What ecstasy would you experience? What essence of God would you feel coming out of Him into you?

Social philosophers since George Herbert Mead have known that there are levels of interaction between persons. According to Mead, there is that kind of a relationship wherein people come to know each other as objects, when they simply learn the facts about each other. This is a kind of self-revelation, and can be especially effective when we interact with a competent psychoanalyst. Sometimes we find the courage to verbalize those things about ourselves that we usually keep concealed. In such depth analysis, if we can bring ourselves to tell about ourselves with no holds barred, it is possible to find a kind of connection that can give us a high as well as a profound sense of emotional relief. And yet, after we have given all the secret facts about ourselves and said to the analyst all those things that we never even admitted to ourselves, we still feel estranged and alone. We somehow sense that, even though the analyst knows more about us than we have ever revealed to anyone before, we still feel that the analyst really does not know us at all. We know that something ultimately vital to who we are still remains secret, and we are more aware than ever of our estrangement. Furthermore, we know that this feeling of anxiety and estrangement cannot be overcome by giving the analyst even more facts about ourselves. We know that, even if we dare to let go of our pride and *let it all hang out*, we will still be horribly alone.

In all of this analysis of self, we sense that there is a knowledge about ourselves that cannot be grasped by assembling the objective facts from the past, no matter how intimate the facts may be or how honestly we might be willing to share them. It dawns on us that there is another way of being known that goes far beyond mere facts and, when we reflect upon it, does not require much in the way of facts at all. Such knowledge is transrational. It comes when we are known in the context of the mystical. Through subjective encounters it comes to us at those *meetings* wherein we not only encounter another at the deepest levels of the soul but, in so doing, experience the love that is God and the God that is love. It is of such an encounter that Paul writes in the great love chapter, "For now we see through a glass, darkly; but then face to face: now I know in part; but then shall I know even as also I am known" (1 Corinthians 13:12).

We never know when such spiritual transrational encounters will occur, for the Spirit bloweth where it listeth, and we cannot know from whence it comes or where it goes (John 3:8). Sometimes they happen unexpectedly, with strangers about whom we know practically nothing—objectively speaking. Yet, when such an encounter is our privilege, we are transported out of the mundane into the sublime. It is only when one of these encounters is over that we realize our hearts burned within us as it was happening, and we wonder just *who* was encountered? Did we meet some stranger, or was it an angel unawares? Perhaps there was something even deeper. Did we taste something of the resurrected Jesus? Do we, like the disciples on the road to Emmaus, realize that our *chance encounters* along life's road may be so much more than that—even a miracle?

After such a profound encounter, we are brought back to earth, and we realize how shallow our former relationships have been. There are those whom we have known for years, perhaps all of our lives, whom we now sense we really do not know at all. We may have known all about them. When it comes to objective facts about their lives, we probably have an abundance of them. But we are deeply aware, once having tasted the depth of the spiritual encounter, that there is a subjective knowledge lacking in anything less than that. Most of the *others* in our lives never let us reach through their eyes and into their souls. We find them inscrutable and therefore distant. We may have looked at these others from all sides and possible angles, but still we know only the illusions about them; we really don't know them at all.

The gospel is the good news that we need to leave the state of estrangement. God also uses the gospel to open us up for spiritual encounters with each other. The Scriptures tell us that by God's grace we can have those *meetings* wherein we not only meet each other, but we meet God as well. It's the good news that by grace we can be saved from estrangement. We know it's by grace, because we know that we can't make such encounters happen by our own determined efforts. We know that all we can do is be surrendered and open so that when God brings such a meeting our way, we can accept it as God's gift. Our salvation from estrangement is not of works, lest anyone should boast. Instead, our salvation overtakes us when we position ourselves to receive it by grace as an undeserved gift. "For by grace are ye saved through faith; and that not of yourselves: it is the gift of God: Not of works, lest any man should boast" (Ephesians 2:8–9).

For those of us who do receive this gift that comes from God through *the other,* such a richness of life flows into our personhood that we are lifted to a new plane of existence. In receiving from *the other*, we are receiving God, and as Scripture says, "But as many as received him, to them gave he power to become the sons of God, even to them that believe on his name" (John 1:12). It is in receiving God that we are empowered to enter into *the other*.

By grace we can receive Jesus into our souls. But we must also be ready to meet Him as He is mediated to us through encounters with others, when by the gift of the Holy Spirit we are enabled to penetrate the soul of the other, even as Christ meets us through the other. The estrangement that is the cause of all of our anxieties is vanquished, and life is experienced more abundantly than ever before. The abundant life is the promise of God (John 10:10).

As you read about the subjective encounters that overcome estrangement, you may feel frustrated because I did not seem to be specific enough nor was I sufficiently clear or concrete in my explanations. But that is the nature of postmodernity. The hard concrete descriptions of reality that characterized the kind of philosophical discussions that were part of modernity (i.e., logical positivism) have been transcended by a new (but then again, perhaps ancient) kind of talk that reaches beyond reason and science. It is talk that tries to *feel* what lies on the other side of the *thin places* of the universe. It is talk that could be poetic, if only I were artistic enough to put it into poetry. Postmodern talk is like that.

And so I leave you with a plea: Go off by yourself and, like Jacob on the mountain (Genesis 32:24–28), struggle with God until you are spiritually exhausted. Then, in that time of resignation that follows giving up (because there is nothing left in you with which to carry on the struggle), the Spirit will come. The Spirit will come by grace. When you surrender, it is then that there may come a rushing in of the One who is *Totally Other*. Then, filled with the Spirit, you will be ready to relate to others in love. You will be able to reach into others and know others in ways that are truly miraculous. You will have, in truth, arrived back at the heart of old-time religion in the midst of our postmodern world.

PART FOUR

When It Comes to

Social Action

How to Deal with Racism

without Being Patronizing

T he story is told of an African-American man standing at the bottom of the steps leading up to a gigantic church building. He was looking at the doors of the church and, at the same time, scratching his head with a puzzled look on his face.

As he stood there in a rather befuddled condition, Jesus Himself came by and, seeing the confused man, went over to him and asked, "What's troubling you, Friend?"

The man, not realizing that he was talking to Jesus, answered, "They told me I can't get into their church because I'm black!"

"Oh, don't be surprised by that," Jesus answered. "I've been trying to get into that church for years, and they won't let me in either."

The point of the story is blatantly clear. A church that shuts out people for racist reasons shuts out the Lord. Racism has a horrendous effect on the church's witness to the world. We will never know how many people have been turned off to Christ because of the racism they found among church people. Racism has also been responsible for social discontent and even revolutions. Those who are oppressed by racism will not accept their oppression forever. Sooner or later, the social conscience of these people will be justifiably raised, and rebellion will follow.

When Mahatma Gandhi was living in South Africa, he once tried to attend a worship service at an Anglican cathedral. It was at a time in his life when Gandhi was very much open to the Christian faith and giving serious consideration to the role that Jesus should play in his life. Shortly after he took his seat in the sanctuary, one of the ushers at the cathedral came over to Gandhi and whispered in his ear that *colored people* were not allowed to worship in that particular church. Not only did this keep the great Indian leader from becoming a Christian, it also had far-flung social ramifications. Commenting on the event years later, Gandhi said, "That poor usher. He thought he was ushering a colored man out of a church when, in reality, he was ushering India out of the British Empire."

Fortunately, Gandhi's form of rebellion against racism and colonialism was nonviolent. Otherwise, we can only imagine how many victims to the evils of racist oppression would have died in the Indian struggle for independence.

I hope that there is no need to convince you that racism is wrong. If you know anything about Jesus, you know that He prayed, and still prays, that His people might be one (John 17:21). If you know anything about the Bible, you probably know that the apostle Paul specifically teaches that all the differentiations once used as reasons for discrimination on the basis of race, sex, and ethnicity have been obliterated for those who are in Christ. "There is neither Jew nor Greek, there is neither bond nor free, there is neither male nor female: for ye are all one in Christ Jesus" (Galatians 3:28).

In another place in his writings, Paul attacks anything that would support racial divisions in the Body of Christ by appealing to events surrounding Christ's death on the cross (Ephesians 2:11–22). Paul alludes to the fact that the Jewish Temple on Mount Zion was divided into three distinct areas. The innermost place was the Holy of Holies. This was the place where, once a year, the high priest offered the blood of a lamb on the altar called the Mercy Seat, thus making atonement for the sins of the faithful. This offering was in anticipation of the coming atonement of Christ, the ultimate Lamb of God, who would shed His blood on the cross for all of us.

The second section of the Temple was called the Holy Place. Here, ceremonially pure circumcised Jewish men were allowed to come for worship. Finally, there was the Outer Court. This was the place of worship reserved for both women and Gentiles—the two categories of people considered to be second-class citizens. A partition in the Temple separated Jewish men from those "spiritually inferior" people. But Paul writes this:

> But now in Christ Jesus ye who sometimes were far off are made nigh by the blood of Christ. For he is our peace, who hath made both one, and hath broken down the middle wall of partition between us; Having abolished in his flesh the enmity, even the law of commandments contained in ordinances; for to make in himself of twain one new man, so making peace; And that he might reconcile both unto God in one body by the cross, having slain the enmity thereby: And came and preached peace to you which were afar off, and to them that were nigh. For through him we both have access by one Spirit unto the Father. Now therefore ye are no more strangers and foreigners, but fellow citizens with the saints, and of the household of God. (Ephesians 2:14–19)

In this passage, Paul makes the point that when Christ died for our sins He simultaneously destroyed the walls that separated genders and races into superior and inferior categories. The collapse of the Temple wall that had divided people into first- and second-class citizens was no more. Through His death on Calvary, all were declared to be one in Christ Jesus. For all the ages to come, there was to be the good news that, because of what Jesus did on the cross, there must be an end to all divisions.

In light of this biblical truth, it would seem that we have a right to expect that the Church of Jesus Christ would be the least racist group of people here on earth. Unfortunately, close to the opposite is true. Sunday morning at eleven o'clock is still the most segregated hour in American life.

I spend a great deal of time on college and university campuses. In such settings, I meet all kinds of people and hear all kinds of opinions expressed. To my dismay, I find that the least racist groups on campus tend to be the secular humanists. When there are racial incidents on campuses, too often it is the secular humanists, rather than the Christians, who are the most concerned. Whenever efforts are made to increase racial reconciliation or to protest racial injustices, I can count on two things: First, the secular humanists will be at the forefront of these efforts; and, second, there will be few, if any, signs that Christians are involved in leadership roles. A sociologist at LaSalle University did a study which revealed that the more fundamentalistic the beliefs of people were, the more likely they were to harbor racist attitudes.

What would happen if all we evangelical fundamentalist Christians were suddenly removed from a given community, and only the secular humanists were left behind? Would racism and discrimination increase or decrease? I think I can guess what the answer will be. If we in the evangelical ranks are going to get right with God on racial matters, we all have a great deal of repenting to do. Perhaps we need to begin with confession. To try to play innocent and say things like, "Some of my best friends are black folks" only perpetuates a state of sick denial. We are socialized into racist attitudes, even if we are unaware of what is happening. We pick up racism from our primary group associations in ways that are too subtle for us even to notice. And what we absorb in our formative years nurtures attitudes and behaviors that offend and hurt others, even when we are not conscious of doing so.

We usually point to white Anglo-Saxon Protestants as the agents of racism, but those who are African-American, Hispanic, or Asian are not innocent. There is a bitterness that comes over the victims of both overt and covert discrimination. That bitterness eats away like a cancer and has a demonic effect on oppressed peoples. The reaction to racism is racism. The oppressed need a special gift of grace to overcome bitterness—a grace that God has promised to those who would receive it (Hebrews 12:14–15).

For me, dealing with this problem begins in the early morning. I try to wake up about half an hour before I need to get up so that I can spend some time in silence letting God deal with me. In the silence of the early morning, I set aside time where I can surrender to His presence. I know that the Holy Spirit is always with me, but I also know how important it is to give the Spirit daily opportunities to penetrate my consciousness and deal with those things that ought not to be there. In my morning solitude I yield myself to what the Holy Spirit wants to do to me. Among other things, I wait for Him to convict me of those evil attitudes and feelings that have been part of my nature for all too long. I wait patiently for the Lord and allow God time to convict and convince.

In those times of silence, I discover things about myself that I might otherwise ignore. I become aware of dimensions of my soul that I didn't know existed. It is in these times of self-discovery and increasing self-awareness that I come to grips with the dark side of my humanity and find the evidences of my latent racism.

As the Holy Spirit invades my personhood, there is not only convicting and confessing going on, there is also cleansing. In those times of deep surrender to the presence of the Spirit, I sense myself being purged of, among other things, my racist dispositions. It is as though the Holy Spirit connects me with Jesus on the cross as I lie in the stillness of the morning. I feel Him draining out of me those demonic spirits that maintain the racisms that have been so much a part of me. I ask the Lord, early in the morning, to create in me a pure heart, free from the dark spirits that would nurture that which never should have been in me (Psalm 51:10).

The cleansing of my consciousness is not the only crucial work the Holy Spirit must exercise in me if I am to be freed from racism. There is the equally important work of the Spirit, which also provides me with a new vision of what I see when I look at others, especially when I look at those who otherwise would have been viewed through the filter of racism. The apostle Paul once told us:

> Wherefore henceforth know we no man after the flesh: yea, though we have known Christ after the flesh, yet now henceforth know we him no more. Therefore if any man be in Christ, he is a new creature: old things are passed away; behold, all things are be-

come new. And all things are of God, who hath reconciled us to himself by Jesus Christ, and hath given to us the ministry of reconciliation. (2 Corinthians 5:16–18)

In this passage, I think Paul is talking about the same changed perception of others that I am trying to describe. In accord with St. Francis of Assisi, I am more and more learning to view others sacramentally. I increasingly see them as a means of God's grace, and through them I encounter the sweet and loving presence of Jesus.

When our Anglican and Lutheran Christian brothers and sisters take holy communion, they believe that the real presence of Christ is inherent in the bread and the wine. Unlike the Roman Catholics, who believe in the doctrine of transubstantiation, Anglicans and Lutherans do not believe there is an essential change in the *elements* of holy communion, but they do believe that *through* the bread and wine it is possible to mysteriously experience the real presence of the living Christ. I'm not sure about that theology, but what I know *is* true is that what the Anglicans and Lutherans say about the elements of holy communion is true about persons who confront us as either neighbors or strangers. "Each person is sacramental," said St. Francis. Each person, while he or she is not Jesus, can be a means of God's grace through whom Jesus is encountered.

To experience other people as Francis did would make racism impossible. How would it be possible for a Christian to hold any animosity toward someone of another race, if the presence of Jesus were sensed in that person? How could a Christian discriminate against a person, if that person were viewed as a sacramental means through whom Jesus could be spiritually encountered? Would not each of us then realize that to reject a person of another race would be to reject Jesus Himself? Would not experiencing Christ in others obliterate in us any effects of the cultural conditioning that creates racism?

Key African-American intellectuals have traced some of the roots of racism back to ways of thinking that have come down to us from ancient Greece. The Greeks had a way of viewing human beings that has far-reaching consequences for those of us in today's world. They viewed people as having two parts to their personalities, a physical body *and* a spiritual soul. The physical body, they said, was evil, because *everything* physical was considered to be evil. To the Greeks all that was physical or material was *totally other* than that which was spiritual and good.

In light of this distinction between body and soul, it's no wonder that the ancient Greeks had difficulty accepting the Christian gospel, which declared that in Jesus, the perfect God took on human flesh. Since flesh was evil in their eyes, it seemed impossible to them that a good God could ever have possessed a physical body. They even had difficulty believing that a good God could be the Creator of the physical universe. Good, as they saw it, could not create evil. That is why it was bold of John to declare to a Greek audience that not only did God create the universe, but God (the Word), in Jesus, became flesh and dwelt among us.

> In the beginning was the Word, and the Word was with God, and the Word was God. The same was in the beginning with God. All things were made by him; and without him was not any thing made that was made. And the Word was made flesh, and dwelt among us, (and we beheld his glory, the glory as of the only begotten of the Father) full of grace and truth. (John 1:1–3, 14)

When the apostle Paul preached to the people of Athens on Mars Hill, he ran into the same problem (Acts 17). He seemed to have his listeners with him as he talked about Jesus until he told them that Jesus had risen from the dead. To the ancient Greeks, having one's spiritual soul freed from the physical body was the final good for which everyone longed. The idea that Jesus was *physically* resurrected from the dead and would have a material body forever seemed to suggest that Jesus would be eternally tied to that which is evil.

Down through the ages, those of us who have been subtly influenced by Greek thinking have unconsciously come to see the physical body as something that is evil and inferior to the spiritual side of our humanity. This has resulted in racist thinking. Whenever one race of people wants to designate another race of people as inferior, the oppressing group tends to view itself as intellectually and/or spiritually superior, while looking down upon the oppressed group as being primarily physical.

This kind of thinking works itself out in our present day. Racists seem to be quite willing to concede physical superiority to African-American people and expect them to concede spiritual or intellectual superiority to their oppressors. Eldridge Cleaver once referred to all of this as "the brawn versus brains dichotomy." For Cleaver, it came as no surprise that white people were willing to accept black people as athletes, as long as the black people were willing to leave the task of *thinking* to white folks. Blacks could do the physical things like running, jumping, and using their brawn in football. But when it came to the thinking tasks that go with sports, like quarterbacking football teams or coaching, then blacks would be expected to step aside and let the whites take over. In rebellion against this tendency in sports, some key African-American leaders have pressed for more coaching and managerial positions to be made available to members of their race.

Whenever there is a discussion about the role of race in sports, there are those who point out what is all too obvious—that African-Americans dominate most professional sports, including the NFL and the NBA and are underrepresented in the halls of academia. "Is there need for any more proof," they say, "that African-Americans are the physically superior and that whites (and increasingly Asians) are the intellectually superior?"

The truth is that physical anthropologists have run huge numbers of comprehensive studies, which prove beyond a shadow of a doubt that there are negligible differences between the races when it comes to IQ. Any talk about the intellectual superiority of one race over another has been proven to be pure myth. Furthermore, the domination of certain sports by African-Americans can easily be explained by racism. If a group of people are told that they are physically superior, it is only a matter of time before that belief becomes a self-fulfilling prophecy.

In the African-American community, many young men spend endless hours on the basketball court, because sports is the only thing they believe they can do well. Many of them see sports as the only real escape route from the grinding poverty of the ghetto. Consequently, they are often conned into spending their time playing ball instead of studying. Is it any wonder, then, that they often do brilliantly in sports and fail miserably in their academic studies?

I argue not only against the claims that some whites make about their superior intelligence, but also against the assertions of many African-Americans as to their physical superiority. We have all heard the African-American claim that "white men can't jump!" Then, at the Olympics, we find out that white men can be just as successful as black men in the high jump. The claim is made that whites can't run, and then we find that some whites from Germany and the Scandinavian countries are able to successfully challenge our African-American sprinters in race after race. Even when it comes to basketball, we discover that white players, from places like Croatia and Australia, with far less experience and practice than our "Dream Team," do much better than anybody expected. Needless to say, I believe that race, in terms of abilities, is a myth; it is social, economic, and cultural factors which really give driving force to racist theories.

Such racist thinking is most likely to rear its ugly head when it comes to sexual matters. Martin Luther King once said, "We want to be the white man's brother, not his brother-in-law." I don't know how many times I have heard people who disclaim any semblance of racism say, "I've got nothing against black people. Some of my best friends are black people. I just wouldn't want my daughter to marry one."

Having assigned physical superiority to African-Americans, racists are caught in a trap. Because sex is a physical thing, they are caught up in the belief that black people are their sexual superiors. With racism come sexual fears that are evil and disgusting. Racists create myths about the sexual appetites of blacks. Sadly, an honest discussion about all of this has yet to take place in the Church.

Against all of this racist thinking stands the Bible. The Bible recognizes nothing evil or inferior about the physical side of life. Quite to the contrary—it celebrates the physical. The Bible makes a moral judgment about the material universe in the creation story and declares that it is "good!" The Bible does not promote the idea that the Spirit is good and the body is evil. Nor does it teach that at death the *good soul* goes to heaven while the *evil body* goes into the grave, as the Greeks believed. The Bible teaches the resurrection of the body, as well as the immortality of the soul. Jesus was not *spiritually* resurrected from the dead. He was *physically* resurrected (Luke 24:36–43). And the same will be true for us. In the afterlife, we will not be disembodied souls but, like Jesus, we will have resurrected bodies. Our resurrected bodies will be qualitatively different from our earthly bodies, but they will be physical, nevertheless.

> Now if Christ be preached that he rose from the dead, how say some among you that there is no resurrection of the dead? But if there be no resurrection of the dead, then is Christ not risen: And if Christ be not risen, then is our preaching vain, and your faith is also vain. Yea, and we are found false witnesses of God; because we have testified of God that he raised up Christ: whom he raised not up, if so be that the dead rise not. For if the dead rise not, then is not Christ raised: And if Christ be not raised, your faith is vain; ye are yet in your sins.
>
> All flesh is not the same flesh: but there is one kind of flesh of men, another flesh of beasts, another of fishes, and another of birds. There are also celestial bodies, and bodies terrestrial: but the glory of the celestial is one, and the glory of the terrestrial is another.
>
> Behold, I shew you a mystery; We shall not all sleep, but we shall all be changed, In a moment, in the twinkling of an eye, at the last trump: for the trumpet shall sound, and the dead shall be raised incorruptible, and we shall be changed. For this corruptible must put on incorruption, and this mortal must put on immortality. So when this corruptible shall have put on incorruption, and this mortal shall have put on immortality, then shall be brought to pass the saying that is written, Death is swallowed up in victory. (1 Corinthians 15:12–17, 39–40, 51–54)

This is not the place to go into an extensive explanation of how the theologians reconcile the biblical truth that immediately upon death we are with the Lord in glory and that, at the same time, we who are dead in Christ shall be resurrected at the day of His coming. However, I assure you that it can be done. I personally make a limited attempt at it in my book, *A Reasonable Faith.*[1]

What must be stressed in this discussion is that the whole way of thinking nurtured by Greek philosophy is negated by the biblical message. Human beings, according to God's Word, do not *have* souls, we *are* souls (Genesis 2:7). Out of the Bible comes a declaration that every human being is a living soul in which the spiritual and the physical are inseparable. And all the racist theories that are built on the idea that body and spirit can be dealt with as separate things, with one race being predominately one and another race predominately the other, are rejected by the Scriptures. Consequently, the more our thinking is controlled by the Bible, the more racism will disappear.

There are signs of hope these days. Christians, both liberal and conservative, are recognizing racism for the sin that it is. Bold efforts are being made to abolish racism, especially in the Church. Promise Keepers, the massive men's movement, has made racial reconciliation one of its primary goals. Major Christian denominations are making great efforts to open up to racial diversity in their leadership ranks. Within the charismatic movement, racial integration of Sunday morning congregations is especially common. The work of the Holy Spirit is increasingly evident as we see God at work making us into one people. We have a long, long way to go. But to say that we haven't started the journey is to ignore what is really happening in the Church of Jesus Christ.

One of my favorite stories was told by Clarence Jordan, the founder of Koinonia Farms in Georgia. At a time in the 1950s, when racism and discrimination were especially rampant in the South, he went into the hills of South Carolina to conduct some revival meetings in a Baptist church. When he came out on the platform to preach, he was amazed to discover that the congregation of several hundred people was thoroughly integrated. White and black people were sitting together all over the place.

Right after the service was over, Clarence got the old hillbilly preacher who pastored the church aside and asked him, "How did you get this way?"

"What way?" answered the preacher.

"Racially integrated!" answered Clarence. "Did you get this way since the decision?"

"What decision?" asked the old preacher.

"The Supreme Court decision of 1954 that struck down segregation of the schools," Clarence responded.

"Supreme Court?" the preacher shot back. "What's the Supreme Court got to do with what we do in church?"

Good question! Maybe the world at large has to be told by law to end discrimination, but we, as the Church, should not need a court to tell us what to do. The Bible has already given us God's marching orders.

Clarence Jordan was not about to drop the matter. "Come on," he said, "You *know* that to have a racially integrated congregation like this is really unusual down here in South Carolina. Tell me how you got this way!"

"Well," answered the old preacher, with a sly little smile on his face, "this church was down to just a handful of people when the last preacher left, and they couldn't get a new preacher no how. So, after a few months, I told the deacons that, if they couldn't get themselves a preacher, I'd be willing to preach for them, and they let me do it."

"The first Sunday I preached to the people, I preached on Galatians 3:28 and told them how everybody becomes one in Christ Jesus. I told them that, with real Christians, nobody pays any attention to things like the color of people's skin. I preached that not to be one in Jesus was not to be Christian."

"After the service, the deacons called me into the back room and told me that they didn't want to hear that kind of preaching no more!"

"What did you do then?" asked Clarence.

"*I fired them deacons!*" the old preacher shouted back. "I mean, if deacons ain't gonna 'deac' like the Bible says, they ought to be fired."

"How come they didn't fire you?" asked Clarence.

"They never hired me!" was the answer. "Well, when I found out what bothered them people," continued the old preacher, "I gave it to them every week."

"Did they put up with it?" inquired Clarence.

"Not really," answered the preacher. "I preached that church down to four. But after that, we began to pick up new members. We wouldn't let people into membership unless they were really Christians either."

"How did you know if people were *really* Christians?" asked Clarence.

"That was easy," said the preacher. "Down here, from when we're knee high to a grasshopper, we're taught that there's a difference between black folks and white folks. But when people become Christians, all of that stuff is forgotten. In Jesus, we overcome all of that racist evil, and we work hard at becoming one in Christ."

After the service, Clarence went home with a university professor who drove forty miles to attend that church. As they rode together in the car, Clarence asked the man, "Why do you go to that church? Why do you listen to that preacher? He can't utter a sentence without making a grammatical error. You're a professor of English. Why would you travel forty miles just to go hear that man preach?"

The young intellectual answered with measured words, "I go to that church because *that man preaches the gospel!*"

The gospel that university professor came to hear is the good news that, in Jesus, racism is defeated. What more can be said?

Chapter 15

How to Be Politically Involved

without Losing Your Soul

I n 1976 I ran for Congress. I won the primary but lost in the general election. Many things happened to me in that run for office that became part of my collection of memorable moments. But few things made more of an impression on me than an interview I had with a top official of my party following the primary.

As is the custom with candidates for Congress, I was brought to Washington for a briefing at the national offices of the party. There I had a variety of conferences to plan strategies for the general election. In one interview, one of the party leaders, for reasons that I could not figure out, gave me an especially hard time. After putting up with barbs and innuendoes for about half an hour, I asked the man, "What is going on here? Maybe you don't like it that I'm a Baptist preacher? Do you think that because I'm a Baptist preacher, I can't be a good politician?"

His response was unforgettable. He said, "Mr. Campolo, you miss the point. The fact that you're a Baptist preacher leaves no doubt in my mind that you're a good politician. What I'd like to know is, do you have any ethics?"

The image that those outside the Church have of church people was painfully clear in that answer. We are viewed as being very political but not always as having our politics guided by high ethical principles. We need to explore why the world thinks of us that way.

First of all, I believe that we have earned a bad reputation because of our "trash talk." We have a tendency to demonize those people whom we oppose politically. When it comes to trafficking in rumors, distortions, and even lies, certain Christian leaders often shock outsiders. If you read the newsletters and listen to many of those on Christian radio and television, you know that some of our leaders can be very careless with the truth. Even worse, they often have a tendency to make allegiance to a particular candidate or party a test of a person's Christianity. They use religion to legitimate a given party or candidate so that many of the faithful come to view anybody opposed to that party or candidate as being opposed to God. Opponents of those whom these leaders define as godly are declared to be agents of the evil forces in the world, who must be defeated by whatever means necessary.

Many religious leaders have made "family values," *as defined by themselves,* the defining issue in American politics. They are quick to portray those who don't agree with them as destroyers of the American family, and will not hesitate to engage in savage character assassination to defeat their political enemies. Even when they don't out and out lie, these would-be crusaders for preserving the American Family often create false impressions by twisting the truth. In their efforts to keep America from going down what they believe to be the slippery slope to moral destruction, they are all too ready to demonize those who oppose what *they* have defined as the Christian agenda.

We must be ever mindful that the Bible tells us to be subject to our public officials and is quite clear about how we are to talk about each other. We are not to make exceptions and speak disparagingly about those who govern. "Put them in mind to be subject to principalities and powers, to obey magistrates, to be ready to every good work, To speak evil of no man, to be no brawlers, but gentle, shewing all meekness unto all men (Titus 3:1–2).

We do the cause of the gospel great harm when we get caught up in the name-calling and the politics of bile that have become all too common among those who use the pulpit for partisan political purposes. The Bible teaches us to "speak the truth in love" (Ephesians 4:15).

When we fail to do so, we not only violate the will of God, but we earn for the Church a bad reputation. When I'm in secular circles, I'm upset by how often I hear people refer to certain preachers and televangelists as "political mudslingers," but that is the way they come across to those outside the Church. Our political conversations should, instead, reflect the character of our Lord. The apostle Paul tells us:

> Finally, brethren, whatsoever things are true, whatsoever things are honest, whatsoever things are just, whatsoever things are pure, whatsoever things are lovely, whatsoever things are of good report; if there be any virtue, and if there be any praise, think on these things. (Philippians 4:8)

The second thing to bear in mind is that we ought to be focused on issues, rather than giving allegiance to any political party. Religious leaders, in their official roles, ought not to endorse candidates or political parties. To do so is not only unwise and hurtful to their witness, it is also illegal. There is a growing awareness among the watchdogs of the political process that many preachers and their churches may be violating the laws that govern nonprofit corporations, such as churches. Nothing in the law keeps churches and church leaders from speaking out on issues, such as abortion or the rights of homosexuals, but to go beyond that and tell congregates exactly how they should vote, or for whom they should vote, is not allowed. Those who cross this line of propriety do so at the risk of having their ministries lose their tax-free status. Right now several mega-churches in Texas are being challenged in the courts by those who claim that they have broken the law and become involved in partisan politics by endorsing specific candidates and legislation.

A particular practice that has generated significant concern and even some outrage is the publishing and distribution in churches of politically biased voter guides. Christian groups on both the political right and the political left have compiled voter guides specifically designed to make the candidates they favor look like knights in shining armor and those whom they oppose look like evil principalities and powers. For instance, one voter guide put out by a powerful Christian political action organization lists Tony Hall (Democrat, Ohio) as a candidate who voted *antifamily*. I found this extremely surprising since Congressman Hall went against his party's platform in championing the pro-life cause at the Democratic National Convention. He had a 100 percent rating from the Family Research Council and several pro-life alliances. Furthermore, Chuck Colson, the leader of Prison Fellowship, who labels himself a conservative Republican, transcended partisan politics to name Congressman Hall "one of the finest Christian leaders in Washington."

When I sought an explanation for the negative assessment that had been made about Congressman Hall, I found that this particular Christian political action organization had made its judgment on the grounds that he had sponsored several pieces of legislation that would have given humanitarian aid to the poor in Third World countries. The convoluted arguments of this Christian political action group that labeled Tony Hall *antifamily* claimed that, even though his bill would have provided food, educational programs, and public health assistance to some of the poorest and most oppressed people of the world, it would have required American tax dollars to do it. They reasoned that, since American tax dollars come from American families, Tony Hall must be antifamily.

Without getting into the pros and cons of foreign aid, I think it is stretching things a bit to conclude that the congressman's concern for desperate people in poor countries made him an antifamily candidate. This, along with a number of other twisted impressions of Tony Hall presented in this particular voter guide, suggests to me that the guide was not designed to help Christians vote their faith commitments as much as it was an attempt to get Tony Hall's Republican opponent elected.

Don't get the wrong idea. It's not just conservative Christian political action groups that are playing this game of skirting the law by developing and distributing biased voter guides. There are liberal Christian organizations that do the same sort of thing. In my opinion, liberal groups don't do it as much or as effectively these days, simply because they lack the means to do so. Politically conservative Christian organizations have huge amounts of money and massive numbers of volunteers to carry out their agendas of partisan politics. Liberal Christian groups do not.

All of this leads me to highly recommend that you raise questions if anyone, but especially your pastor, arranges to have voter guides distributed in your church. Remember, it's not enough to fulfill the letter of the law; Christians should avoid even the appearance of evil. If a voter guide is handed out at your church, ask the following questions:

- Is the voter guide partisan or biased in such a way as to break the law and jeopardize the tax-free status of the church?

- Does the voter guide deal with the issues in an *honest* way?

- Is the voter guide an attempt to raise concerns that should be important to Christians, or is it a veiled attempt to get certain candidates defeated?

- Some issues that concern all Christians are usually raised by conservatives (i.e., abortion, parental rights, and prayer in schools), and other Christian concerns are usually raised by liberals (i.e., the environment, protection for the poor, and healthcare). Does the voter guide deal with *all* of these concerns or just those of one political group?

God is not a Republican or a Democrat. Neither party has a corner on virtue or vice. A fair voter guide will reflect this.

When it comes to politics, we often take matters too seriously, or, conversely, not seriously enough. On the one hand, politics is important. But in America, politics is not as important as some religious leaders make it out to be, even if it is too serious to be left in the hands of politicians. On the other hand, we ought not to delude ourselves into thinking that the realization of the kingdom of God in history is dependent upon the outcome of a given election in America. God is still the Lord of history, regardless of who controls the Congress or who occupies the White House. Furthermore, religious leaders who seem to put all their hopes for the country in the political process are prone to be extremist in their predictions. They promise that we will live in the Promised Land if only the party and candidates that they favor get elected. Conversely, they often threaten us with the end of all that is good if those whom they oppose win out. Who gets elected *is* important, but not as important as some would lead us to believe. Whether our country rises or falls depends more on the character and spirituality of our people than on which political party holds governmental power. The Bible says: "If my people, which are called by my name, shall humble themselves, and pray, and seek my face, and turn from their wicked ways; then will I hear from heaven, and will forgive their sin, and will heal their land" (2 Chronicles 7:14).

Winning elections is important, but we must not be so intent on winning that we behave in ways that make us into liars, slanderers, and distorters. Defeating those whose ideology or character runs counter to our personal interpretation of what Christianity is all about is an effort worthy of our energies. But we must ask ourselves over and over again, "What does it profit if we win elections and, in the process, lose our souls?" Even when we feel we must work to defeat a particular candidate or party, we must remember the warning of the existentialist philosopher Frederick Neitzsche: "Beware when you *fight* a dragon, lest you *become* a dragon."

In addition to being a voter or a campaigner, you may want to consider becoming a candidate for office yourself. Contrary to what many believe, holding political office is truly a noble Christian calling. Edmund Burke, in a famous quote, once said, "All that is necessary for evil to triumph, is for good men to do nothing." You may choose to run for public office for no other reason than to keep evil in its place. Should you do so, here are a few things to keep in mind:

First of all, minor offices can be of major importance. Ralph Reed, the leader of the Christian Coalition, has told his followers that the person who lives in the White House is not as important to their movement as those who control local school boards and township councils. In his understanding of how things really work in politics, Reed correctly points out that the majority of the decisions that most directly impact the lives of most Americans are made on the local level.

Decisions on the following will, in all likelihood, be made by local school boards:

- How much money will be put into our children's education?
- What kind of sex education will our children receive?
- Which books will our children read?
- Who will teach our children?
- What religious activities will occur in school?
- What racial policies will be established?
- Will girls be treated differently from boys?
- What role will sports play in education?
- What provisions will be made for the physically and mentally impaired?
- What values will be taught?

A partial list of other things to be decided on a local level would include:

- What standards of public decency will be established?
- What drinking establishments will be allowed in town?
- What housing will be available for the poor?
- How will public assistance be provided?
- What provisions will be made for the elderly?
- Will there be gambling or blue laws?

Reed is right when he contends that the political decisions that mold our communal values and most impact the quality of our lives are made by seemingly minor officials elected on the local level. Given this reality, we should readily acknowledge that holding public office in local government provides a good position from which to influence your community with the values of the Kingdom of God.

In light of the importance of holding office on the local level, it is surprising just how easy it is to get elected to office. Since those who occupy local offices seldom receive any financial remuneration worth mentioning, yet must give significant time to service, few in the community ever seek to run for election. The possibility of seizing an opportunity to make a big difference for good is, consequently, very real.

If you do get elected to office, there is one mistake you must work hard to avoid. Don't use your office to impose your own religious beliefs and commitments upon others in such a way as to violate their rights and sensitivities. We live in a pluralistic society. When elected, you must recognize that you are supposed to represent all of the people in your political area, not just those who share your own particular religious values. That doesn't mean that you ought to be governed by polls. Too many politicians are nothing more than thermometers who, in their voting, do little more than register the prevailing political temperature.

In 1976, when I ran for the U.S. Congress, part of the ritual of being a candidate was to show up at fund-raising dinners with the express purpose of building up the enthusiasm of the party faithful. At one such function, the party chairman introduced me by telling the crowd, "Tony is the kind of candidate who will listen to the people. He will stay in touch with his constituency and when he votes, he will vote the will of the people!"

It all sounded so good that I was tempted not to disagree with his kind words about me. But these were the party faithful, and they would vote for me no matter what. With an audience like that, it's easy to be a bit daring and even to get into some risky rhetoric. When I stood up to speak, I decided not to say what my supporters expected of me. I said to the crowd, "What the chairman said isn't quite true. I really won't vote my constituency. Instead, I will vote my conscience. If I know that something is right, I will vote for it, even if my constituency is against it. And if I think something is wrong, I'll vote against it, regardless of how many voters I might alienate in the process."

I went on to say, "In the Bible we read about a politician who voted his constituency rather than his conscience. His name was Pilate. When Jesus was on trial for His life, Pilate knew that He was innocent.

But instead of going with a judgment based on what his conscience was telling him, Pilate polled his constituency. Then he told the people, 'I find no fault in Him. But I leave it up to you. What do you want me to do with Him?' And his constituency roared back, 'Crucify Him!' And so Pilate did!

"Jesus was crucified," I said, "because Pilate was into polling and voting his constituency."

I'm not so sure that, if I had won that election, I would have been as much of a paragon of virtue as I seemed to be that night as I pontificated with such pompous piety. But people who would put what I said at that dinner into action are the kind we need in public office.

Voting your convictions does not have to mean pushing your beliefs down someone else's throat. Two thousand years ago, the apostle Paul established a brilliant model in expressing his convictions in the context of a pluralistic society. When preaching to the people of Athens, he sought common ground. Paul pointed out that some of his own convictions were mirrored in the ideas of certain Athenian philosophers and poets (Acts 17:17–34). Paul's message was that Christians are not the only ones with truth and that, together with people of other faiths and philosophies, it is possible to discover the truth and values that God makes known to all people through His *general revelation*. This is what Paul was talking about when he pointed out that even those who had never received the laws of God through missionary endeavors had a knowledge of the truth and a godly sense of right and wrong.

> For not the hearers of the law are just before God, but the doers of the law shall be justified. For when the Gentiles, which have not the law, do by nature the things contained in the law, these, having not the law, are a law unto themselves: Which shew the work of the law written in their hearts, their conscience also bearing witness, and their thoughts the mean while accusing or else excusing one another. (Romans 2:13–15)

In politics, you ought to assume that down deep inside of people there is a common sense of what we ought to do, and what we ought not to do. The philosopher Immanuel Kant called this the "categorical imperative of the transcendental unity of apperception." That's just a high-brow way of saying that there is a common sense of what is right and wrong, and if we work on it hard enough, we will find that common sense among the people we are trying to serve.

"But what happens if I have to vote on something, and I believe that what the Bible says is at odds with the will of the people?" you ask. That is when you have to obey God (as best you understand God) rather than the people (Acts 5:29). Don't try to hide your unpopular vote or excuse it. Just tell people that they have the option of voting you out of office if they cannot tolerate your stand. That's what democracy is all about. Voting your conscience is not what upsets people. What does tick them off is when they feel that you're trying to be everything to everybody, just to get reelected.

Whenever Christians impose the Gospel on non-Christians, the cause of Christ is hurt. Sometimes *not* declaring the Gospel in a public way is a great way to declare it, as strange as that may sound. As a case in point, there was a news story awhile back about a high school in the rural South which had a tradition of singing a hymn as part of its high school graduation program. One year, a couple of non-Christians in the graduating class objected and said they didn't want anything religious during the commencement.

The school board held a meeting and concluded that, since the singing of the hymn was something requested by the students, it was legal. A court decision upheld the school board. But then one of the school board members, who was known to be a strong Christian throughout the community, made a plea to the members of the graduating class and asked them if they would be kind enough *not* to sing the hymn, even though they had won the right to sing it. After all, he explained, it would not be a matter of compromising their faith if, out of loving concern for a couple of their classmates, they gave up something that would make those two high school seniors feel seriously uncomfortable.

The other students agreed. The hymn was not sung. And two high school kids were sent a message that their feelings were important to their classmates. Now that's what I call a good witness for Christ, even though some would probably not agree with me.

The apostle Paul once said that things that were *lawful* for him were not necessarily *expedient* (1 Corinthians 10:23). I think he would have been pleased with the recommendation of that school board member and the decision of that senior class.

The biggest problem Christians face in their involvement with politics is that politics is about power, while being Christian is about love. In trying to use power to create the values of the kingdom of God within the present social order, the danger is that we will set aside love. As we work to establish righteousness via political means, it is sometimes too easy to think ourselves justified when we hurt those who oppose us or run roughshod over those who stand in the way of our own personalized version of the kingdom of God. If we fail to demonstrate love for others in the process of creating our version of the kingdom, then, even if we win, we lose.

In truth, if we follow Jesus, we can be political winners without being spiritual losers.

Chapter 16

How to Be an Environmentalist

without Becoming a Tree-Hugger

I
t was on one of those clean-up-your-neighborhood days that I
was driving through Camden, New Jersey, and spotted a little
boy—he couldn't have been more than eight years old—pulling
behind him a huge plastic bag filled with trash.

"What are you doing?" I called at him from my car window.

The boy, not knowing me from Adam, looked up with pride and
called back, "Mister, I'm cleaning up America!"

Now *there's* a noble calling.

Every summer an army of collegiate volunteers joins me in ministry to urban children across America. We try to help them through
special programs that include sports, Bible study, and academic tutoring. We also try to make the kids who live in these urban slums into
environmentalists. If you had to look at the trash and junk strewn
along the streets and piled up on the vacant lots where they live, you
would understand why this is so important. If you could see the empty
beer cans and discarded needles from drug users in every direction
you looked, you would grasp the significance of what we are trying to
get the kids to do. It's difficult to experience God in the midst of a
filthy environment. It's hard to feel spiritual when you are surrounded
by garbage. And it takes a real effort to sense God's abiding presence
when the graffiti of angry people is everywhere you look.

I believe that one of the reasons God created everything beautiful is because God wanted to nurture our souls through beauty. When we mess up God's beautiful world because of our sin, God calls us to repent and to do the works of repentance. That means to make everything like new in His name (Revelation 21:5). It was to that end that the volunteers and staff of our ministries in Camden—perhaps the most messed-up city in America—called upon the hundreds of kids with whom they work daily to give one day a month to cleaning up their neighborhoods. This involved picking up cans, collecting paper for recycling, gathering up discarded tires, and sweeping up the omnipresent broken glass.

Any careful reading of the Bible provides a lot of evidence to support the claim that trying to make all things good and beautiful is very much a part of being God's people. When Jesus saved us, He called us to be partners with Him in the work that He wanted to do in the world. There is little doubt that our Lord very much wants to recreate this world through us and make it like new. Part of the reason why Jesus came into the world and saved us from sin was for just that purpose. Through us who are saved and sanctified by His grace, He wants to renew the earth. God's will is that everything, ourselves included, should be made new and beautiful again. The Bible says as much in Romans 8:19ff:

> For the earnest expectation of the creature waiteth for the manifestation of the sons of God. For the creature was made subject to vanity, not willingly, but by reason of him who hath subjected the same in hope. Because the creature itself also shall be delivered from the bondage of corruption into the glorious liberty of the children of God. For we know that the whole creation groaneth and travaileth in pain together until now, And not only they, but ourselves also, which have the firstfruits of the Spirit, even we ourselves groan within ourselves, waiting for the adoption, to wit, the redemption of our body. (Romans 8:19–23)

I wonder how much of the despair and how many of the threats of violence that lurk on our city streets are nurtured by ugly surroundings?

I wonder how many tough kids see nothing good in themselves because they see nothing good in the streets and alleys of their neighborhoods? I wonder how many people trash themselves and the others around them because they live in a world of trash? Questions like these beg for answers, and I'm sure that knowing the answers would inspire a lot of us to wish we could join that little kid in Camden and help to clean up America. But whenever we get into discussions about the environment, some strange ideas come to the surface.

MY CONCERNS

For me, concern for the environment didn't come from the alarmists who talked about the consequences of the growing *holes* in the atmosphere at the north and south poles, nor from the scary news that we are being exposed to increasingly dangerous cancer-giving radiation because chlorofluorocarbons are destroying the ionosphere. Nor did it come from those granola-types that hang out at natural-foods stores. Instead, my own awakening came from going to see the whales!

For almost twenty-five years, my wife and I have annually visited Provincetown, Massachusetts, to go whale watching. In case you don't know what a whale watch is, let me simply describe it as a group of ordinary folks like me who go out on the ocean in a boat hoping to find some whales to watch. To enjoy whale watching, you have to be the kind of person who is willing to patiently wait, sometimes for hours, for these huge leviathans of the deep to surface. When they do, they send spouts of mist into the air as they expel their breath. Whales never seem to stay in sight long enough, but at least the humpbacks we watch off Cape Cod do usually reward us with a good display of their tails as they dive into the deep and disappear.

Once, in the midst of a whale watch, I was taken by surprise when a whale did something quite unexpected. She swam up alongside the boat and poked her head out of the water. Incredibly, that whale just stayed there, for what must have been at least thirty seconds, and for thirty seconds she looked straight at me. Call me "off the wall" if you want to, but I know that her gigantic eye focused on me and, in turn,

I was transfixed and riveted on her. It was truly something that Martin Buber would have called an "I-Thou encounter." I *felt* something, and the emotion took me by surprise. What I felt was mystical. I wish I could come up with words to share with you the sense of awe and wonder that came over me in that encounter. I knew that I had connected with something more than a gigantic mammal. I felt myself being addressed—spoken to—and even loved. I sensed that there was a plea coming from my *sister* from the deep, and that there was a *pathos* in that plea. There was, in that encounter, a message sent and a message received. That message from my sea-bound friend was that she, and her kind, were dying off. I felt her pleading that I should enter into her sufferings and join her and the other members of her species in their struggle for life.

I know that most people will argue that I have read more into that encounter than I should have, and that I had no reasonable basis for reaching the conclusions I did about being *spoken to* by that humpback whale. But what happened to me happened. Sometimes a person knows something even when logic would say it's all imagination. And in that unforgettable moment, I knew, and I still know, what the whale was all about.

Since that mystical encounter off the shores of Provincetown, I have reflected long and hard on how the saving of the whales and the rescuing of nature from devastation is a divine calling. I have tried to figure out ways to carry out that calling. I have found no better guide in this venture than St. Francis of Assisi. Centuries ago, Saint Francis earned the reputation of being a man who could preach to the birds and have them understand what he was trying to tell them. This premodern follower of Christ sensed a spiritual kinship with nature and gives us a hint in poetic form of what that kinship was like. There is no better expression of what it is like to view nature with a heart that is alive to the Holy Spirit than in Francis's miraculous poem, *Canticle to the Sun*:

> *Most high, all-powerful, all good, Lord!*
> *All praise is yours, all glory, all honor*
> *And all blessing!*

To you alone, Most High, do they belong.
    No mortal lips are worthy
    To pronounce your name.

All praise be yours, my Lord, through all that you have made,
    And first my lord Brother Sun
    Who brings the day; and light you give to us through him.

How beautiful is he, how radiant in all his splendor!
    Of you, Most High, he bears the likeness.

All praise be yours, My Lord, through Sister Moon and Stars;
    In the heavens you have made them, bright
    And precious and fair.

All praise be yours, my Lord, through Brothers Wind and Air,
    And fair and stormy, all the weather's moods,
    By which you cherish all that you have made.

All praise be yours, my Lord, through Sister Water,
    So useful, lowly, precious, and pure.

All praise be yours, my Lord, through Brother Fire,
    Through whom you brighten up the night.
    How beautiful he is, how gay! Full of power and strength.

All praise be yours, my Lord, through Sister Earth, our mother,
    Who feeds us in her sovereignty and produces
    Various fruits and colored flowers and herbs.

All praise be yours, my Lord, through those who grant pardon
    For love of you; through those who endure
    Sickness and trial.

Happy those who endure in peace,
    By you, Most High, they will be crowned.

All praise be yours, my Lord, through Sister Death,
From whose embrace no mortal can escape.

Woe to those who die in mortal sin!

Happy those She finds doing your will!
The second death can do no harm to them.

Praise and bless my Lord, and give him thanks,
And serve him with great humility.

As I have sought to make sense out of the message that I received from the whale and have tried to understand why rescuing God's creation is so important, St. Francis has been my constant guide. Francis, more than any man I know about since Jesus, was gifted with an intimacy with nature that enabled him to understand the divine purposes of all God's creatures. The insights that come from his words and his life help me to understand the reasons why I was called to join in the struggle to save the whales, as well as the other creatures that God *spoke* into existence.

It was through Francis that I first discovered that the purpose of all of God's creation was *worship*. He, more than any of the other saints, helped me to realize that God did not create the animals, birds, trees, and everything else in heaven and earth simply for our own personal enjoyment and use. Francis made it clear to me that everything was created to glorify God and "to sing His praises forever." This theology is nowhere more clearly supported than in Psalm 148.

Praise ye the Lord. Praise ye the Lord from the heavens: praise
him in the heights.
Praise ye him, all his angels: praise ye him, all his hosts.
Praise ye him, sun and moon: praise him, all ye stars of light.
Praise him, ye heavens of heavens, and ye waters that be above the
heavens.
Let them praise the name of the Lord: for he commanded, and
they were created.

He hath also stablished them for ever and ever: he hath made
a decree which shall not pass.
Praise the LORD *from the earth, ye dragons, and all deeps:*
Fire, and hail; snow, vapors; stormy wind fulfilling his word:
Mountains, and all hills; fruitful trees, and all cedars:
Beasts, and all cattle; creeping things, and flying foul:
Kings of the earth, and all people; princes, and all judges
of the earth:
Both young men, and maidens; old men, and children:
Let them praise the name of the LORD: *for his name alone is*
excellent; his glory is above the earth and heaven.
He also exalteth the horn of his people, the praise of all his saints;
even of the children of Israel, a people near unto him.
Praise ye the LORD.

The message of this psalm was so clear to Francis that he knew that the death of any creature was the silencing of a voice that was meant to sing praises to the Creator. In his daily life Francis lived out this creed, doing all that he could to protect all of God's creatures. When the shepherds around Assisi decided to hunt down and destroy a vicious wolf that had been killing off their sheep, Francis intervened to save the wolf. He begged the shepherds to give him three days to make friends with the wolf and to call him away from his predatory ways. Out of respect for the saint, the shepherds of Assisi agreed. Francis then went out, found the wolf, and loved this once dangerous creature through a kind of conversion and tamed him. When Francis returned to Assisi, the people were amazed to see the wolf following him into town. So gentle was the wolf that he became a much-loved pet to the town's children.

Francis taught that a spiritually regenerate man could become an instrument of salvation for fallen creation, an instrument through whom God can initiate the conversion of the earth into the Peaceable Kingdom. Nature waits for the sons and daughters of God to rescue it from its travail (Romans 8:19–23). Francis heeded that call, and in the loving power of the Spirit began to do what Jesus will do in glorious fullness for the rest of creation when He returns (Ephesians 1:18–23).

I want to be like Francis! I, too, want to rescue God's creatures from unnecessary destruction so that they might join with the elect of God in singing praises to their Creator.

St. Bonaventura tells how Francis not only rescued God's creatures from death but also called on them to praise their God and Creator. Francis invited the crickets that he heard at eventide in the open fields of Umbria to sing hymns of praise to God and assured the crickets that God loved to hear their rhythmic songs of love to Him. Francis would ask the sheep grazing on the hills surrounding Assisi to lift up their heads and to "baa" unto their Creator, according to Bonaventura.

It is to preserve their songs of praise that God's creatures must be saved, contended Francis. That is a lesson I learned from him as I studied his spirituality. I learned that the songs of the humpback whales are nothing less than hymns of praise to the Lord. Furthermore, I believe that to interfere with those songs by killing off the humpbacks is blasphemy because, by so doing, we interfere with the worship of the Creator by creatures created to worship God.

If all of this seems absurd to you, I can only say, you didn't meet my friend in the ocean of Provincetown. You didn't have her look you straight in the eye and plead for life. You didn't feel the sacredness of that creature, whose brain may be able to think thoughts about God that are beyond the scope of our understanding. In the words of Bob Dylan, "Don't condemn what you don't understand."

In the midst of all of this mystical talk, let us remember that there are also utilitarian reasons for being environmentally concerned. Unless we clean up the air and the water, our planet will eventually become uninhabitable. Unless we do something about the destruction of the rain forests in the tropics, we will mess up the balance of nature. By interfering with the causes of rainfall, we will bring on disastrous weather patterns. Unless we do something about the hydrocarbons we are pumping into the atmosphere, we face the danger of global warming. If we don't do what must be done to preserve nature, we may be rendering extinct those animals and plants whose extracts could provide the cures for such illnesses as cancer and Alzheimer's disease.

We must recognize that it is from the organic world that most of the miracle cures (i.e., penicillin) of modern medicine are gleaned.

POLITICAL ACTION

If we want to save the environment, Christians must realize that we *must* become involved in politics and economics. Each one of us can do a lot to help save the environment by recycling, conserving water, saving electricity, and cutting back on the use of fuel oil. But we also must recognize the fact that efforts by individuals alone are not enough. Collective action is also needed. Together we must work to pass the kinds of laws that will stop environmental destruction. Just a handful of people can ruin God's creation, even while the bulk of the population behaves in an environmentally responsible way. An industry dumping chemical waste here, a lumber company deforesting a rain forest there, and an oil tanker carelessly piloted somewhere else can do irreparable damage that will leave us all the victims of an ecological disaster. We must take collective action to stop such practices. Even the most *laissez faire* capitalist has to concede that, without some kind of government regulation on those who would abuse the environment, there isn't much chance that we will be able to turn back the horrendous tide of waste and ugliness that has resulted from environmental irresponsibility.

We can't let those who put profits ahead of our collective well-being unravel the Clean Air and Clean Water Acts. These laws were put in place over the last couple of decades because some legislators realized that those who would destroy the environment had to be stopped. Laws such as the Endangered Species Act must not be repealed.

It is the epitome of naïveté to assume that industrialists and business leaders will, out of the goodness of their hearts, act as responsible custodians of God's creation. Being environmentally responsible is expensive, and those who are driven to optimize the bottom line of their commercial enterprises inevitably will cut corners when it comes to being environmentally responsible. Concerns for preserving nature are quickly relegated to being matters of secondary importance when profits become all important. If we are to fulfill the biblical imperatives to care for and preserve the environment, we must collectively work through governmental regulations to constrain those who pose a threat to a clean, healthy, and beautiful world. The Environmental Protection Agency (EPA) may sometimes seem to be a pain in the neck, and some of its rules and regulations probably need serious changes. But we need something like the EPA until human nature is changed and people can be depended upon to do the will of God, rather than seek their own self-interest.

BEYOND POLITICAL ACTION

Responsible Christian social action for saving the environment requires collective political regulations. But political action alone will not get the job done. Some creative efforts beyond politics are also needed. That's why I joined with some of my friends to start the Christian Environmental Association (CEA). CEA is hard at work finding practical ways to save nature and does so in ways that often go beyond political action.

As a case in point, CEA has a plan to buy up vast acreage in the endangered rain forests. We have begun to do this in Belize, a small nation in Central America, once known as British Honduras. A private company that owns most of the rain forest in Belize has entered into a contract with us in which they are offering to sell their land for thirty-five dollars an acre. CEA has gone to work seeking out church youth groups and Sunday school classes, as well as interested individuals who are willing to buy one or more acres of the rain forest in Belize. CEA has met with great success in this effort, and I believe that our program of *buying* up the rain forests may prove to be the only way to save them.

Practically speaking, it does little good to set forth the very valid argument that the natives who inhabit the rain forest are the rightful owners of that land. That argument will save the rain forest for the natives who live there about as well as it protected the native North

Americans from the seizure of their lands by European invaders. We have to recognize that those investors who, justifiably or unjustifiably, have laid claim to the rain forests (often paying huge fees to secure legal titles) will determine the destinies of both the rain forests and those who live in them. Facing this reality, the members of CEA are determined to become the lawful owners of this land, for the express purpose of developing it in ways that will bless the indigenous people who live there.

CEA also has established a base camp in the rain forest of Belize. They have built living quarters and meeting rooms so that visitors from North America can come and learn what rain forests are all about and what the destruction of them means for our earth. Visitors get to meet with the people who live in the rain forests and to hear firsthand what threats to their ways of life are posed by the indiscriminate slash-and-burn clearing of the land by exploiting investors.

During their visit to our base camp in Belize, the visitors learn about ways in which the resources of the rain forests can be responsibly developed and how the trees can be harvested carefully so as not to destroy the habitat of both people and animals. CEA provides a chance for visitors to discuss what it means to be building a loving sense of community with native peoples who, for better or for worse, are forced to become a part of the global village.

EARTH DAY

CEA is doing a great deal, but there is one thing that I have not been able to get its members to do, in spite of their conceptual agreement with the idea. I very much want for CEA members, most of whom are college students, to become an evangelistic presence at Earth Day celebrations. Once a year when Earth Day rolls around, environmentalists gather together in cities and villages across the country both to celebrate nature and to learn what can be done to prevent its destruction. I believe that Christians should be a prominent presence on these occasions, bearing witness to the God who so loved the world that He sent His only begotten Son to deliver it from the ravages of sinful humanity. I have proposed that CEA members show up and distribute tracts with their own version of the Four Spiritual Laws that might look something like this:

1. God loves you and all of creation and has a wonderful plan for both.
2. Sin disrupted God's plan for you and for the rest of creation.
3. Jesus, God's Son, came into the world and did what was needed to restore both you and all of Creation to what God willed from before the world began.
4. God calls us to be transformed by Jesus Christ into persons who will work to carry out something of His plan to make all things new.

It seems to me that people who love Creation ought to be ready and willing to love its Creator. We must not abandon Earth Day celebrations to those New Age gurus who regularly show up and try to dominate these occasions. Christians ought to be on hand for these special days, and there and then declare that Jesus Christ is the Lord of *all* creation through His death and resurrection. I want Christians to learn how to do evangelism in the context of Earth Day celebrations.

A few years ago my wife and I were on a train traveling through the southwestern part of England towards Essex. The train was packed with Earth People heading for Stonehenge, where a big celebration of nature was underway. To give you some idea of the *flakes* who were on that train, consider the *chap* who was sitting opposite me, obviously spaced out on something. He had that Alfred E. Neuman blissed-out smile that communicated a "What? Me worry?" mind-set. I happened to notice that my off-the-wall friend was wearing only one shoe. This led me to ask him if he was aware of the fact that he had lost one.

To my question he sweetly smiled, looked at me through his glazed eyes, and slowly said, "I didn't lose a shoe! I found one!"

Whether I should have or not, I couldn't help but laugh. Gatherings like the one to which this young man was headed need an army of

Christian soldiers to invade them, bear witness to what God wants to do to make the world new, and offer our invitation to whosoever will join the God of Creation in the great task of rescuing the earth from the evil that would pollute and destroy it.

THE POOR

Recently CEA has focused on another primary reason for Christians to be environmentally concerned—the poor. As the environment has been decimated by human folly and irresponsibility, the poor have been the primary victims. This is not to say that the poor are innocent victims, for they, out of ignorance or out of need, often have joined with the rich and powerful in acts of environmental destruction. When it comes to deforestation, the peasants in places like Haiti are the primary culprits. It is the Haitian peasantry that cuts down mahogany trees in order to turn this precious wood into charcoal for their stoves. But even as blame is laid upon them, there has to be a growing consciousness among the rest of us as to how the destruction of our environment is felt disproportionately by the poor of the earth.

As trees are cut down without any program for replanting, and as the soil erodes, land is rendered unusable for growing food. The results are predictable. Less and less food can be produced in these places, in spite of the fact that a population explosion makes the need for food increasingly more desperate. In Haiti during the last twenty-five years, food production has dropped 40 percent while the population has increased by nearly 25 percent. It is obvious that mass famine lies waiting just down the road for the poorest of the poor in Haiti.

Even evangelical missionaries in Third World countries, who know they risk losing some of their more conservative supporters when they become proponents of environmentalism, are beginning to speak out. They are stepping forward and declaring that being environmentally responsible is very much a part of living out the gospel of Christ to the poor that they are seeking to save.

In the summer of 1987 I stood on the edge of the Senegal River in West Africa. With me was a tribal chief who was the leader of a nation of nomads. His people were dying off from a lack of water. The herds of goats that had provided his people's livelihood were all but gone, and most of the able-bodied young men of the tribe had left to seek a new life in the city of Dakar.

As we talked, the chief said, "This is not a drought that we must endure. It is far more serious than that. My people know how to survive the droughts. For a thousand years we have survived the droughts. But this is not a drought."

When I asked him why he thought what was happening was more than a drought, he simply answered, "The world is changing."

That tribal chief was no environmental scientist or meteorologist, but he was right. As we have destroyed the rain forests, filled the atmosphere with dirt, and otherwise disfigured the earth, we have changed the weather patterns of our planet. Rain that was once produced in rain forests like that which surrounds the mighty Amazon is disappearing at an incredible rate. Acreage of rain forest the size of the state of Washington is being wiped out each year. When rain forests are no longer there to create the rain that is needed, desertification begins to occur in places like Senegal. Desertification is happening around the world, but particularly so on the continent of Africa. The Sahara Desert there, which is roughly the size of the United States, is expanding southward at the rate of almost two miles a year.

It takes no genius to figure out that the first victims of this changing world will be the poor. As food production declines, and the world's population expands, shortages in food and water will take their first toll on the poor. Thus, those who have a heart for the poor must surely see that environmental concerns must not be left to idiosyncratic tree-huggers. The God of History who said, "Blessed are the poor," does not have to provide a specific calling for us to be aware that caring for the environment is an essential part of Christian discipleship. Jesus had a special concern for the poor. That's why I know that, if He were here in the flesh, He would do something significant to withstand the destruction of the environment. Our Lord would do this not only because He wills for nature to be rescued and freed to worship the Creator, but because His concern for the poor necessitates keeping the earth fruitful for all of His creatures, but especially for the poor.

GET INVOLVED

There are so many things we all must do to live out discipleship with respect to the environment. There is a multiplicity of books that spell out all kinds of things you can do that will help save the earth and preserve it for the next generation. But a good place to start in the quest for environmental responsibility is to join one of the solidly Christian environmental groups that are mobilizing Christians to act collectively as well as individually to save the planet and all of its creatures. I've already told you about CEA. Write to us at:

The Christian Environmental Association
1650 Zanker Road, Suite 150
San Jose, CA 95512

Another good option is the ecumenically grounded Green Cross. Their address is:

Green Cross
10 Lancaster Avenue
Wynnewood, PA 19096

But do *something!* Hugging a tree is okay, if that's what turns you on. But responsible Christianity requires collective action to save the environment, before it's too late. Time is slipping away on this one!

Chapter 17

How to Be Positive about Women

without Being Negative about Men

The other day I heard about a woman who, when asked about her husband leaving her for a younger woman, answered, "Of course he left me for a younger woman! Anyone his own age would have seen right through him."

Women have a lot of reasons to be angry. They often sense that, in our society, their primary value is wrapped up in their physical appearance, especially in the shape of their bodies. Out of fear that not looking young anymore could cost them everything from their jobs to their marriages, many women live with a preoccupation about their weight. Some of them, in desperation, go from one fad diet to another at great risk to their health. Anorexia is becoming more common as women increasingly suffer from anxieties about becoming fat. Many women live in constant fear that men will punish them by losing interest to the extent that they fail to measure up to the physical dimensions prescribed by the centerfold playgirls in *Playboy* magazine. Most of all, women are afraid of getting old. They fully comprehend the sarcasm of the secular feminist Kate Millet, who said, "A forty-year-old man is *mature*. But a forty-year-old woman is *obsolete*."

Being on the speaking circuit, I sometimes find myself in unusual settings. From time to time (for reasons I can never figure out), I end up as a speaker for women's groups. I usually enjoy these opportunities. But I remember one such gathering that really left me feeling depressed. It was a meeting for a nationwide Christian organization that sponsors luncheon meetings attended, for the most part, by white, middle-class, suburban housewives.

When I arrived at the hotel for the luncheon, I was pulled aside by the Mistress of Ceremonies, who gave me a variety of warnings about what I should and should not talk about. In the midst of her exhortations, which I tried to endure patiently, she blurted out, "And for goodness sakes, don't mention anything about age or weight!"

I fully understood why she felt it was necessary to warn me. From my years of pastoral counseling, I had gained an understanding of what women go through as they daily try to escape the awareness that the years are passing them by and that, with the passing of time, there is also a passing of those physical traits which women have been made to believe are the basis of their self-worth. Women don't just *imagine* that they are too often judged on the basis of their physical appearance. There are constant reality-checks to remind them that we live in a sexist culture and that its values have been readily absorbed, even by their own husbands.

Sitting on the beach is not my thing. In addition to my concern about getting skin cancer and an aversion to feeling hot, I just don't like the dirty feeling of sand sticking to my body. But to humor a friend, Peggy and I joined him and his wife for a few hours of basking in the "glories" of a beach on the Jersey shore. As I sat on my towel, trying to be cool about the whole thing, a young woman in a bikini walked by. She was one of those hard-bodied creatures in her late teens, who was well aware that her exhibitionist tendencies were getting her the desired results. My friend, obviously caught up in the passing display, elbowed me and said, "Hey Tony! Look at *that!* Now *that's* really something."

I'm a pacifist. Otherwise I might have killed him! If that bikini-clad woman strutting her stuff was "something," what was he indirectly saying to his fifty-five-year-old wife? Was it not the message "You're nothing"? If you contend that my friend's wife shouldn't react that way to his insensitivity, I have to ask the question Why not? Why shouldn't she feel diminished by her husband's sexist remarks?

Why shouldn't she feel ashamed for being fifty-five and showing it? And why shouldn't she feel just a little resentment toward her husband who, to be objective about it, wasn't exactly an Adonis?

The apostle Paul tells us that, when we become new persons in Christ, we are not to regard each other "after the flesh, but after the spirit" (Romans 8:1). Obviously, my friend had not gotten this particular Pauline message. He certainly had not lived it out that day. He had failed to let his wife know that the spiritual depth she had developed over the years, and the character she had carefully nurtured, made her incredibly desirable and far more interesting than some self-absorbed teeny bopper in a bikini.

It is each marital partner's responsibility to so affirm the other that each is convinced that the other can say with integrity what Sir Thomas More once said to his wife:

> Believe me, if all those endearing young charms, which I gaze on so fondly today, were to change by tomorrow, and fleet in my arms, like fairy gifts fading away, Thou wouldst still be adored as this moment art, let they lovliness fade as it will; And around the dear ruin, each wish of my heart would entwine itself verdantly still.

In the Workplace

In the work-a-day world, women also encounter attitudes from men that offend and hurt. Too often, women are expected to shrug off sexual innuendoes and inappropriate touching without making any complaints about sexual harassment. They find that equal pay for equal work is still far from being a reality. And women trying to climb the corporate ladder find that, in most settings, a *glass ceiling* keeps them from going all the way to the top.

One woman executive said, "To get anywhere in the corporate world a woman has to do the same work a man would do in the same job, but she must do it twice as well." Then she added wryly, "Fortunately, that is not difficult."

Another woman said, "We deserve more pay than men. After all, anything Fred Astaire could do, Ginger Rogers could do backwards and on high heels."

In May, 1997, a highly successful female sales executive from a prominent Christian company was interviewing for a position with another, smaller Christian company that specialized in the same products as the larger firm. She was seeking an executive-level position comparable to the one she was planning to leave. However, the glass ceiling slapped her in the face when the president of the smaller company said, "Well, in our company our *ladies* are only managers, not executives." And this is, supposedly, a Christian company. I guess he missed that part of the Bible that says "neither male nor female in Christ Jesus."

In America, there have been some correctives in the system that have, for the most part, benefited the college-educated, junior-executive female. This is the type of woman who can readily be encountered on airplanes as she flies off to her meetings. With affirmative action plans in place in many sectors of the business world, there may even be advantages for some women who, in certain situations, can actually earn *better* pay than men who have greater ability or who have better qualifications for their jobs. This is because, in today's societal system, it is often essential for appearances' sake that companies practice a kind of tokenism that gives a few women access to certain leadership roles.

What we have to recognize is that, while there have been some correctives in our society that have made things better for *professional* women, very little has been done to remedy the oppressive conditions often endured by working-class women and those women who fall below the poverty line. Foremost among the problems faced by these less fortunate women is the problem of deadbeat fathers. These are men who leave their wives and children and then do everything in their power to evade the responsibility of financially supporting them. Unfortunately, men who want to get out of paying child support have an easy way of doing it. They often can escape the authority of the family court in one state simply by moving to another. Why isn't there a federal system that would simply take support payments out of these guys' salaries and then pass them on to the families they left behind? Why isn't there an automatic reciprocity between states to hold these deadbeat husbands accountable?

Being underpaid and having to work in undesirable conditions happens more often to unskilled working women than to their professional sisters. Why aren't more efforts being made to see to it that women who work on assembly lines or in other low-skilled jobs get the same kind of economic compensation that men get for the same kind of labor?

The new welfare reform laws are going to make things even more difficult for economically disadvantaged women. A lot of welfare mothers are going to be forced off the dole and into the workplace. Many have long argued that the old welfare system had to go because it created dependency and destroyed dignity. But the same people who cheer such changes in the welfare system are very likely to be opposed to the government's providing adequate day care for the children of working-class mothers or seeing to it that they have guaranteed healthcare. In a society where one-third of all our children are living in single-parent homes headed by mothers, women who live near or below the poverty line have a right to be angry about this. There's injustice here! The women's rights movement may have delivered some limited goodies to those professional, upper-middle-class women who complain so articulately on television talk shows, but it has all but forgotten the poorer women of America. Working-class women have a right to be ticked off, not only at the male-dominated *establishment*, but at a women's movement that seems to be concentrated on the concerns of highly educated professionals to the neglect of *their* basic needs.

It is time for Christians to stand up and speak out for oppressed women. We should be doing everything possible to lift the heavy burdens they bear. To start with, every church that can should provide good, inexpensive day care for working mothers. Churches should be committed to securing fair pay for working women, and no church should pass off the concerns of working-class women and those who are on public assistance as though they were unimportant. The Bible has piles of verses that call upon the people of God to defend the orphans and the widows (Isaiah 10:1–2). In today's world, that would have to include all those single mothers and children who live at or below the poverty line. When it comes to justice in the workplace, the Church should echo the apostle James who, in his epistle, calls down God's judgment on those who underpay their employees, both male and female.

> Go to now, ye rich men, weep and howl for your miseries that shall come upon you. Your riches are corrupted, and your garments are motheaten. Your gold and silver is cankered; and the rust of them shall be a witness against you, and shall eat your flesh as it were fire. Ye have heaped treasure together for the last days. Behold, the hire of the labourers who have reaped down your fields, which is of you kept back by fraud, crieth: and the cries of them which have reaped are entered into the ears of the Lord of sabaoth. Ye have lived in pleasure on the earth, and been wanton; ye have nourished your hearts, as in a day of slaughter. (James 5:1–5)

It's bad enough that most churches don't fight against the economic oppression of women, but there are some churches that actually add to it. There are churches in this land that allow *evil* preaching against women to come from their pulpits. For instance, there ought to be outrage against any preacher who, in a misguided understanding of Scripture, suggests that women ought to endure physical abuse as part of their obligation to be biblically submissive. Since it's usually our fundamentalist churches who have these kinds of preachers, it's up to conservative groups, like the Christian Coalition, to speak out against such distortions of God's Word. To tell women that they ought to endure abusive husbands is to ignore the fact that even the apostle Paul suggests that there have to be limits to what a woman puts up with in a marriage. Paul writes that marital partners ought to do their best to stay together, but a reading of 1 Corinthians 7 tells us by implication that there may come a point at which the only thing to do is to leave.

Just recently I read about a battered woman who had been urged by her pastor to leave the shelter where she was hiding out, return to her abusive husband, and be in *subjection* to him. She did, and he killed her! All that the minister could say in response to the news of what happened was that the husband would have to answer for what he had done on Judgment Day. There was no hint on the pastor's part that he himself had done or said anything wrong. Such a pastor not only makes himself an enemy of women, he also makes the gospel, as Paul would say, "of none effect among many."

One of the reasons that the Church—a community of faith brought into existence by the greatest and most balanced women's advocate of all time—has not spoken out more boldly on women's issues is that it has not gotten its own house in order. As women strive to change society and make it more just toward them, the Church should be their greatest ally. "Instead," says one of my Christian feminist friends, "I don't think the Church has ever met a *status quo* in regard to women that it didn't like."

The Church not only has failed to speak up for women, but it has, in its own way, maintained practices that put women down. Perhaps more than most institutions in the world today, the Church has kept women out of key roles of leadership and has deemed them, in many instances, unfit for the gospel ministry. As an evangelical Christian, I have found that it is in my own circles that the tendency to hinder women and keep them out of leadership roles is most pronounced. Some of my evangelical colleagues quote from 1 Timothy 2 to support their case against women preachers, and have even led church schisms in opposition to any attempt to circumvent these words of Paul: "Let the woman learn in silence with all subjection. But I suffer not a woman to teach, nor to usurp authority over the man, but to be in silence" (1 Timothy 2:11–12). I might take the concerns of those opposed to woman preachers just a little more seriously if there were some consistency between what they *say* and what they *practice*. But the same men who deny women pulpits here in the United States seem quite willing to send them overseas as missionaries to preach the gospel in desperately difficult situations. How many of our evangelical missionary societies do you know about that refuse to allow women to preach in Africa? Don't most of those who are against women preachers readily send women out to preach in foreign missionary settings?

There is a kind of sexist/racist hierarchy at work here. At the top of that hierarchy are white males. Then, going down the ladder, next come white women. Below white women are black men. And below black men and at the bottom of this hierarchy are black women. Given this arrangement, each group is allowed to preach to those groups that are below it. This means that the white males can preach to anybody, but white women are not allowed to preach to them. White women, on the other hand, can preach to black men, as well as to black women. Black men, in this system, can preach to black women. And black women, I suppose, are left with their children—at least their daughters—as those to whom they can give the gospel.

Recently, I read a history of missionary work among Native Americans during the nineteenth century. To my surprise, I found that most of those who carried the good news of Christ to tribes in such hard places as the Dakotas and the remote corners of Montana were *women*. While men occupied the good paying pulpits back East, these pioneer woman missionaries braved the frontiers, sometimes wading in snow up to their waists, in order to preach the salvation story to the lost. Back in the nineteenth century, the Church seemed willing to let women preach, as long as they ministered in those hard places where professional male clergy types were not as willing to venture.

An angry colleague of mine once called me down in public by asking what he believed was an embarrassing question. He said, "There is no question as to whether or not women should be allowed to speak in church. What would we do for Sunday school teachers if we forbade their speaking?" (Now there's an interesting question.) He then went on to say, "I don't mind them teaching Sunday school, but the real question is whether or not we should ordain them for the pulpit ministry. Where do you stand, Mr. Campolo? Where do you stand on the matter of the ordination of women?"

My response was simple. "I thought that *everybody* was ordained to the ministry! Isn't that what Paul is talking about in Ephesians 4:9–12? Aren't we all, through the Spirit, given gifts for ministry? And aren't we all told not to neglect the use of the gifts that we have been given? (See 1 Timothy 4:14). Where in the Bible does it say that the gifts of the Spirit, which include the gift of preaching, are only for men? And do you not agree with my contention that *all* are ordained regardless of race and gender? In Christ," I contend: "There is neither Jew nor Greek, there is neither bond nor free, there is neither male nor female: for ye are all one in Christ Jesus" (Galatians 3:28).

The passage in 1 Timothy once posed a very serious problem for me, because I am one of those who believes in the infallibility of the Scriptures. It is inconceivable to me that Paul could have made a mistake when he wrote these words because I'm convinced that the Holy Spirit guided Paul and kept him from errors. However, recent biblical scholarship has shown me that my former reading of this passage was limited by a failure to understand what was going on in the Church of the first century. Lately I have come to read this passage with a whole new interpretation.

It seems as though the women in the early church were abusing their newfound Christian freedom. The realization that in Christ there was "neither male nor female" (Galatians 3:28) and that women stood before God as equals to men led them to be carried away into excesses, which were both shocking and unkind. Many evangelical scholars contend that these women, emancipated by their new status in Christ, were standing up in church meetings and putting down their husbands, giving them lectures on how they should behave. The humiliation of husbands, whose shortcomings were being publicly exposed, apparently had become scandalous. These scholars believe that Paul was trying to put an end to this embarrassing behavior when he wrote, "And if they will learn any thing, let them ask their husbands at home: for it is a shame for women to speak in the church" (1 Corinthians 14:35). He was simply declaring that domestic problems should be dealt with in private and that women should not abuse the privileges they had found through Christ's liberation by behaving in an unseemly fashion. Church was not the place for them to try to teach their husbands what those husbands should and should not do.

BEING CAREFUL ABOUT GOING TOO FAR

Even those who support women in the preaching ministry have among them many who contend that this feminist thing is on the verge of going too far. As a case in point, they cite attempts to rewrite all the old hymns of the Church using inclusive language. "And it doesn't stop there," they say. "They want to go back and rewrite the Bible so that male language is wiped out of the Holy Book."

On the one hand, I have to admit that there is something arrogant about the suggestion that when Jesus prayed the "Our Father," His understanding of God was somewhat lacking about the nature of the Almighty. The idea that feminists, with their inclusive language, have a better theology than the Son of God kind of leaves me more than a bit skeptical.

On the other hand, there *is* a strong case to be made in regard to language, and it is a case that I believe is difficult to ignore. Add to that the fact that I, as a male, cannot really understand the emotional reactions that many women have when they experience a sense of being shut out and reduced to second-class citizenship in the kingdom of God by religious language that is not gender-inclusive.

My wife, Peggy, who hardly can be labeled as an extremist on women's issues, has joined a church where inclusive language is used in every part of the worship services. Peggy says that once she got used to the inclusive language of her church, she realized just how much the old male exclusive language had given her the feeling that the gospel, God, and the Church were not meant primarily for her. Peggy now chooses to use no pronouns for God when she writes and speaks. She tells me that the gender-inclusive language of her church has helped her to identify more personally with God, even though she still prefers that the old familiar hymns be left as they are, and is uncomfortable with changing the Scriptures.

We men have to recognize that we have done a job on God, and in idolatrous fashion have redefined God in a very male-human form. We need to recognize our tendency to do in our own minds what Michelangelo did on the ceiling of the Sistine Chapel—that is, to make God into a physical creature who evidences all the traits we ourselves would have in idealized form. The God of Michelangelo, and of most of the rest of us striving-to-be-macho men, has bulging muscles and all the other accessories that characterize what we think a *real* man should possess.

When I first encountered Mormonism, I was shocked to learn that they believe that when we get to heaven we should expect to see God the Father in the form of a man, looking very much like a human being. "After all," they say, "if God made Adam in His image, should we not expect to find God looking like Adam?" I'm not sure that our own theology is far removed from that. Between those who think of God in Michelangelo fashion and those who buy into Mormon theology, it's easy to figure out one reason why the inspired Scriptures command us to make no graven images of God (Exodus 20:4). It is because there is a tendency for people in any given society to create images of God that incarnate the idealized traits of their own idealized selves. The God of those societies dominated by men will probably come across looking like a powerful male. In America, that means we are likely to end up with a God that looks a lot like Charlton Heston! There's no doubt about the evidence that the God contrived by male-dominated societies results in an idolatry much like the one the apostle Paul condemned in Romans 1:19–23.

I have gradually come to understand that there is a feminine side of God. On a subconscious level, I probably always knew this. Even before the feminist movement demanded that I use inclusive language to publicly declare it, I saw this side of God in the Jesus who approached the world with what we would call a feminine sensitivity and appreciation. The way our Lord considered the lilies of the field and the way He gave pause to the smallest bird that might fall dead from a tree made me see in God some traits our culture has conditioned me to think of as feminine. If the male side of God's character was expressed by Jesus' strong declarations of truth and pronouncements on morality, the side of God that I tend to think of as feminine was clear in His gentle sense of wonder while enjoying what the less perceptive would call the simple things of life.

The more I think of this other side of God, the more I think that if I could have been around in Jesus' time, I would not so much have wanted to see Him perform miracles and defy the self-righteous religionists in macho manner as I would have enjoyed sneaking along after Him as He took His private walks. I would have loved peeking at Him from behind some boulder on a hillside near the Sea of Galilee and watching Him be charmed by all the sights and sounds that surrounded Him. I would have liked watching the way Jesus looked at all the people He met and seeing how He delighted Himself with simple food and the taste of water.

The side of God that I have been socialized into calling masculine is something to be admired. But it is the *feminine* side that draws love out of me. It is this *feminine* side of God that I find in Jesus that makes me want to sing duets with Him. When I think about the *feminine* side of Jesus, I want to throw out my arms and be loved.

When I was younger and tougher and trying to be a dead serious prophet (And what young preacher doesn't have some desire to play such a role?), I was offended by a hymn that was dearly loved by many of the elderly members of the congregation I pastored. During the hymn singing in our Sunday evening services there was a time for requesting favorites, and I used to hate it when some elderly lady would ask for "I Come to the Garden Alone." But the older I get, the more I understand why they requested that hymn. As I outgrow my own messianic tendencies and more and more simply surrender to the Messiah in love, this hymn becomes increasingly meaningful to me. More and more I enjoy about Jesus what I earlier would have condemned as feminine sentimentality, and I love to sing these words:

> I come to the garden alone,
> While the dew is still on the roses;
> And the voice I hear, falling on my ear;
> The Son of God discloses.

He speaks, and the sound of His voice
Is so sweet the birds hush their singing,
And the melody that He gave to me,
Within my heart is ringing.

I'd stay in the garden with Him
Though the night around me be falling,
But He bids me go; through the voice of woe,
His voice to me is calling.

And He walks with me, and He talks with me,
And He tells me I am His own;
And the joy we share as we tarry there,
None other has ever known.

Not only do I love what might be called the feminine in Jesus, but the more I know Jesus, the more I realize that Jesus loves what might be called the feminine in me. In a day and age in which so many women are trying to rediscover the side of their humanity that the world deems masculine, I find that Jesus is helping me to appreciate those dimensions of me the world calls feminine.

For instance, I find myself understanding the concept of being the bride of Christ. I want Jesus to find in me and to *create* in me a sweetness and a sensitivity for all things and all people. I want more and more for Him to find in me, or to create in me, a gentle heart and an awareness of the goodness that lies in the people around me, especially the goodness in my enemies.

Once I wanted to be the enemy of the enemies of Jesus. But, little by little, I have come to realize that Jesus refuses to declare *any* of us to be His enemies, even though there are those who would like to dignify themselves by assuming such a title. And the more I become aware that Jesus does not view His enemies as enemies, the more it becomes difficult for me to define them as *my* enemies. I want to learn to love those people who stand on the other side of the struggles in which I am engaged. I pray that Jesus will bring out in me that blessed trait (which some disparage as feminine weakness) that will enable me to find the good in the racist, the homophobe, the fascist, and the militarist. The side of me that the world calls masculine would want them destroyed. But as Jesus draws out the so-called feminine in me, He makes me want to see them rescued by having the goodness that is in them overcome the evil. There is that feminine side of me that must be recovered and strengthened if I am to be like Christ. And it is in the recovering of that side of my humanity that I find myself more and more willing and less and less afraid to be called "a bride of Christ."

Society brought me up to suppress the so-called feminine dimensions of my humanness. But as Jesus makes me whole, both sides of who I am meant to be are coming to be fully realized. Only when I am delivered from the cultural distortions of my humanity will I be fully able to love Jesus and fully able to accept His love for me. Until I accept the feminine in my humanness, there will be a part of me that cannot receive some dimensions of God's love. Until I feel the feminine in Jesus, there is a part of Him with which I cannot identify.

What I long for in the end is to know the way He can love Himself through me and I can love myself through Him. Only when I know Him in His wholeness and am myself made whole will this happen. And when it does happen, I will be fully alive in Him and He in me. It is not yet, but it will be.

Having made the case as best as this male, socialized into a chauvinistic culture, can do, I have to go on to say that there is some validity to the claims of those who contend that this whole inclusive language thing can get out of hand. My friend, Peter Gomes, the chaplain of the Harvard Chapel, is one of them.

Peter strongly advocates the use of inclusive language, and such language is evident in all the prayer services and worship services at the Harvard Chapel. He fully recognizes that the Holy Spirit is leading us to talk about God and to think about God in new ways. However, Peter also has a strong appreciation for the past, and with that appreciation goes a kind of reverence for the way God is referred to in the old hymns of the Church. He is not about to see them rewritten to please his radical feminist friends in the Harvard Divinity School, any more than he is willing to see Shakespeare rewritten in order to fit the requisites of a radical feminist agenda.

Peter points out that when Oliver Cromwell took over England with his Puritanism, he set out to eradicate any semblance of what he believed to be the false theologies of the past. This led him to wipe out all traces of Catholicism. His troops, following his orders, went into the cathedrals of England to lop off the heads of any statue of a saint in sight. Today we mourn the loss of a great deal of Medieval art and the understanding that the spirituality of that age through its art could have provided. Cromwell, in his zeal to purify the Church, destroyed much that was precious. It just might be, contends my friend Peter, that radical feminists are doing something like that right now in their efforts to rid the Church of any evidences of male domination in liturgy, hymns, and Scripture. Peter calls for a treasuring of what *has been* and an appreciation of the good in the old forms, even as he calls for all new religious art and writing to reflect the inclusiveness that full citizenship for women in the kingdom of God requires.

Even as I have argued for a Christian feminism as a man, I have to say that women are not the only ones who have been oppressed by the role definitions that society has prescribed for the sexes. We men have taken it on the chin too. We ask why, when the *Titanic* was going down, fathers of children were expected to go down with the ship, while old ladies who had no one depending on them were given seats in the limited number of lifeboats? We ask why forty thousand men died in Vietnam, but only a handful of women had to lay down their lives in that war? We ask why men are required to take the risk roles in our society while women are allowed to play it safe? And we ask why men die younger than women, and why women receive three times as much healthcare as men do?

Across America, men are standing up and asking women, "Why are you so down on us?" We sweat our heads off in the workplace to feed our wives and families, often putting up with indignities that no one should have to endure. We are willing to lay our lives on the line to protect our wives and our kids. "We're tired," we say, "of being unappreciated and held responsible for everything that's wrong in the world. We are fed up with constantly being referred to as victimizers, when in reality, we are often victims."

In my own case, there is much that traditional gender role prescriptions denied me. For instance, what society defined for me as a social role cut me off from my kids. I watch my son change diapers for his children and play with them in ways that, in my generation, were reserved for mothers. I watch him share in the raising of his kids in ways that were not expected of fathers in my generation. My son's emotional involvement with his children is something I never enjoyed. All of which is to say that the old system not only oppressed women, it also oppressed men. It denied us the opportunities to experience the kind of intimacy and emotional gratification that can come from those roles and activities that until recently seemed to have been reserved only for women.

What I'm trying to say is that women shouldn't be too hard on us men. We undoubtedly have victimized women by our actions, ideologies, theologies, and attitudes. But we ourselves have been victims of The System, and few of us, if any, have given voice to the oppressions we have suffered and the emotional losses we unconsciously endured because society kept us out of certain roles. Weep for us men too. We also got the short end of the stick. Men need liberation from socially prescribed roles that have hindered us from realizing the fullness of life as it was planned for us in accordance with the providence of God.

Let both women and men together declare the fullness of a gospel that liberates both sexes into that completed humanity that we find in Jesus Christ.

PART FIVE

When It Comes

to Family Life

How to Raise Kids

without Going on Guilt Trips

I f our kids only knew what they put us through! They have no idea of the sleepless nights we spend wondering where they are and what they're doing. They haven't the slightest inkling of the anxieties they create or the chest pains we feel when they stand on the verge of making decisions that we're certain will ruin their lives. They don't have a clue about what we're really feeling when we hear them mock the values and principles we believe to be the only basis for a good and fulfilling life.

It's so hard to idly stand by and watch our children self-destruct, knowing that there really isn't much we can say about it. We are sadly aware of the truth in the old song from the sixties in which Bob Dylan sang defiantly, "Mothers and fathers throughout the land, your sons and daughters are beyond your command." But that doesn't stop us either from caring or feeling responsible.

We know that our young adult children are making decisions that will determine the course of their lives, but we feel increasingly powerless to intervene and save them from serious mistakes—many of them the same mistakes we made ourselves. Between the ages of eighteen and twenty-five (just seven short years) our daughters and sons are likely to determine whom they will marry, the careers they will follow, the sort of education they will acquire, where they will live, and most importantly, what part God will play in their lives. Destiny is largely determined for them by what they choose during these decision-making years. We are painfully aware that they lack the wisdom to know what dangers there are and which caution signs to notice as they navigate the treacherous waters that separate them from the relatively fixed patterns of later life.

Things are different now than they used to be. For most of human history, people lived in what sociologists refer to as "traditional societies." Children grew up in the footsteps of their parents. Boys accepted as their lot in life the vocations of their fathers, and girls took on the roles that had been prescribed in another generation for their mothers. There were fewer choices in life, and therefore not as many chances for serious mistakes.

Everything is changed now. The opportunities and choices for young people increase dramatically by the year. And those of us who grew up in a different time and in a different world hardly know how to guide our children. Furthermore, when we do speak, they sometimes act as though we don't know what we're talking about, and we latently fear that they might be right. Our parents instructed us with a degree of certainty because they believed that we would live in a world that was run by the same rules that governed their lives. But when we speak to our children, we're not so sure. We know that their world is so different from the one in which we were reared that the same rules don't apply. Being in such a state of anxiety, we are prone to ask, "What's a parent to do?"

In Hasidic Judaism there is the story of a group of lost souls encountering their rabbi in the middle of a huge dark forest. They say, "Rabbi! We're lost." And then they ask, "Can you show us the way out of the forest?"

"No!" answers the rabbi. "But I too have been lost. I have been lost longer than you have been. And in my wanderings I have learned many ways that do *not* lead out of the forest. Perhaps if you share with me the ways you have learned that do *not* lead out of the forest, and I share with you the ways that I have learned that do *not* lead out of the forest, we will together be able to find our way out of our lost condition."

Granting the truth of this ancient rabbi, perhaps you will allow me the privilege of sharing with you some of the ways that I find do *not* work when it comes to trying to give direction to our children in their crucial decision-making years. Hopefully, between what I can tell you about what has not worked for me, and what you have discovered has not worked for you, we can, through a process of elimination, figure out some viable paths to offer us all some escape from the confusions of parenting. With this approach in mind, I will proceed to name some of the methods we ought not to adopt and cite some of the things we ought not to say as we try to help our kids get set for life. Here is my list of "Don'ts."

Don't Nag

You might not consider it nagging, but it *is* nagging when you keep on making the same point over and over again, continually trying to drive home the same message. It doesn't take long for children who are under a steady bombardment of repetitious directives to *turn off.* In some cases, nagging even drives children to do the opposite of what they know their parents want. That, of course, is what Paul was talking about when he wrote, "Fathers, provoke not your children to evil" (Ephesians 6:1). Or, as one scholar translates this verse: "Parents! Don't overcorrect your children so that you end up driving them to do the wrong thing." Let me cite two examples of the sort of situation that is hard for parents of kids that aren't little anymore.

Your daughter is involved in a relationship that you believe could lead to disaster, but you realize that harping messages of disapproval could create intense defiance. Young women have been known to marry the wrong people for just that reason. What drives young people up the wall even more than up-front nagging are the not-too-subtle *hints* that parents try to drop as they resort to indirection in their efforts to send their messages. If you try to tell your daughter about the marriage of one of your relatives that didn't work out because she married the wrong man, whom you describe as unmistakably like the guy your daughter is dating, it will only make matters worse. Your daughter will probably be more *ticked off* than ever because she thinks you believe she's dumb enough to fall for your covert message.

Still, you know it isn't right to just do nothing. After all, parents have a responsibility to do their best to let the truth be known to their children. It would be a truly tragic thing if, after a painful divorce, your daughter or son accusingly asked, "Why didn't you ever tell me?"

The problem becomes especially troubling when you feel that your child is about to marry someone who has a different faith commitment or, even worse, no religion at all. The Bible tells Christians, "Be ye not unequally yoked together with unbelievers: for what fellowship hath righteousness with unrighteousness? and what communion hath light with darkness?" (2 Corinthians 6:14). To say nothing when a son or daughter who is a Christian seems headed for marriage to a nonbeliever is certainly to fail in what God requires of parents.

Here is another situation in which a child is headed for trouble, and parental silence on the matter would be evading responsibility. Suppose your son has gotten in with a group of friends who drink heavily, or into something even worse. You see signs that he is setting aside any pretense of being a Christian. You may have brought him up in the ways of the Lord and watched proudly as he made his profession of faith and joined the Church. But now you seriously doubt if any of that had real meaning for him. You wonder if his former expressions of being a Christian were nothing more than some rite of passage that you and the Church foisted upon him. What makes matters worse is that you haven't the slightest clue how to talk to him about any of this. It always seems awkward to bring up the subject.

In both of these situations, and in a host of comparable ones, I suggest a different, but very direct, approach. Make *an appointment* with your child to deal with what is bothering you. Set up the meeting away from your home, perhaps for breakfast or lunch at a restaurant. Choose a place where you won't run into people who know you, and arrange this when the two of you have at least a couple of hours to talk. Saturday morning is often a good time. Tell your son or daughter that there is something important that you need to talk about and ask him or her to give you the time as a special favor.

After the two of you finish eating, get into your concern without beating around the bush. Simply say something like, "What I want to talk to you about is . . ." As you begin the discussion, it's important that you tell your child that you wanted to be up-front about this matter here and now so that it won't be lurking below the surface of every conversation the two of you have. Let it be known that after "today" you will not be bringing up the matter again, not that you will not continue to be concerned, but because you don't want to be a nag.

Plan what you're going to say carefully. Remember, your words are likely to be repeated to your child's friends or to his or her might-be partner. You may have to live with what you say for the rest of your life. I know of a situation in which parents said some very negative and hurtful things to their son about a young woman he was about to marry. What they said was repeated to her, and those parents are still suffering the consequences. The son married the woman anyway and, because she is still hurt and angry, she makes sure that those parents seldom get to see their son or their grandchildren. So be careful! Pray long and hard for guidance about what you ought and ought not to say.

Sometimes it's a good idea to begin with some confession on your part. It is always less difficult for children to be open with a parent who has made himself or herself vulnerable. People always find it easier to confess shortcomings to someone who doesn't come across as superior. Talking about your own mistakes, especially the mistakes you have made in your relationship with this child, is a good way to reduce any defensiveness and have your child consider his or her own faults.

Make it clear to your son or daughter that you are expressing how *you* feel, rather than pronouncing judgment on what is really going on. In reality, things may not be what they appear to be from your subjective point of view. It may be that there is more to the situation than meets the eye. Over and over again remind your child that you are expressing your feelings and that you might be wrong. Be ready to *listen* to his or her response to your concerns. And above all, don't argue! Once you have made your case, let it rest.

I hope I don't have to tell you not to threaten. We all know horror stories of parents who issued ultimatums that resulted in broken relationships. No Christian parents should say things like, "If you do what I think you're planning to do, don't think you can come back home after your life is ruined!" Like the father in the story of the Prodigal Son (Luke 15:11–32), you must let your children know that, no matter what happens, and no matter where they end up, you will always be there to welcome them back with love. Christian parents must always do their best to model the unconditional love of God.

On the day of this important meeting with your child, make sure you are rested. Tired people are easily irritated. You cannot afford to lose your temper. Give yourself plenty of time to become spiritually prepared. Try to spend a day in prayer and fasting, but don't tell everybody about it (Matthew 6:6–18). It really ticks off a child to find out that *everybody knows* that he or she has been a special subject of prayer, as loving a thing as prayer really is. In silence, yield to Jesus and invite Him to give you wisdom and words. Remember, He promised that at crucial times He would put the right words in your mouth (Matthew 10:19–20). This doesn't mean that you should not plan each word you are going to say with exacting care. But it does mean that the more you surrender to being penetrated by the Holy Spirit, the more the tenor of your words and the way you come across will be conditioned by His love. If Christ has permeated your heart, mind, and will prior to the meeting, you will not come across as judgmental or superior.

As you end the discussion, make it clear that the next step is in the hands of your child. Say to him or her that *you* are not going to bring the matter up again. It will be a matter of discussion in the future only if he or she wants to talk about it.

DON'T BE HARD ON YOURSELF

After you have given it your best shot, don't condemn yourself when you inevitably think of the ways in which you could have handled the situation better and the things that you *should* have said. You're not

God! None of us ever does things perfectly. In retrospect, every one of us, in just about every situation in life, can see how we could have done better. Instead of lying awake thinking about what you might have said and done better, simply put the whole matter in the hands of God.

Jesus once told this story:

> And he said, So is the kingdom of God, as if a man should cast seed into the ground; And should sleep, and rise night and day, and the seed should spring and grow up, he knoweth not how. For the earth bringeth forth fruit of herself; first the blade, then the ear, after that the full corn in the ear. (Mark 4:26–28)

The message of this passage of Scripture is quite clear. After you have done all that you can do, try to relax in the confidence that God will take it from there and bring about the good that He wills (Romans 8:28). Simply look to Jesus and say, "It's in Your hands now!"

In many instances, if parents are patient, they will find that their kids eventually come around and embrace the very things their parents taught them in their younger days. To parody the words of Winston Churchill, "We can always count on our children to make the right decisions, after they have tried all the other options!"

DON'T THINK OF YOURSELF MORE HIGHLY THAN YOU OUGHT TO THINK

This is a directive that comes right out of the Bible (see Romans 12:3). What we need to remember is that when our kids turn out to be wonderful in the eyes of the world, we tend to take far too much credit. And when they miss the mark, we tend to take far too much blame. You are not the only influence impacting the lives of your children. They grow up in a society in which television, rock music, educational institutions, and a host of other "principalities and powers" are powerful forces with which your children must wrestle as they try to sort out what their lives will be all about (Ephesians 6:12). In the end, our children are individuals with their own decision-making powers. *They* are the ones who must decide which of these "principalities and powers" they will allow to dominate their minds and hearts. They are the ones who will determine *how much* and in what ways each of these value creating societal agents will influence their lifestyles.

Our children are not Pavlovian dogs, conditioned simply to become whatever we train them to be. Rather, they filter the many messages that they receive in the context of their daily experiences and then decide what they will believe and do. Only they, as free individuals, can choose what they will allow to be relevant to their lives and what will be discarded as "hay, wood, and stubble." As parents, we may send all the right messages, but it is our children who ultimately will decide what to do with those messages. As parents, we might wish at times that we had this power in *our* hands, but if we did, our children wouldn't really be human. Their power to make decisions does make them capable of choosing evil, but it's also what enables them to choose what is good. In the end, it is the freedom to decide that enables our children to love and become what God wants them to be.

Remember, God created two perfect children and raised them in a perfect environment, yet both of them rebelled against the will of God. But if God had to do it all over again, I believe God would do the same thing. Why? Because if and when we do decide to do God's will, and if and when we do choose to love God with all of our hearts and souls and minds (Matthew 22:37), our Creator experiences a joy that infinitely abounds.

At those times when you regret that your children have wills of their own and the power to rebel, consider that without free will they could never really love you. That's what God wants to teach us. *Don't despair!* Remember, as that great American philosopher Yogi Berra once said, "It ain't over 'til it's over!" Even when we think all is lost, it really isn't.

The story is told of Monica, the mother of St. Augustine. This fourth-century woman had a son who was so perverse that almost anyone else's child would have been considered to be no problem at all in comparison. But through Augustine's difficult years of rebel-

210

lion, Monica never stopped praying for her son and she lived for the time when he might give his life over to God.

One day, Augustine announced to his mother that he was leaving his home in the city of Hippo to live in Rome. He wanted to go to the big city where the action was, and he let it be known that Hippo was no place for a lover of nightlife, like himself. When she heard the news, Monica's heart broke. She was sure that by going away to Rome her son would be lost to her and to God forever. She begged Augustine not to do this and, in an act of desperation, pleaded with him to go and sit with her in the church while she prayed about it. He yielded to his mother's request that he go to church with her, but while Monica was on her knees in prayer, Augustine sneaked off to the harbor and boarded a ship sailing for Rome. When Monica discovered what had happened, she was deeply hurt, but she never despaired; she just kept on hoping and praying.

While in Rome, Augustine quite miraculously came to Christ through the witness of St. Ambrose. Under Ambrose, he was nurtured into Christian discipleship, and when it was learned that the city of Hippo needed a new bishop to lead their church, Ambrose recommended the once wayward son of that town for the office.

Can you imagine the surprise and joyful amazement of Monica the day she went down to the dock with others from her church to meet their new pastor? None other than her own son Augustine walked down the gangplank! The mother who never gave up on her son had been rewarded. Monica's story is a reminder to mothers everywhere that where there's life, there's hope. It may be that, even when the life of your loved one is ended, there is still hope.

A year or so ago I was scheduled to speak at a small Christian college in the South. Following the first evening meeting, a middle-aged woman lingered in order to have some personal words with me. She had driven several hours to visit with me because she had an important story to tell. When I had been to this particular school a few years earlier, her daughter had made a decision to give her life to Christ. Prior to that, this young woman had been going through a particularly difficult time. She had rebelled against the claims of Christ and the value system given to her in childhood. In simple language, this woman's daughter had been living a wild life. Everything from the color of her hair to her sex life seemed to be a rejection of all that her parents had prayed for her to be.

On the second night of my speaking series during my previous visit to the college, this young woman had responded to the invitation to receive Christ as her Savior and yielded to Him as Lord of her life. Following the meeting, she had gone back to her dormitory room and written her mother a lengthy letter describing what had happened to her that night and how she had committed herself to becoming all that Jesus wanted her to be. She wrote of her desire to be reconciled with her parents and begged for forgiveness for all the heartaches she had caused them.

After writing the letter, this new convert had gone out to mail it, and while returning to her dorm, she had been hit by a car and killed. Her parents, not knowing what had transpired in their daughter's life just hours before her death, had gone through the funeral with little more than wishful thinking. They had hoped against hope that their daughter had been more in touch with Jesus the night of her accident than they were aware or had any reason to believe. It wasn't until several days after the funeral that the letter she had posted to them on the night of her death arrived in the mail. While the tragedy of their daughter's death still pained her parents enormously, they found much consolation in the good news that she had reached out for a right relationship with God on the very day that she was called to meet God face to face.

Those parents had the wonderful certainty of their child's faith because of her letter, but I am reluctant to make any final judgment about what goes on with even those young people who leave no evidence that their lives are in Christ when they are taken out of this life. Who really knows what can happen on the other side of the grave? What did Peter mean when he wrote this in his epistle:

> For Christ also hath once suffered for sins, the just for the unjust, that he might bring us to God, being put to death in the flesh, but

quickened by the Spirit: By which also he went and preached unto the spirits in prison; Which sometime were disobedient, when once the longsuffering of God waited in the days of Noah, while the ark was a preparing, wherein few, that is, eight souls were saved by water. (1 Peter 3:18–20)

Might it be that God, as one poet describes Him, is "the Hound of Heaven" who pursues us down the labyrinths of time and even into eternity in order to bring the lost sheep into the bonds of God's love? I cannot speak with any kind of authority about such things. I can only say that God is able to do abundantly more than we can ever hope or think (Ephesians 3:20). So never despair!

Chapter 19

How to Raise Mentally Healthy Kids

without Getting Messed Up

by Pop Psychology

G randchildren are God's reward for not killing your children. One of my friends told me that, if he had known grandchildren were so much fun, he would just have had them instead of children, because rearing children was really hard. Indeed, rearing children *is* hard, and it seems to be getting harder all the time. In the good old days parents had a lot of help in rearing their children. Back then, parents were usually surrounded by members of an extended family, many of whom had much experience in raising children.

In the nineteenth century, people didn't move about as they do in today's urban-industrial society. People reared children in stable communities. Their children grew up, got married, settled down, and reared their own children all in the same locale. In villages and towns across the country, people found themselves living in the context of blood relatives and neighbors, some of whom were as close to them as their own relatives. In those days, a network of kin and friends was always there to assist new parents in their tasks. There were sisters and brothers nearby to baby-sit. There were grandparents readily at hand to answer questions and lend assistance to parents who might feel overwhelmed by child-rearing responsibilities. If a child got sick, there was always a grandmother handy to give the concerned mother wise advice and help. When it came to child rearing, the grandmothers had been through it all before and knew what should be a cause for alarm and what was nothing to worry about. Young parents in the old days were seldom confused about what to do *for* their children, or *with* them. The traditions and supporting advice that came from the extended family provided directives on what was good for kids and how they should be reared.

That collective guidance system of friends and kin that made up the support systems for parents then is all but gone these days. The mobility required of those who want to be fully viable on the ever-fluid job market has made us a people on the move. In any given year we can now expect some 20 percent of the nation's population to move. It is more likely than not that a young couple and their children will find themselves stashed away in some apartment house surrounded by strangers and very much on their own. And when it comes to rearing children, these isolated parents have nowhere to turn, except the childcare shelf in local bookstores. There they find a host of books written by *pop* psychologists and shoot-from-the-hip preachers who claim to know much more about rearing children than they really do. Some of the advice that comes from these books is more than off-the-wall; it is downright dangerous. As this advice gets circulated on television talk shows, from *Jenny Jones* to *Oprah*, it begins to take on the character of truth, and those who challenge the premises on which this advice is based are treated as though they are questioning what everybody *knows* is true. Well, what these pop psychologists tell us *isn't* always true. What's worse is that sometimes what the would-be experts claim to be sound advice turns out to be downright dangerous. Their conventional wisdom is sometimes counterproductive in efforts to rear emotionally healthy children.

Let me start my questioning of delusive child-rearing theories by going after one of the most popular: It is the idea that everything having to do with a child's success, whether it be in school or in any other endeavor in life, is totally dependent on the child's level of self-esteem. Some educators tell us that they believe that the academic achievement of children is almost completely tied up with self-esteem. If kids are failing, or if they are getting into trouble, parents are told that the problems are all because the children suffer from low self-esteem. What's worse is that there is often an unspoken message that somehow it's all the parents' fault. Parents are left believing that, if they just had been better parents and had properly built up little Johnny's self-image, he wouldn't be having such a bad time in school.

What fascinates me about all of this is how we fail to ask some basic questions about such assumptions. For instance, social research reveals that Japanese children have very low levels of self-esteem. As a matter of fact, they can be rated as some of the most unhappy children in the world, because they are so down on themselves. The depression that pervades teenagers in Japan renders them among the people most prone in the world to commit suicide. Nevertheless, Japanese children certainly are doing well in school, and their behavior is usually marked by good manners and obedience, notwithstanding their poor self-esteem.

Those of us who know anything about how children were reared a couple of generations ago will readily concur that parents in those days were not great adherents of the cult of self-esteem. They didn't work overtime trying to build up their children's self-concepts. As a matter of fact, they often worked overtime doing just the opposite. Parents a couple of generations ago worried that their kids might get "too big for their britches" if they were overly praised. They concerned themselves with the possibility that their kids might go on ego trips and end up as prideful persons and conceited egomaniacs. They constantly reminded their children of this biblical admonition: "For I say, through the grace given unto me, to every man that is among you, not to think of himself more highly than he ought to think; but to think soberly, according as God hath dealt to every man the measure of faith" (Romans 12:3). And if that didn't work, they laid on their children this fear-generating warning: "Pride goeth before destruction, and an haughty spirit before a fall" (Proverbs 16:18).

Scholars such as Phillppe Aries, who have studied the history of family life, would likely acknowledge that parents in the past used to *put down* their children because they thought that this was what good parents did. Yet their children, who were seldom given the self-esteem treatment that modern educators believe is so essential, were well behaved and learned how to read and write very well. Certainly, children came out of school with a better knowledge of English and math than most of those who graduate from our present-day schools with their self-esteem philosophy.

There is a real danger in the belief that the whole secret of rearing successful children is in the building up of their self-esteem. Actually, overdoing this may actually be *creating* some of the very problems we have been led to believe high levels of self-esteem should cure. For instance, exaggerated and ungrounded self-esteem may actually encourage violent reactions from some young people.

Along with some of the most dedicated urban missionaries in the world, I have been hard at work trying to develop ministries for inner-city kids. In the name of Christ, we have been involved with thousands of children and teenagers through a variety of programs. We not only want them to come to a saving knowledge of the gospel; we also want them to succeed in life. Therefore, we have paid close attention to those things that are molding them into adults. From our careful observations, we have increasingly come to see that the cult of self-esteem can be extremely counterproductive.

Take the case of an urban kid who is constantly bombarded with the message that he is special. He is told day in and day out that he is *somebody*. From motivational speakers in school assemblies to special courses designed to build up his self-image, he is told that he should never let anybody put him down or show him any disrespect. Then one day he's called upon in class to answer a question. When he gives the wrong answer and is corrected, he blows up. Why shouldn't he? "That teacher didn't show me any respect," he tells us.

I heard a news report about a teenager coming back after school and pumping a half-dozen bullets into the chest of his teacher because, as he said, "My teacher flunked me, and that made me feel like nothing." If you create a sense of distorted pride in a youngster, then anything that brings that inflated self-concept into question is going to be intolerable. Increasingly, teachers, who are afraid of what might happen to them if they tell their students what failures they really are, simply inflate grades to avoid the hassle. This only adds to the charade that we call education in many city schools. Students graduate with decent grades convinced that they are as smart as anybody else only to find out that they cannot function in the real world. And God help anybody who challenges their self-deception and precious self-esteem.

For the first time, a group of social scientists in the Philadelphia area are calling into question the self-esteem approach for curing the educational and behavioral problems of children in public schools. They are trying to tell educators that self-esteem should not be a given. It should be earned. They want to convince educators that kids should feel good about themselves *because* they have worked hard and should be praised *because* they have behaved in good and constructive ways. To say that self-esteem comes first is to get it backwards and gets kids off on the wrong track.

Instead of playing with self-esteem as a means of getting kids to do better in schoolwork and in their behavior, why not try having high expectations for them? Why not let them know that we will settle for nothing less than their best? There are all kinds of studies to show that young people and children tend to measure up to great expectations. If little is expected, little will be achieved. If much is expected, much will be achieved. Don't worry about kids getting discouraged and giving up. It is absolutely mind-boggling what kids can achieve, if they believe it is expected of them. Sometimes the difference between an achiever and a nonachiever is just that the nonachiever is slower. In such a case, good schoolwork *can* be done by a slow student; it will just take him or her longer to do it.

For ten years I taught at an Ivy League university where my students were next to brilliant. Their SAT scores ranked them in the upper 5 percent of the nation. When I gave up my teaching in that high-powered school and concentrated on teaching at a small Christian liberal arts college, I was told that I should lower my expectations and not expect the average students at the Christian college to measure up to what the Ivy Leaguers could do. I didn't heed that advice. I taught my courses with the same reading lists that I had used at the big prestigious university, and gave tests at the same level of difficulty as the tests I had designed for my Ivy League students. Some of the students at the Christian college balked at first, but once they got the message that I wasn't going to back down on what I expected of them, they settled into a work schedule that made them very successful. Some of them may have had to work harder and longer to do what some of the Ivy Leaguers did, but they did it. And the more they achieved, the more their self-esteem grew.

There's nothing wrong with self-esteem. It's just that real self-esteem is something that *results* from accomplishments, rather than being the primary *cause* of accomplishments. Expect great things from your kids, and don't let them off the hook when they whine about the work being too hard. In the end you will show respect for them by letting them know that you believe in their ability to do great things.

PUNISHING WITH REWARDS

The second pop psychology myth I want to explode is that you get your best results from children by rewarding them. Most of us got the idea somewhere along the line that we should accept the behavioristic theories of B. F. Skinner and offer rewards to kids to encourage them to do what we want them to. We were told that, as with Pavlov's dog, rewards elicit from children the behavior we deem desirable.

The practice of tempting kids to do what we want them to do by promising them rewards is being carried to absurd extremes these days. Kids are getting rewards all over the place. To go into the bedrooms of most teenagers is to enter trophy rooms. They seem to be awarded trophies for just about everything. In many cases, they seem to get trophies just for showing up. And in the end, getting trophies and other rewards becomes their primary motivation for everything they do.

Some graduate students in a poor neighborhood near the University of Pennsylvania, lived next door to a grumpy old man who was disliked by just about everybody in the neighborhood. There was a gang of boys who took delight in irritating this obnoxious man in just about every way imaginable. They threw water bombs on his porch. They rang his doorbell and ran away. They threw junk in his yard, and they undoubtedly did a lot of other things that only their demonic little minds could dream up.

The university students decided to perform an experiment. One day they called over these delinquent kids and told them that they would be rewarded for what they were doing. The kids were told, "We don't like that old man either, so we'll pay each of you a dollar a day for doing all the mean things that you're already doing to him on your way home from school." The teenagers couldn't believe their good fortune, and they got into their harassing of the old man with more enthusiasm than ever. They were relentless over the next couple of weeks.

Then the graduate students changed things. They called the teenagers together and told them that they couldn't keep up the high payments, and so they were lowering the pay to fifty cents a day. The kids kept up their mean harassment for another week.

And then the grad students made the sad announcement that payment would be reduced still again to just twenty-five cents a day. That did it! One teenager responded, "Hey! Do you think we're going to work for nothing? If you can't pay us better than that, we're not going to do it anymore." And they didn't!

That story was told to me; I haven't yet been able to trace it down to be sure that it really happened that way. But the overall principle of the story is true. If you take something that kids do just for the fun of it and begin to reward them for doing it, things change. Instead of doing it for the joy of doing it, they will make the reward the important thing. Then, if the reward is removed, they will stop doing what had previously been a joy to them.

Sometime ago, I was part of a conference with the Speaker of the House of Representatives, Newt Gingrich. The discussion ranged over a variety of social problems related to the poor and socially disadvantaged people who live in urban America. Of particular concern to the Speaker were the reading problems that seem to plague inner-city children. The speaker, a strong advocate of the economic motivations that make the free enterprise system work, came up with what he believed was a workable idea. He suggested that the kids be paid to read books. He asked, "What do you think would happen if we rewarded children in city schools for reading books? Suppose a child was paid a dollar for every book that he or she reads? What do you think would happen?"

"It might prove counterproductive," was my response. "The child who now *enjoys* reading would begin doing it, not because he or she loved books, but because there was money to be made. What's worse is that the children probably would search through the school library looking for the shortest books they could find so that they could read as many as possible. They would choose books that were of little interest to them, instead of books they would find exciting, just to make more money. They would end up reading primarily for economic rewards, and when the rewards were ended, they would lose interest in reading. That's not what we want."

Over the past couple of decades, trying to motivate kids with rewards has become a vital part of the child-rearing philosophy being proposed by some pop psychologists. Children are financially rewarded for cleaning their rooms, getting good grades, and even for *not* hitting their brothers and sisters. What must be granted is that *initially* rewards as incentives work quite well. There is almost always an upsurge in the desired behavior when a reward system is first introduced, but the gains are short-lived. After the initial burst of enthusiasm that the rewards create, interest slowly dies down, and it isn't long before the rewards lose their luster; the only question left for the child is how little has to be done to continue to get the promised payoffs. If the reward is money, we're teaching the child materialism. We're saying to the child that the only value anything has is in the money you can get from it. That's hardly what we want our children to think. Yet this is the way we're leading children to think, by using this kind of a reward system.

It's no surprise to me, in light of all of this, that by the time they get around to choosing a vocation, most young people make money the dominant consideration. It's not whether or not a life-vocation serves God and other people that is of primary concern to teenagers when choosing a vocation. Nor is it even the personal fulfillment or the psychological gratification that might come from their life's work. That kind of thinking belonged to the sixties. Today the overriding question when choosing a vocation is simply, "How much does it pay?" Is it any wonder that so many people end up in vocations that give them little sense of satisfaction? After all, the joy that might come from doing something significant for others is seldom given as a reason for choosing a life-vocation. Young people are led to believe that financial rewards are what really matters.

I have a deep conviction that there are a host of other motivations that we should be giving our children for what they do. One of these is to let them know that what they do, they ought to do out of love. Jesus once gave a parable that communicated loud and clear that love is best expressed not with words but with actions:

> A certain man had two sons; and he came to the first, and said, Son, go work today in my vineyard. He answered and said, I will not: but afterward he repented, and went. And he came to the second, and said likewise. And he answered and said, I go, sir: and went not. Whether of them twain did the will of his father? They say unto him, The first. (Matthew 21:28b–31a)

Little Johnny Ballard asked his preacher father what he could do to help, and his father told him that on Saturday nights he could shine his father's shoes so that they would be ready for Sunday church. Little Johnny did what he was asked to do. His father was so delighted that he put two quarters on the table next to Johnny's bed, along with a note that read, "This is for being such a good boy and shining my shoes."

The following week little Johnny shined his father's shoes again. But on Sunday morning when the preacher tried to put them on, he found a quarter in each of his shoes, along with a note that read, "I shined the shoes because I love you!"

We dare not corrupt motivation like that with economic incentives. All children should learn to express love by being obedient and by doing good things that please their significant others.

GIVING CHILDREN A SENSE OF MISSION

If we really want our children to become all that God wants them to be, we ought to motivate them with something better than some system of reward. We need to give them a sense of mission, to build into their consciousness an awareness that every Christian has a high calling from God (Philippians 3:14).

I grew up in a family that did just that. Ever since I can remember, my mother told me that I had been brought into this world to serve other people in the name of the Lord. "Your life is not your own," was her constant message to me. She regularly told me that when I was just a baby she had taken me to church and dedicated me to God's work in the world. Sometimes people ask me, "Tony, when were you called into the gospel ministry?" and I have to answer, "I was never called: My mother decided!"

There are those who will argue that parents have no right to define for children what they should do with their lives. But I ask, "Why not?" Everybody else is telling our children what to be and what to do. Certainly the media, especially television, is telling them. School counselors tell them. They usually run a battery of tests on our kids to figure out where their interests and abilities lie and then advise them from the test results what vocations would best suit them. Even the music that they listen to gives them values and pre-scribes a lifestyle. So please, tell me why it is not the prerogative of parents to stand up and say, "As for me and *my house,* we will serve the Lord!"

Some will say that kids are going to react negatively to our telling them what to do with their lives. They will warn us that, "If parents do that, then children will rebel!" Of course they'll rebel! That's what children do for a living. They rebel! The task of parents is to clearly define for them what it is they are to rebel against.

I am quite serious about this, because I hold to a theory of child rearing that involves dialectics. I believe that it's the parents' responsibility to clearly prescribe a way of life and to establish a definite set of values to which a child should adhere. That's what is called the thesis of the dialectic process. According to philosophers since Kant and Hegel, every thesis generates an antithesis. What this means in child-rearing theory is that it is only a matter of time before the child reacts against this prescribed way of life (the thesis) and tries to assert his or her own individuality with an alternative and often opposing way of life (the antithesis).

There will be tension between what the parents want the child to be (the thesis) and what the child himself or herself wants to be (the antithesis). This will be particularly true during the teenage years. But out of this tension there will emerge a synthesis, which will bring together the best elements of both.

Synthesis
(the best elements of both)

Thesis   **Antithesis**
(parents' desires)   (the child's will)

It's not a good thing for parents to succeed in imposing their wills on the child. There have been too many instances of children who are unfulfilled and painfully frustrated because they have had their individuality stifled by overbearing parents. Good parenting doesn't result in children being clones.

It is also not a good thing for a child to be into self-expression without limits. We have all seen the tragedies of young people who have been able to do their own thing without the restraint of parentally established standards and values. What's really best is the synthesis that incorporates all that is good from the traditional values of the past (as promoted by the parents) with the spontaneous and innovative ways of the child. This synthesis is what creates the kind of balanced, wholesome, and creative persons who have the best possibilities for good and fulfilled lives.

All Christian parents should clearly define the mission in life that they believe expresses the will of God for themselves and their children. In our family, we let it be known that we were called to reach out to the poor and the oppressed. As we read Scripture to our children, we emphasized what the Bible says about the *have-nots*. We reminded our children constantly of the words of John, who wrote,

"But whoso hath this world's good, and seeth his brother have need, and shutteth up his bowels of compassion from him, how dwelleth the love of God in him? My little children, let us not love in word, neither in tongue; but in deed and in truth" (1 John 3:17–18). We let it be known that we expected them to recognize that their privileges (and our kids lived very privileged lives) carried with them a heavy responsibility to do good for others who were less fortunate. We tried to define that the mission of our family was to serve those who were poor and oppressed.

The missionary organization with which I have been involved over the years tries to reach out to economically disadvantaged urban children and teenagers. These at-risk children are mostly African-American, and their environment is painfully oppressive. Our missionary staff workers don't try to motivate these youngsters with rewards. Instead, they try to give them a sense of mission. They tell them that Jesus saved them and has lifted them up so that through them He can change things for good in their communities. Day in and day out our workers tell the kids to study hard and keep themselves pure, not because there will be financial rewards for all of this, but because they will then be people who can change the neighborhoods where they live into the kinds of communities that God wants them to be. Our workers tell these inner-city kids that they are called to be agents of change who will end racism, poverty, and the kind of hell created by drugs. It is in this context that we tell the kids that they ought to pick up the trash that's on their streets, obey their parents, stay off of drugs, not engage in premarital sex, and do well in school. Motivation, we believe, should come out of a sense of mission and not from the self-interest that lies in motivation generated by rewards.

A reading of the New Testament will reveal that Jesus motivated His disciples with a high sense of mission. The essence of His message to them was that they had been called to work for the kingdom of God. With parables, our Lord gave them pictures of that kingdom. And as He taught them to pray, He told them to pray for that kingdom to come on earth, as it was in heaven (Matthew 6:10). When a couple of the disciples tried to jockey for positions of power, hoping that they would be rewarded for their faithfulness by getting to sit on the right and left hands of the Lord when He brought in His kingdom, Jesus let them know in no uncertain terms that this was not what His kingdom was all about. He let them know that in His kingdom loving service was its own reward, and that the joy of life comes for all of His followers from the same thing that gave Him joy—doing the will of the Father. Jesus took a bunch of ordinary people and turned them into saints, not with promises of rewards, but with a vision of a kingdom that they could join Him in creating for all of God's people.

Now we come to the big question that every parent has to answer: Will you buy into pop psychology and try to motivate your kids with material rewards? Or will you inspire your children to do what is good and right by giving them a godly vision? Will they end up reluctant to do anything good unless they are convinced that they will get "paid off" for it, or will they become people who will do good for goodness's sake?

How to Be Sexually Attractive

without Being Obscene

One of my friends sarcastically said, "I was brought up to believe that sex is a dirty, filthy thing—and you should save it for the person you marry!" Is it any wonder that we Christians are so ambivalent about sex? Many of us have been brought up in a puritan-type religion that puts down all sex as "the lust of the flesh" and makes it difficult for us to face up to the whole matter of being sexually alive persons. People who love us tell us how sinful sex is in the hope of keeping us out of trouble. So much of what we are told about sex is clothed in a kind of hush-hush secrecy that suggests sex is something bad. Then, after we are thoroughly indoctrinated with negative messages about our supposedly *unclean desires,* we come to the altar to say, "I do!" Somehow, with those simple words, sex is supposed to be transformed into something holy and beautiful. It's no wonder that for many of us this sudden expected transition just doesn't happen, leaving us feeling guilty about sex, even when we're involved with our own marital partners. Only God knows how many have been rendered frigid and impotent by the psychological consequences of the bad attitudes about sex engendered by distorted religion.

Duffy Robbins, my colleague at Eastern College who teaches the courses in youth ministry, told me about being on a church retreat for teenage boys. One boy was deeply disturbed about his preoccupation with sexual fantasies and the fact that he was into masturbation. At the same time, this troubled kid was desperate to have a close relationship with Jesus. To him, it seemed obvious that his hunger for deep spirituality could never be satisfied unless he got rid of his sexual desires. This confused and troubled teenager came to the Saturday night campfire service determined to set things right in his life once and for all.

Duffy described how he, along with the other boys on the retreat, were sitting on logs arranged around the campfire when this kid started to pray, "Oh God, deliver me from all sexual desires! Please change me so that girls don't turn me on anymore! Take away all my sexual appetites!"

Duffy said, "I didn't know whether to laugh or cry. But I did know I had to stop him in the middle of his prayer."

"Wait a minute!" Duffy called out. "That's not really what you want. And even if it is what you want, it's not going to happen. Having sexual desires is no sin. Don't you think Jesus had them?"

The idea that Jesus might have had sexual desires was a brand-new thought to this kid. His Christian education had probably so emphasized the deity of Jesus that he had lost sight of Jesus' humanity. The very idea of Jesus having sexual desires seemed like blasphemy to this kid. Our uptight attitudes that ignore the humanity of Jesus are too often transmitted in a million-and-one subtle messages to kids like him.

It's hard for us to accept that the Bible actually teaches that Jesus was tempted in all ways even as we are tempted, but it does. The difference between Jesus and us is that He never sinned (Hebrews 4:15). When one contemporary author suggested that Jesus might have been sexually drawn to Mary Magdalene, most of us went ballistic. As a matter of fact, if He knew nothing of what it means to be sexually *turned on*, Jesus could be of little help to those of us who struggle with sexual temptations daily.

I've got some good news to report. If you go to Jesus and say, "Lord, I'm sexually *turned on* and your property is in danger," the Lord will not say in response, "I haven't the slightest idea what you're talking about. I've never been where you are." The good news is that each time you are tempted, Jesus knows exactly what's going through your mind, because He had the same kind of hormones that you do. Even more important, Jesus can show you how to get sexual things under control so that they don't destroy you. He's done it! Not only can He show you *how* to do it, but for those who are willing to be possessed by His Spirit, He can provide the power to *do* what He did (John 1:12). For those of us whose sexual appetites can be destructively out of control, Jesus can be a strengthening presence that will save us. That's what that troubled kid at the campfire meeting needed to know.

The story of that teenager is kind of funny, because all of us know that in his innocent prayer, he was putting into words what all of us feel at one time or another—or perhaps with ongoing regularity. All of us have known what it's like to sense that our sexuality can be at odds with our desire for spirituality. Most of us know that what turns us on can destroy our families, ruin our reputations, and ultimately drive us to despair. Out-of-control sex may have already messed us up, or we may have come so close to having this happen to us that we wonder how we ever got out of certain dangerous situations undamaged.

We regularly hear sermons telling us that sex is a gift from God and that it is God's will that we enjoy it. But sometimes when our sexual desires seem out of control, and we sense their destructive potentialities, we, like that teenager, wish they would all go away.

Of course, those sermons that tell us that sexual desires *are* a good part of our humanity are right. God made us so that we want sex. We have to recognize that God deliberately made that whole erotic trip one of the most pleasurable trips we can take. And any form of religion that takes the fun out of sex has to be bad religion.

Down through the centuries there have been those in the Church who have rejected the legitimacy of the fun side of marital sex. They have tried to tell us that sex is some kind of necessary evil that we have to engage in to perpetuate the human race. Some of the Church's theologians have gone so far as to suggest that sexual desire was the original sin. Such killjoy theologians have done their best to make us feel guilty for wanting to have sex and have labeled as *dirty* anybody who dares to make sex into fun and games.

SEX FOR FUN AND BONDING

Maribel Morgan, a thoroughly fundamentalist Christian woman, sent shockwaves through conservative church circles when she published her book, *The Total Woman*.[1] She told her sexually uptight readers that sexual pleasure is something God wants for us. And while feminists may have a lot of legitimate criticisms of Morgan's book, there is something that has to be admitted by even her severest critics. She helped a lot of straight-laced women to feel a sense of freedom when in bed with their husbands. *The Total Woman* enabled a lot of Christian women to relax and enjoy the fun of being sexy with their husbands.

God is not against fun. God is not a killjoy. God is not against play. And God is not against the joy of sex. I regularly meet Christians who act as though, if we aren't suffering for Jesus, we must not be in the will of God. This makes them feel guilty not only about enjoying sex, but about enjoying anything. Just remember that God enjoys having a good time, and God is into sensate pleasures. That's why God created the world and everything in it. It gave God pleasure. It turned God on. I think God had a lot of fun making pandas and gets a real kick out of watching penguins waddling across the ice. And I believe that God enjoys having people share all the pleasures of life that God means for them to enjoy within marriage, as long as they enjoy them in the ways in which God intends for them to be enjoyed. Sex for the sake of fun is no sin. In reality, the fun of sex is one of the things that makes being married one of the greatest joys God offers us in this life. So don't be afraid to play at sex in your marriage.

The fun that we have in sex helps to get us into it big-time. Sexual relations, in most instances, have a bonding effect on the relationship between husband and wife. To regularly have sex with the same partner is to be conditioned to associate one of life's greatest pleasures with one special person. And that, in turn, plays a big part in making us want to be with that person all the time. That is why I believe that birth control is a good thing. It delivers sex from simply being a means for creating babies. It frees us up to use sex in this bonding manner. Sex helps marital partners to build more intensive relationships with each other. Many opponents of birth control miss this point completely. Once we understand that sex was meant for pleasurable bonding, we are likely to give more attention to how to make sex work for us. Specifically, we are more prone to figure out how we can use sex to more effectively do all that God intended it to do for us. Here are some suggestions that may help.

First of all, give sex some of the best hours of the day. With our busy schedules and exhausting lifestyles, we are all too likely to leave sex to those last few minutes of the day just before we drop off to sleep. That's not right! We ought to realize that sex should not be something to be left for those last moments of consciousness before we pass out. To those who have sex as an afterthought after an exhausting day, I have to say, "Couldn't you get into it earlier in the evening, or even in the morning when you are rested?"

Don't rush through sex. Sex deserves more time and better time than most people usually give it. Good sex takes time. And for us older types, it's important to realize that, as we get older, we have to allow even more time for it. Frankly, it takes longer for us to get going. Instant turn-ons are for kids! Furthermore, the older we get, the more psychological and emotional and the less physical the whole sexual thing becomes. When it was all physical, then it was just a quick thing we might do. But the older we get, and the more we as couples are together in love, what we want from sex is something that far transcends just a biological explosion.

Second, those who study such things tell us that men and women are different in their approaches to sexuality. Nobody is quite sure to what extent these differences are biologically grounded or to what extent they are the result of social conditioning. However, the experts *are* sure of this—that women are much more sensitive to the surroundings in which lovemaking occurs, and men too seldom understand this. The physical setting is of great importance to most women. They want a romantic atmosphere that might include everything from the right lighting to the right kind of sheets on the bed. And they are *very* conscious of odors. Many men would get a lot more responsiveness from their wives if they took the time to shave and shower before climbing into bed.

Third, with sex, as with the rest of life, we are all called to be persons who do not seek simply that which is in our own interests, but rather put the interests and pleasures of our mates above our own gratification (Philippians 2:4). This certainly holds true when it comes to sexual relations. Each of us must be mindful of what the other is experiencing. Each must realize that insuring the gratification of one's partner is of utmost importance. As a case in point, scientific studies indicate that sexually men turn on quickly, while women come into a state of arousal in comparatively slow fashion. That means that men have to be careful not to rush things. For men, especially, love must be patient (1 Corinthians 13:4–7). It is also important for men to realize that they experience a rapid decline in sexual interest immediately after sexual climax, whereas women come down from a sexual peak much more slowly. In light of this difference, the tired male needs to realize that it comes across as relatively insensitive and animal-like behavior when he simply rolls over and goes to sleep once his biological needs have been satisfied. A loving husband needs to do better than that if he wants his wife to be an enthusiastic partner in the future.

At the same time, women need to recognize that, for whatever reason (and again, it may be social conditioning), men often just *don't get it.* They have to be told. If there's something about what a man is doing or about the setting that is a turn-off, the wife may need to tell her husband how she feels so that he can make things right for her.

For those who are sensitive to these matters over the long haul of a marriage, there will come the wonderful realization that, when it comes to sex, the greatest gratification comes from making sure that one's partner is gratified. Christians ought to be good at sex, because one of the gifts of the Holy Spirit is a sensitivity to the needs of those we love, and another is a deep desire to meet those needs.

GENDER DIFFERENCES

If husbands and wives are going to show each other the kind of thoughtful consideration befitting Christians, then they must be aware of some other important differences between men and women. They should know, for instance, that, for men, sexual hungers are most intense from the middle teens to about the age of twenty-five. After that, a man's sexual potency gradually declines. That is not to suggest that men *lose it* by middle age. Actually, husbands can stay sexually active right into old age, providing their marital partners work at keeping them interested. But that's the point. As the years roll by, the wife has to do more and more to keep things going, and must be increasingly aware that the days of *instant* turn-ons will gradually fade with the passing of time. Sex can be better as the years go by, but it takes more and more creativity and initiative on the wife's part to make that happen.

Women, in contrast, reach the pinnacle of their sexual interest somewhere around the age of thirty-five. That's ten years later than for men. Recognizing the fact that women tend to marry men two to three years older than themselves, it becomes obvious that something here must be addressed. A wife may find that in her late thirties she has sexual desires that her husband, who has passed his pinnacle of sexual potency twelve years earlier, may find difficult to satisfy. Efforts and concessions must be made by both partners if a good marital adjustment is going to mark their relationship. The kinds of efforts and concessions we're talking about here are not going to happen unless husbands and wives can talk honestly and try to explain to each other their individual feelings and longings. I have known of too many cases wherein wives have responded to this situation by making their husbands feel sexually inadequate. Once this happens, the sense of humiliation that this creates for the husband makes him even less able to perform, and their relationship goes into a downward spiral. It is not surprising that, in this situation, many husbands turn to extramarital affairs with other women who don't threaten their sense of being masculine.

COMMUNICATION IS KEY

Those who do marital counseling tell us that the sexual maladjustment that comes from a lack of communication over sexual matters is often covered up. For instance, I once knew a husband who somehow managed to get into a fairly strong argument with his wife every night just before bedtime. It turned out that he was feeling less and less capable of measuring up to her expectations of him as a sex partner. So, in order to avoid being put to the test, he made sure to have a nightly argument with her so they could go to bed so mad at each other that sex would not even be considered. The marriage broke up completely unnecessarily.

It wasn't until after the divorce that this poor guy got some good counseling and figured out why he was always fighting with his wife. The good news is that this couple got together again. But it wasn't what the counselor told them that got them together again; it was the fact that the counselor got *them* to talk to each other that started them back on the road to being happy together.

Talking about sex within a marriage is hard. Men have been socially defined as persons who ought never to have problems having sex, and women are sometimes made to feel that they are devoid of quality Christian spirituality if they turn on too easily. Christian women are often taught an inhibiting kind of modesty that makes them feel that sex is a necessary evil rather than something that God meant for us to enjoy.

Maybe you've heard of the bride who mistook Victorian uptightness for Christian virtue, and on her wedding night took a sedative that knocked her unconscious. She left a note for her new husband on the bedside table that read, "Do with me what you must!"

That poor wife not only misunderstood what Christian virtue is all about, but she was actually transgressing the will of God. Our God is into eroticism within marriage. That's why both men and women are instructed to sexually meet each other's needs:

> Let the husband render unto the wife due benevolence: and likewise also the wife unto the husband. The wife hath not power of her own body, but the husband: and likewise also the husband hath not power of his own body, but the wife. Defraud ye not one the other, except it be with consent for a time, that ye may give yourselves to fasting and prayer; and come together again, that Satan tempt you not for your incontinency. (1 Corinthians 7:3–5)

Sexual uptightness can have dire consequences. In one case I know about, a woman who had been brought up in a religious value system that made her feel that sex was something dirty was, quite understandably, frigid in her marriage. But that wasn't all. Beneath the surface of her uptightness was an intensive yearning for sexual gratification. Tragically, she became horribly messed up in an extramarital affair. Psychologically, she became two different persons. A "good" woman who disdained sex within her marriage, and a "bad" woman who could go out with a despicable man she really didn't know and go wild. This poor victim of bad religion could not reconcile her idea of goodness with the sexual side of her personality; so she decided to keep them separate, collapsing into a psychological disaster that ruined her life.

FRANKNESS IS NEEDED

I am well aware that there will be some who, upon reading this chapter, will feel that what I have to say is somewhat inappropriate. They will say to themselves something along the lines of, "I was looking for something that would help me spiritually, and I was *not* expecting to get into all of this X-rated material."

My primary response to such objections is simply to claim that sex is at the heart of spirituality and to warn that *sexual* hang-ups are *spiritual* hang-ups. If we are to be spiritually whole, then careful attention must be given to the development of a healthy disposition towards our sexuality. Contrariwise, there are few things that can compare with unhealthy attitudes and beliefs about sex when it comes to those forces that can spiritually destroy people and marriages.

How many churches have been destroyed over sexual scandals? How many ministers have lost their pulpits because of sexual indiscretion? How many Christian marriages have been destroyed because of misconceptions about sexuality? How many relationships have failed because of the inability of marital partners to talk openly about their sexual needs and problems?

There is a place for modesty in our lives. Sometimes we are *too* open about things that should be dealt with in private. At the same time, unless we Christians can find ways to properly discuss sexuality, we are setting ourselves up for disaster. Unless we can share with one another our insights from theology, the social sciences, and the Bible on this crucial matter, we are in danger of being blindsided by demonic forces that seek to use sexuality to destroy us. Misconceptions about sex not only can set us up for spiritual, psychological, and social destruction, they can also distort everything about our understanding of the gospel.

Our very understanding of God is at stake when it comes to understanding the proper role of sex in the lives of Christians. It is sometimes difficult for Christians to understand that eroticism can be, or should be, a part of their involvement with God. Communion with God, to most Christians, too often becomes a thing of the mind, and only to a lesser degree, of the emotions. To suggest that a loving God might be the Creator of the erotic feelings that excite our emotions and send vibrations though our bodies seems almost obscene to many of us. Yet such things are very much a part of the devotional lives of both biblical characters and the saints of the Church.

David dancing before the Lord as he leads the parade that brings the Ark of the Covenant to the House of God is an example of this (2 Samuel 6:12–23). In the story, David's wife, Michal, is appalled by David's erotic behavior, especially since it was so public. But David condemns Michal for her attitude and declares that such physical responses to God are at the very heart of true worship.

David's son, Solomon, certainly knows something of the relationship between the erotic and the spiritual. Over and over, in the *Song of Solomon,* he writes that being involved with God is like a sexual love affair:

> I am the Rose of Sharon, and the lily of the valleys. As the lily among thorns, so is my love among the daughters. As the apple tree among the trees of the wood, so is my beloved among the sons. I sat down under his shadow with great delight, and his fruit was sweet to my taste. He brought me to the banqueting house, and his banner over me was love. Stay me with flagons, comfort me with apples: for

I am sick of love. His left hand is under my head, and his right hand doth embrace me. (Song of Solomon 2:1–6)

The connection between the erotic and the spiritual is evident throughout the life stories of the saints. Perhaps few, if any, capture this relationship as well as St. Catherine of Avila. This devotional giant talks about her surrender to Christ in ways that would certainly raise eyebrows with neo-Freudian psychoanalysts and run shudders up and down the backs of puritans.

The poet John Donne writes about his love for God in sexual language and writes about his sexual partner in religious language. When Donne writes about God he says such things as:

> Divorce me, untie, or break that knot again,
> Take me to you, imprison me, for I
> Except you enthral me, never shall be free
> Nor ever chaste, except you ravish me.

And when he writes about the woman he loves, he says,

> Off with those shoes: and then safely tread
> In this love's hallowed temple, this soft bed.
> In such white robes heaven's angels used to be
> Received by men; thou angel bring'st with thee
> A heaven like Mahomet's paradise; and though
> Ill spirits walk in white, we easily know
> By this these angels from an evil sprite,
> They set our hairs, but these our flesh upright.

Donne was not confused or distorted in his thinking. Instead, he found what we all should find. He found the presence of the holy in his sexual life, and he found the erotic in his spiritual devotions with God. Would that we all could do the same.

It is not simply some of our latent Victorian attitudes and our distorted versions of Puritan religion that nurture our inability to relate anything spiritual to the erotic side of our lives. There are other factors. Most of us, say the psychoanalysts, have negative feelings about our bodies. Ernest Becher and others tell us that we develop contempt for our bodies because they remind us of our mortality. Our bodies connote a side of our humanity that is doomed to corruption and death, and we work overtime to try to suppress this dimension of who we are. Certainly the apostle Paul reminds us of the fact that our bodies *are* the corruptive side of personhood (1 Corinthians 15).

Given these realities, it isn't too hard to understand why sex, one of the primary reminders of our physical nature, should generate emotions ranging from fear to shame. However, our God wars against this kind of thinking. Over and against the suppressed contempt for our bodies that leads to sexual repression, there is the biblical declaration that what God has created is "good" (Genesis 1:31) and that it is God's command to us that we should enjoy everything that was created for us to enjoy. Our bodies are gifts from God and the Bible suggests that God wills for us to enjoy them to the fullest.

It was the Fall (i.e., the consequences of the sin of Adam and Eve) that changed everything. It was because of sin that the first couple suddenly viewed with shame what they had previously enjoyed as innocent pleasure (Genesis 3:1–14). Negative attitudes towards sexuality don't come from God, according to the Bible, but instead come from sin. It is a distortion of God's plan for us that has led us to associate sexuality with the dark side of our humanity. Negative attitudes towards sex have been around since the tragedy in Eden. Christianity has constantly had to struggle against this negativism towards the physical side of life. The tendency to look on anything that has to do with the body as dirty and sinful has been so pervasive that one of the primary cultural barriers the early Christians had to overcome was the belief that anything to do with God could not have physical traits. Consequently, first-century Christians had a hard time convincing people of their day that Jesus, Whom they claimed was God incarnate, really did have a human body.

The people in the Hellenistic world of the first century had been led to believe that the spiritual side of their humanity was pure and good, while the physical side was essentially evil. Such thinking was derived from the Greek philosophy that pervaded the Mediterranean region. Not surprisingly, the first Christian heresy was one in which questions were raised not about the *deity* of Jesus, but about the *humanity* of Jesus. For some of the early hearers of the gospel, their greatest difficulty came in accepting the fact that Jesus was a real human being with a physical body. After all, if all flesh was essentially evil, how could God have a body? Our tendency to despise our bodies stems from the beliefs of these early Christians. Their attitudes have been transmitted down through the ages to us. But such thinking is not from the Bible. The Bible declares that what God created is good—the physical is not inherently evil. The Bible tells us that Jesus had a body even as we do and that the desires of our bodies are by no means evil.

Jesus affirmed marriage when he attended the wedding at Cana. The Bible compares the ecstasy of the relationship that can exist sexually between a husband and a wife to the ecstasy that can exist between Christ and the Church. To know the fullness of the freedom from fear and guilt that can come from a personal transforming relationship with God is to be delivered from the fear and guilt that often surrounds our sexuality. To know the truth about Jesus is to know the truth that sets us free to fully explore and enjoy all that God meant for sex to offer us.

How to Hold Your Family Together

in a World That's Falling Apart

I'm Italian, and I was raised in a family that was into the Italian way of life. That meant that I grew up eating. Italians are organized around eating. It's not that we are a people who *pig out* from morning until night, but rather we are a people who love to sit around a dinner table and talk and talk and talk.

The art of storytelling was turned into an art form when the *whole* family got together to eat. That meant that all my uncles, aunts, and cousins had to be there—especially my Uncle Tom. Uncle Tom and my mother were the best storytellers of them all. I never tired of the tales they told, even though we all knew that, as the years went by, they were embroidered and embellished to make them more dramatic and funnier. Part of the reason I never tired of them is that the stories were never the same. Some new dialogue was added here, and some colorful descriptions of the circumstances and facial expressions were added there. In the words of my son, "The Campolos never lied; *they just remembered big!*"

The stories we told were about family. Long before social scientists began to talk about the need to pay attention to oral tradition in family life, the Campolos were into it. I heard the tales of how my mom and dad had met and about all the mix-ups and *faux pas* in their dating. I listened to the details of all that happened on their wedding day and who said what to whom and why.

It was not enough to *tell* these stores; the stories had to be told so as to reduce the audience around the table to hysterical laughter and to generate a sense of high drama. There were stories about what I did as a little boy and others about all the daring things I did in my growing-up years. It never occurred to me to tell my own story at these get-togethers, because I knew it would never come out as good as it would when Mom told it. By the time she finished telling my story, I was bigger than life, and not even Tom Sawyer or Huckleberry Finn could measure up to what Mom had made of me.

There were stories about my sisters, too, and those stories made me feel that I was lucky to be in our family. W. I. Thomas, the great American social psychologist, once said that if things are real in the imagination, they are real in their consequences. When the stories about my teenage sisters were told, I was led to imagine them to be the most interesting, datable, fun-loving personalities that had ever walked through the portals of West Philadelphia High. I never found out what their high school experiences were really like. What was real to me was what I heard in the imagined reality of my family's stories.

Robert Bellah, the University of California sociologist and coauthor of *Habits of the Heart*,[1] contends that stories are the essence of a social unit. Stories are what define a group. They determine who is *in* and who is *out* when it comes to belonging. As a case in point, when Mary anointed Jesus' head with precious perfume, He instructed His disciples that, wherever His story was told, this thing that she had done would be part of that story. In so doing, Jesus defined her as an integral part of the kingdom of God and of the fellowship of the saints. The story that included her ensured that she would belong to Christendom forever.

When my wife joined my family, it took awhile for her to belong. Acceptance always takes time. In the beginning, Peggy was just a good listener—a silent observer at the Campolo family gatherings. She listened in as the stories of those who belonged to the family were told, took them for the exaggerations they were, and enjoyed them. But there came that time when the relatives gathered to tell our stories and stories about Peggy came to be included as well. When she became part of the family legend, I knew that she had become one of us. In the minds and the hearts of the Campolo clan, her story had become part of our story. Stories about a family give that family spiritual substance. They give a group of relatives a mystique. They set the family apart from the rest of the world and establish a tradition that gives the family pride and glory. But if we are going to have family stories, then we have to have regular times when families get together for the stories to be told. That's why dinnertime is so important. When a family eats together and makes the dinner hour a time of sharing stories, the solidarity of the family is given reinforcement and vitality.

One of the sad realities of modern life is that families don't eat together as often as they once did. Sometimes when I am lecturing on the subject of family life, I ask the audience questions like, "How many of you, as you were growing up, had a set time for dinner? How many of you had dinner with your family every night?" I'm not surprised when most of the hands in the room go up.

Then I ask, "How many of you nowadays have dinner with your family every night at the same set time?" And I'm always sad, but not surprised, when very few hands go up.

Our helter-skelter rushed lifestyles in today's world have destroyed those precious storytelling dinner hours, and we have had nothing to put in their place. The typical American father talks to his children only about four and one-half minutes per day, and the typical husband and wife talk to each other only about eleven and one-half minutes a day. There's no time for storytelling, and the art of storytelling is dying.

The end of the family hour around the table is, I believe, a major factor contributing to the disintegration of American family life and of America itself. It was at the dinner table that parents used to share their values with their children. When the news of the new African-American family that had moved in down the street was discussed, for better or for worse, crosscultural attitudes were formed. What was said and how it was said around the dinner table did more to formulate beliefs and feelings about race than anything that was formally taught in school or church.

How those who *beat the system* through clever deceptions at work, school, and play were judged, and either condemned or praised, was most decisive in determining how much integrity the children would have in later life. Children learned what was right and what was wrong during the dinner hour.

It is interesting to note just how often eating together was part of the teaching time in the life of Jesus' disciples. It was as they sat together eating that our Lord had some of His best times of telling parables, teaching doctrines, and sharing His values. Dinnertime was when those things that were most essential for them to remember were most likely to be told to the disciples. When we realize how much of what Jesus said while at dinner was recorded in Scripture, we get some idea of how much more impressionable the disciples were when they broke bread together with the Lord than at other times. It was in the eating together and in the talk around the table that intimacy and belonging was created between Jesus and those who followed Him.

Throughout history, the importance of the dinner hour can be seen over and over. For instance, Martin Luther's *Table Talk*,[2] as recorded by his followers, has been published and circulated as an essential part of Lutheran theology. My teacher at the University of Pennsylvania, James H. S. Bossard, searched through the biographies of great men and women and gathered up hundreds of instances wherein family table-talk was decisive in forming character.

If we want our families to hold together in this world that is falling apart, then we have to make a renewed commitment to having regular dinner times, marked by family storytelling. We cannot allow our busy schedules to destroy this primary means of generating family solidarity. We cannot afford to lose this most important time for sharing who we are and what we believe. Our families and our nation will be poorer if we do not hold on to the tradition-building that comes through storytelling around the table. Every family *must* make the time to eat together and talk together!

GREAT EXPECTATIONS

As I reflect upon my upbringing, I realize that my family did more for me than establish a strong sense of belonging and give me a Christian value system. My family impacted my life by letting me know, in no uncertain terms, that they had high expectations for me. Being "the boy" of an Italian family, I was told that it was my duty to "carry on the family name." With that came the responsibility and obligation to distinguish that name through my personal achievements.

Neither my father nor my mother was able to go beyond the eighth grade, and the effects of their limited education were all too obvious. Anyone who knew my mother would tell you that this strong Italian woman had incredible capabilities that were never fully developed or adequately used. At another place and in another time, given the proper opportunities, my mother undoubtedly would have risen to some prominent role of leadership and fame. My father had great artistic gifts, and though untrained, had mastered the ability to put on canvas oil paintings that looked professional. My parents were not bitter over the limited opportunities that poverty had placed upon their aspirations in life. Members of immigrant families didn't complain in those days. Mom and Dad were just glad to be in America, a land where their children might rise to levels of success that they could only dream about. My parents worked hard and did their best to make life better for me and my sisters than it had been for them, but they let their children know that we were obligated to make them proud. There was no denial on their part, nor on the part of any of the parents in our Philadelphia neighborhood, that parents had a right to get their satisfaction in life by living vicariously through their children.

That was a heavy load for us to carry, and I knew that some of the kids on Delancy Street, where I lived, resented carrying it. But I, and all of the kids in our neighborhood, were well aware that the happiness and sense of success our parents might enjoy were wrapped up in our achievements. I knew that I was expected to *make something of myself.* My mother constantly told me that I had to "go over the top for Jesus!"

In our neighborhood, we would joke about two mothers meeting on the street and the first mother asking the other, "How old are your children?"

Then the second mother would answer, "The doctor is four, and the lawyer is three."

As far as I could figure out, none of this hurt us. We bore the responsibilities that go with great expectations in good humor and accepted as a truism that we were more fortunate than our parents, who had never had the opportunities we were being given. Rather than messing us up psychologically, these great expectations actually seemed to call out of us a sense of pride and a desire not to disappoint the parents whose high hopes for us made us believe that we were special. Fear of disappointing them was an unspoken concern for me and my friends. When we failed, as we did from time to time, we were driven to repentance by the shame we brought upon our parents and the disappointment we saw on their faces.

Arun Gandhi, the grandson of Mahatma Gandhi, told me a few months ago a story that illustrates how the desire not to disappoint parents can affect children and make them better people.

Mahatma Gandhi spent a good bit of his life in South Africa, where he first understood the evil consequences of racism. When he left South Africa and went to India to lead the struggle against English colonialism, he had every intention of returning. His expressed purpose was to go back and strike a death blow to the horrendous apartheid that existed in that country. As you probably know, Mahatma Gandhi was assassinated before he could live out that intention. But after his death, his son and his son's family moved back to South Africa so that the son could carry out his father's uncompleted mission.

"One day," said Arun Gandhi, "my father told me that he had to go into Johannesburg to attend an important meeting with some lawyers. He asked me if I would drive him into the city, take the family car for some needed repairs, and then pick him up at a designated street corner at 5:30 p.m. I dropped off my father at noon, got the car to the repair shop by 12:30, and had the rest of the afternoon in the big city to myself. Having a penchant for American movies, I went to the theater. That afternoon a double feature was showing, and I had a great time. But when I came out of the movie theater and looked at my watch, I realized that it was 6:30. Not only that, it was raining.

"I ran to the corner where my father stood waiting. I rushed up to him and apologetically said, 'My father, forgive me! It has taken them longer to repair the car than I expected. But I believe it is ready now. Wait here and I will go and get it and come back and get you.'

"My father slowly lowered his head and then said softly and with great sadness, 'I phoned the repair shop, and I was told that the car has been ready since 4:30. Now I must ask myself how I have failed as a father, and what I have done so wrong that I should have a son who would lie to his father. I will have to have some time to think about this. Therefore, I shall walk home, and on the way, I will ponder my failure.'"

Arun Gandhi said, "I drove the car slowly following my father all the way home, with my headlights allowing him to see where he was walking in the darkness and the rain. That night the seventeen miles to where we lived seemed like a thousand miles. For six and a half hours, as I followed my father on that muddy road, I constantly banged the steering wheel and said over and over again, 'I will never lie again! I will never lie again! I will never lie again!'"

It was not the fear of a physical beating or the loss of some privileges that made Arun Gandhi into a good man. It was the great expectations that his father had for him and the pain that he knew he would feel if he did not live up to those expectations that had molded his character.

Strange as it might seem, one of the greatest gifts that we can give to each other in a family is high expectations. Parents ought to have high expectations of their children, and children ought to have high expectations of their parents. Husbands and wives ought to have high expectations of each other, even as God has high expectations for all of His children. "I therefore, the prisoner of the Lord, beseech you that ye walk worthy of the vocation wherewith ye are called" (Ephesians 4:1). The high expectations that we have of each other call out of us the best that we have. We become good people and faithful family members, in part, because we are expected to be so. All of us tend to try to measure up to what the significant others in our lives expect us to be. The high expectations of those we love are responsible for much of the good that we find in ourselves.

There is a possible down side to all of this. That is, we can expect too much of those we love, and thus pressure them beyond what they are capable of becoming. This can cause a child to give up out of fear that he or she can never measure up to what the family expects. Kids have been known to run away from home because they feel that they are constant disappointments to the rest of their family. Paul warns in the letter to the Ephesians about pressuring children too much and recognizes that this can drive a child to evil (Ephesians 6:4).

The same can be said about marital relationships. I wonder how many men have turned to sinful and destructive encounters because they were made to feel that they didn't measure up to their wives' expectations. I have a specific minister in mind whose wife expected him to be the ultimate servant of God, winning lost souls to the kingdom by the hundreds and living out the gospel with perfection. He ended up hating being with her because he always sensed that she was disappointed in him, and that if she *really* knew what was going on in his heart and mind she would despise him. His marriage fell apart, and his church was blown apart when it was discovered that he was regularly visiting one of those houses which Sören Kierkegaard once described as a place where "You pay a woman so that you can experience your own despicableness." I'm sure that if I could have interviewed this brother in depth, he would have told me that in those clandestine encounters he had been able to escape from the feelings of unworthiness that had haunted him when he was with his wife. His illicit sex partners had probably looked at him in very earthy terms, and he could escape from the expectations that always seemed too high for him to meet.

However, nothing about the possible down side can destroy the general truth that great expectations can be a precious gift from the family to each of its members, as long as care is taken so that no one is left feeling defeated because of them. An important function of the family is to always make each member feel loved and appreciated. It has been said that home is the place where, when you go there, they have to take you in. Within the family, every person must be made to believe that he or she will always be valued no matter what.

Conversation is the primary means by which a family can maintain great expectations for its members, yet avoid the pitfall of expectations so impossibly high that family members feel hopelessly defeated because they can never quite measure up. We have to be constantly talking to each other and listening to each other with great sensitivity if we are to get this right. Conversation is the only way for any of us to get a sense of what another is feeling. Does the child feel affirmed because Mom and Dad believe that he or she is capable of good and great things? Or does the child feel crushed by the belief that he or she can never achieve what is expected? The only way to figure out which is which is to talk and to listen. Not expecting enough is to fail to bring out the best in children, and expecting more than can be delivered can drive them to despair. Only by *feeling out* a child through constant talk can parents have any idea whether or not they are striking the right balance.

Jesus models the right balance in His relationships with each of us. What could be higher in terms of expectations than Jesus' admonition to be perfect, "even as your Father in heaven is perfect" (Matthew 5:48)? Yet, the grace of Jesus is infinite, and when we are forced to face our failures, Jesus notably rebukes those who would condemn us and lets us know that He does not condemn us. When a woman is brought to Him disgraced because she has been caught in adultery, Jesus does not join her accusers. Instead, He condemns the condemners and then tells the woman that He does not condemn her. But Jesus also tells her that He expects her not to sin in this way anymore. He holds up new expectations for her. For me, this story is one of the most memorable in the Bible.

And the scribes and Pharisees brought unto him a woman taken in adultery; and when they had set her in the midst, they say unto him, Master, this woman was taken in adultery, in the very act. Now Moses in the law commanded us, that such should be stoned: but what sayest thou? This they said, tempting him, that they might have to accuse him. But Jesus stooped down, and with his finger wrote on the ground, as though he heard them not. So when they continued asking him, he lifted up himself, and said unto them, He that is without sin among you, let him first cast a stone at her. And again he stooped down, and wrote on the ground. And they which heard it, being convicted by their own conscience, went out one by one, beginning at the eldest, even unto the last: and Jesus was left alone, and the woman standing in the midst. When Jesus had lifted up himself, and saw none but the woman, he said unto her, Woman, where are those thine accusers? hath no man condemned thee? She said, No man, Lord. And Jesus said unto her, Neither do I condemn thee: go, and sin no more. (John 8:3–11)

THE IMPORTANCE OF FAMILY RITUALS

A third thing that we can do to enhance family solidarity is to establish strong rituals. In addition to creating an oral tradition through storytelling and establishing healthy balanced expectations for each of the members of the family, it's important to give some serious consideration to the role that family rituals have in building a strong family life.

The great French sociologist Emil Durkheim gave classic definition to the way in which collective rituals build group solidarity, but it remained for my university teacher James H. S. Bossard to apply Durkheim's insights to what goes on in family life. It was Bossard who most clearly spelled out for us how family rituals are at the core of what builds loyalty and commitment between members of a family. Ultimately, however, it was Jesus who fully understood the importance of rituals, and our Lord used them well to maintain the values and truths essential for the survival of His Church. Central to Jesus' mission in the world was His death and resurrection. Crucial to His Church is the remembrance of these saving acts of grace. Because of the importance of these things, Jesus did more than just *tell* His followers to remember His death until He returned in glory; He wrapped up the memory of the cross in the ritual of Holy Communion. Whenever the Lord's Supper is celebrated, the followers of Jesus are reminded that His body was broken for them and that His blood was shed for the remission of their sins.

Jesus was asking for literal obedience when He said, "This do ye . . . in remembrance of me. For as often as ye eat this bread, and drink this cup, ye do shew the Lord's death till he come" (1 Corinthians 11:25–26). Our Lord knew that if His followers did not ritualistically celebrate the Lord's Supper, they would be likely to forget what His death was all about. The frequent repetition of the ritual would keep the cross central in their memories.

Some families are so into ritual that they have elaborate prescriptions for how holidays and birthdays should be celebrated. They have rules and expectations about behavior and conversation at meals. They may even establish a pattern of vacationing in the same places or doing the same things each year. Those families that have a great deal of ritual are usually the ones that are the most solid and secure. They seem better able to impart to their children the values and truths which they believe to be of ultimate significance. Ritualistic families have proportionately fewer juvenile delinquents, and their children are psychologically more healthy. Rituals are good for families, and instituting rituals makes family life more fun for everyone.

BIRTHDAY RITUALS

In our own family, birthdays are very special. It's a major sin among us for anyone to fail to send a card to the birthday person. There are presents given at breakfast and a birthday cake at the evening meal. The birthday person can choose what food the family will eat for dinner, and there is always the singing of the "Happy Birthday" song. Our children grew up believing that everybody celebrated birthdays this way. It came as something of a surprise to them to learn that for some children a birthday is just another day and passes with little recognition. They could not believe that for some of their friends, birthdays were not a big deal.

CHRISTMAS RITUALS

Christmas has always been a ritual-filled day in the Campolo family, especially when Lisa and Bart were growing up. Our children always woke up earlier on Christmas morning than any other day of the year, and once awake, they could not wait to get on with the opening of presents. However, there was a prescribed ritual for the opening of gifts. The children were not allowed to leave their rooms until my wife and I got up, which was never until eight o'clock. Until eight o'clock, Lisa and Bart could play with the little things we had stuffed in the stockings that were hung by their beds. But they could never get to the *good stuff* under the Christmas tree until later. Even when Peggy and I called them out of their rooms, they knew that before we could open presents, they would have to march right past the tree and presents (in the living room) and into the kitchen to have breakfast. If you wonder how it was possible to get excited children to have breakfast before opening presents on Christmas morning, I can only say, "We *always* did it that way." It was a ritual.

After breakfast, we would take our places in the living room, and Bart, our youngest, would go to the pile of presents under the tree, pick one, and give it to his mother, who would read the tag aloud. Then Bart would give it to the person whose name was on the tag. The recipient would slowly open the package while the rest of us looked on, cheered, and made guesses as to what the gift might be. Then we would go through the same ritual with the rest of the presents.

Our gift-opening sometimes took hours, but it was wonderful. What I think is really sad is when children are allowed to dive unceremoniously into their presents, tear away the wrappings, and end the surprises of Christmas in just a couple of minutes. When that happens, they miss all the drama that ritual can create. There is none of the delicious anticipation as everyone wonders who will be getting the gift in the big box at the bottom of the pile.

In the afternoon, we always visited my mother and Peggy's parents. Visiting our children's grandparents was deliberately made into a ritual because we knew that someday Peggy and I would be the grandparents eagerly awaiting visits from our children's families. Now, when our son and daughter bring their children to see us, part of the reason is that visiting parents on Christmas Day has always been part of our family ritual.

THANKSGIVING DAY RITUALS

The most ritualistic day in American life is Thanksgiving Day. More people return home to be with their families for this day than for any other holiday of the year. Those who travel as much as I do know that travel reservations must be secured well in advance for Thanksgiving time. Planes are jammed with people longing to get home to their families in order to ritualistically reaffirm their commitments and once again revitalize their sense of belonging.

On Thanksgiving Day the typical American family eats the big dinner at the same time each year. The menu is always the same, with turkey, dressing, and cranberry sauce heading the list. Every year people seem to make the same comments about the food, the table, and the children. It may all seem a bit corny and repetitious, perhaps even unnecessary, until that time when the ritual comes to an end.

One day your son phones from college, and you call your wife to the extension phone as you always do. After the usual pleasantries and the customary bit of joking, you say, "Well, kid, three more weeks and you'll be home for Thanksgiving."

There's a long pause and then he says, "That's one of the reasons I'm calling, Dad. It's been a tough semester—a lot of tension. I've really been hitting the books hard. So some of the guys and I thought we'd take off to Fort Lauderdale for the Thanksgiving break. We just want to relax, have some fun, and take in some rays."

The news is greeted with silence. And then your wife says, with hurt in her voice, "But we *always* have Thanksgiving together."

"Look," he says, "it's not the end of the world. I'll be home for the long Christmas break in just a few weeks."

But it *is* the end of the world! It's the end of that precious world called "the immediate family" that you and your wife have neatly and carefully constructed over the years. You and your wife have probably not read Emile Durkheim's books about the role of ritual in the maintenance of group solidarity, but you both know that something of great significance is happening; something precious is about to end.

That Thanksgiving the whole family, save one, will come together. You will sit down at the same table to eat the same food, prepared in exactly the same way. And yet, deep down inside you will know that nothing will ever be the same again. You will eat the meal, pretending that nothing has changed. You will try to keep the talk light and happy, but it just won't work. Halfway through the meal, a pall of silence will fall over you all, and someone will say, "You know, it's just not the same." Nothing could be closer to the truth, and you will know it. There will be a painful awareness that nothing will ever be the same again. The ritual has been broken, and the end of the ritual signals the end of an era. It's time for new families to begin with their own rituals. It's time for parents to recognize that they are approaching that stage of life when they will have only each other in the house. The breaking of the ritual is a rite of passage that produces inner pain, even though it is both right and necessary for it to happen.

RITUAL REVITALIZES THE PAST

Ritual makes what happened a long time ago contemporary. It helps us to recall feelings that otherwise would get lost in the past. Nowhere is the revitalizing of the past through ritual more evident to me than in wedding ceremonies.

At Eastern College, the Christian liberal arts school where I teach, I am often asked by students if I will perform their wedding ceremonies. When my schedule permits me to do so, I take great pleasure in participating in these important occasions. However, I get a bit testy if the couple tells me that they have abandoned the traditional wedding rituals and have invented their own ceremony. Whenever I marry people, I try to persuade them to use the old forms and words that are set forth in the *Book of Common Prayer*.[3]

There are those who say, "We are the ones getting married. We should have the kind of ceremony that is meaningful to us." I always respond by saying that such a perspective shows far too limited an understanding of what weddings are all about. While it is true that the couple in the front of the church is being married, it should be understood that, if the ceremony is properly constructed, those in the pews may go through a symbolic process of being *remarried* at the same time. When we attend weddings in which we hear repeated the same words that we ourselves uttered when we were married, we experience a sense of marital renewal.

Whenever I hear a young man saying the same words that I myself said almost forty years ago, I seem to go through that same ceremony of commitment once again. When he says, "I, John, take thee, Mary, to be my lawful wedded wife; and I do promise and covenant, before God and these witnesses, to be thy loving and faithful husband . . . ," I can hear myself saying, "I, Tony, take thee, Peggy, to be my lawful wedded wife; and I do promise and covenant . . ." It all comes back to me in the ritual. The past is renewed. I feel again what I felt on my wedding day. I sense the commitment I made on that day, and my marriage is renewed.

As a boy growing up in a very ethnically conscious Italian family, I was required to attend countless weddings and funerals. Both were great fun—yes, even the funerals. Looking back on my upbringing, I know that I was affected greatly by my constant participation in those ceremonies. Those gatherings at weddings and funerals helped establish my identity as an Italian and endowed me with a value system of love and respect. Those long-ago rituals played a great part in the formation of who I am.

RITUAL AND CHRISTIAN NURTURE

When I was part of the sociology faculty of the University of Pennsylvania, an atheistic colleague once said to me sarcastically, "The family that prays together stays together, even if there is no God." In spite of his antireligious world-view, my colleague recognized that rituals, such as regular family devotions, enhance the solidarity of a family. While he didn't believe that there was a God who heard prayers, he was convinced that a family that had a set time for prayers and maintained a set pattern for Bible reading was engaging in ritualistic patterns that built family loyalty. Furthermore, he knew that rituals like family devotions provide one of the most effective means for encouraging children to make a commitment to the basic values of the Christian faith.

It is important for Christians to take note of the unbiased observations of my atheistic friend. Children seldom learn from such direct approaches as lecturing and admonishing. Parents who have ever tried to tell their children what is right and what is wrong can attest to this.

I can remember telling my son, in no uncertain terms, why his failure to straighten up his room each day would lead to his downfall in life. He would sit with his head bowed and his eyes fixed on the cat during my tirade. After I had told him fervently of the importance of being a responsible person and not having to be reminded constantly to do what he should do, he would ask meekly, "Can I leave now?" And I would realize that nothing I had said had sunk in.

Family rituals, on the other hand, because of their latent effect on children, have the power to commit them to family values and make them subconsciously want to do the things that good family members do. Children from highly ritualistic families have an intense longing to identify with their families, and this longing leads them to find pleasure in doing those things that their families deem right. From a sociological point of view, parents who do not have regular family devotions fail to take advantage of a practice that might mean the difference between having children who *want* to be loyal to the values and beliefs of their parents and children who readily abandon such values and beliefs.

Sometimes parents try to justify not having regular family devotions. They claim that their children do not enjoy family devotions and always give them a hard time when asked to participate in Bible study and prayer. I respond to such arguments by pointing out that the participants do not have to *like* a given ritual for that ritual to have a positive psychological effect upon them. Rituals can build loyalty and commitment to family values, regardless of the attitudes of those who are involved in performing them.

RITUALS AND PSYCHOLOGICAL WELL-BEING

I don't want to convey the impression that disliking ritual is a normal reaction among children, for the opposite is true. Family rituals, particularly those which are religious in nature, are enjoyed by most children. Usually, family rituals create for children a sense of well-being that helps them to feel secure.

When Lisa and Bart were small, there were special rituals accompanying their bedtime. My children loved these rituals and would have been very upset if they had not been observed. Every night, after tucking them in, we listened to their prayers. Then, as Peggy and I would begin to leave their room, they would yell, "Drinks!" I have found that there is no way to prevent children from asking for drinks after they have been put to bed. You may pour a gallon of water into them prior to tucking them in, but they will still beg for drinks. It is a ritual, and rituals are based on psychological hunger rather than on physical need.

When my wife had gotten glasses of water for each of them, she would ask, "How much?"

The children would then shout, "Two gulps and a swallow!" You could count on their saying just those words because they were part of the nightly ritual.

After each one of them had taken "two gulps and a swallow," Peggy and I would say good-night and head for the door. Once again the children would call us back, but this time they would want us to sing "Wiggle Down." "Wiggle Down" is a little song we made up to the tune of a university fight song. It goes like this:

> Wiggle down, Bart and Lisa, wiggle down.
> You can sleep, Bart and Lisa,
> If you'll only wiggle down.
> You can sleep, Bart and Lisa,
> You can sleep, Bart and Lisa,
> You can sleep, Bart and Lisa,
> If you'll only wiggle down.

When we finished the song, the children would always cheer, and my wife and I would leave their room for the night. They then went off to sleep, convinced that God was in His heaven and all was right with the world. Our rituals had generated a level of psychic well-being that diminished the possibility of nightmares and gave our children a sense that their world was just as it should be and that nothing essential had changed.

A child may have had a shattering day. He or she may have been scolded by a teacher, suffered unbelievable humiliation at the hands of some bully, or been rejected by a friend. Who can tell what really goes on at school? Asking any child what happened at school on a given day will usually elicit the answer "Nothing." And yet that child may have been wounded emotionally.

The good thing about ritual is that it can put a child's shattered world back together again. A ritual before the lights are turned out, such as the one just described, can convince a child that the world is still in order and that everything is OK. There are so few things that can be controlled in a child's life these days that parents who neglect the use of ritual are failing to use one of the few available instruments for building emotional security and engendering loyalty to family values.

When parents ask me how they can help their children to overcome insecurities, I answer, "Ritual!" When they ask me how they can get their children to embrace the right kind of behavior patterns, I say, "Ritual!" When parents ask how they can give their children good feelings about themselves, I say, "Ritual!"

Tevye, the father in that wonderful Broadway musical *Fiddler on the Roof* was right. Without ritual, children forget what they should remember and become confused about what they should believe. Without traditions, children fail to learn how to behave, and may become as shaky "as a fiddler on a roof."

I am an evangelical Baptist. Because mine is a nonliturgical religious tradition, I sometimes underestimate the value of ritual in church. Yet I know that is a serious error in judgment. Those of us in nonliturgical traditions would do well to discover the importance of ritual, in our worship as well as in our family life. What we do not understand may lead to our downfall.

Holding families together in a world that is falling apart is one of the most important responsibilities we have as Christians. Sociologists can help with their insights as to what makes for family solidarity and well-being. But the Bible anticipates what social science is still discovering and gives us guidance that social science can never provide. In the end, we must use all the resources available because the stakes are so high.

How to Care for People

without Being Exploited

E very year at Eastern College, I can count on some student coming to my office and with joyful enthusiasm telling me how God is working through him or her to reach some troubled soul in the dormitory. The stories have a kind of sameness to them. I always feel as though I have heard them before. I listen as I am told something like this: "John said he never had anybody reach out to him with God's love until I did it last night. Doc, we sat for hours and talked together and prayed together, and he made some important decisions for Christ."

As I listen to the story, I hope that everything my student thinks was accomplished turns out to be as good and as wonderful as he or she believes it to be. What I know is that, in more cases than not, this young man or woman will have another appointment with me in a week or so, in which there will be a marked change in demeanor.

The second conversation usually goes something like this: "You know that kid I was telling you about last week—the one who said he knew nothing of God's love until I gave him some time? Well I've had a little problem with him lately. He wants to talk with me every night. And every time he goes on for hours. He's exhausting me. I don't know what to do. I don't have time for anybody else or to do anything else. That guy is eating me up. I don't even have time to get my homework done. And when I try to suggest that he lighten up and give me some space, he looks at me with disappointment in his eyes and says something like, 'I thought you were different. I thought you really cared. I thought you were a real Christian.' Then I don't know what to do except to give him another couple of hours."

This kind of exploitation by an emotionally hungry person can get especially sticky when the person being exploited is of the opposite sex. There are far too many instances in which an attractive young woman shows some Christian concern for some unhappy guy who seems lost, only to find that in response she gets more than she bargained for. The guy becomes a leech.

One particular case that stands out quite vividly in my mind occurred when I was the pastor of a suburban church. We had a college and career youth program that brought together a couple of dozen older youth for a get-together. There was a stunning young woman in the group whose commitment to Christ in service to others was obvious to everyone. She was intent on being the kind of person who loved people in a Christlike way. This made her particularly vulnerable to the attentions of a lonely young man who started regularly attending our weekly meeting.

The young woman made a special point of seeing to it that this sad and lonely young man was included in everything that went on, both during and after the meetings. If some of the youth group went out for ice cream afterwards, she made sure that this guy was included. If a special outing was planned, she made an effort to urge him to be a part of the fun.

Unfortunately, this young man began to *demand* that she give him more and more of her attention. If she spent time at the meetings paying attention to any other person who might seem to be in need of some conversation and interest, he would sulk. If she did not get into the same car when the youth group went out somewhere, he took it as a sign of personal rejection. Eventually, this forlorn young man started showing up at her apartment and began to intrude into her private life.

She tried talking to him about all of this and endeavored to get him to understand that her refusal to give him the kind of exclusive attention he demanded was not evidence of her lack of Christian concern for him, but nothing worked. The unfortunate end to this story is that the young woman eventually quit coming to that church, just to get away from what had become the sick attachment that this young man had to her.

A friend of mine said, "The Church is the light of the world. And like all lights, it attracts bugs." I don't like the idea of calling people whom God loves *bugs,* but I do know what my friend was talking about. The Church, in spite of all its failures, still tends to be made up of people who welcome those who too often are rejected by other groups. Those who would be ignored, if not excluded, in other settings often find Christians in a church setting who will make them feel cared for and important. People with personality problems, some of whom verge on being neurotic, often take advantage of the loving acceptance extended to them by the Christian community. The vacuum in the lives of these people leads such dysfunctional personalities to try to absorb those who show them even the slightest sign of interest. The romantic feelings that can come into play when the needy person demands attention from someone of the opposite sex can make the situation especially dangerous. The love-hungry person may demand a romantic response as evidence of Christian concern. That was certainly the case with the guy who was *hitting* on the young woman in my church.

Don't be too hard on the troubled people in such scenarios, despite the fact that they can become more of a nuisance than most of us can bear. Life is hard on these people and leaves them with deep emotional hunger. Whenever they find anyone willing to provide the caring that will feed that hunger, these emotionally starved individuals come back for *fixes* time and time again. We cannot simply push them away from us when we sense their insatiable appetites for attention. Instead, we need to figure out how to help these incredibly sad people without either exhausting ourselves or nurturing their sicknesses by encouraging unhealthy fixations on us.

Problems like the ones I have been describing arise, in part, because our approach to ministry has been far too individualistic. We create situations in which we expect individuals to do what God intends for groups to do. There is a big difference between an *individual* endeavoring to rescue an emotionally famished person from loneliness and a sense of alienation, and *a whole group* undertaking the task. Acts 2:47 reads, "And the Lord added to the church daily such as should be saved." I take that verse to mean that God intended for a whole church, rather than an individual, to bear the burdens of those who need help. To paraphrase a statement made famous by a first lady, "It takes a *church* to raise a child."

The scenarios in the two cases of *friendship abuse* which I have just described would have been far different if, instead of *individuals* assuming the responsibilities that go with caring for lonely persons, a whole group of Christians had taken on the task. A Christian fraternity at the college or an entire youth group at a church could have discussed such an obligation and become committed to creating together a sense of fellowship for every newcomer. Then, when someone came along who had intense and perhaps distorted needs for loving concern, such a group would recognize that meeting such needs had to be a collective responsibility.

We ought also to recognize that some of us are victimized by those who are starved for attention because we ourselves are flawed personalities. Some of us have Messiah complexes and see ourselves as special saints who *really care*. With an air of superiority, we present ourselves to serve as personal saviors whenever some emotionally dysfunctional person shows up. Putting on our Junior God badges, we rush in "where angels fear to tread," and try to convince ourselves and others that we are much more loving and far better Christians than anyone else. To use the term *co-dependency* in such arrangements is both fair and accurate. There are those of us who become victims of abuse friendships because we have ego needs that are fed by such abuse. When this is the case, we ourselves need some counseling to help us come to terms with what makes us this way and to find ways to overcome such an exaggerated sense of our own importance.

One of the reasons that each of us ought to be a part of a small support group that meets regularly for prayer, spiritual reflection, and the sharing of mutual concerns is that such a group can help us discern any signs of an inordinate hunger to play savior to persons in need. It's easy for anyone to be blind to this kind of personality flaw, because it can so easily be disguised as a virtue. We simply kid ourselves into believing that our sick-minded Messiah complex is a Christlike characteristic. Young men who are ministers are prone to this kind of delusion and all too readily get sucked into co-dependent relationships with women in their churches. Too often, such relationships destroy these pastors, the unfortunate women with whom they are involved, and their churches too. I suppose the same kind of danger is posed for women pastors as they try to minister to emotionally hungry men in their congregations. That is why I plead with every Christian, clergy included, to become participants in a small support group whose members get together weekly to give mutual spiritual support. A Christian support group can be a gift from God in terms of providing discernment regarding the dangers in certain relationships— dangers which the individual member might be unable or unwilling to see.

Everybody comes to us carrying some kind of emotional baggage, and early on a decision has to be made as to what kind of *handles* should be put on this baggage. We know from the writings of Paul that there is some baggage that requires *two* handles. This is what Paul is talking about in Galatians 6:1–2. "Brethren, if a man be overtaken in a fault, ye which are spiritual, restore such an one in the spirit of meekness; considering thyself, lest thou also be tempted. Bear ye one another's burdens, and so fulfill the law of Christ."

First, there are those who come to us because they are unable to meet their emotional needs on their own. When God created bodies of believers, called the Church, I believe that God had such needy people in mind. God knows that there are situations in which a needy person cannot carry alone the heavy load that life has laid on him or her. Alcoholics Anonymous has long been aware of this and has set the example that should have been set by the Church as to how a group can carry an individual through difficult times. AA offers a safe fellowship for those individuals who need to lean on others in their times of need. In AA, the group works on keeping the needy person from targeting just one member of the group as a support person, but instead spreading the responsibility around. It can easily be said that AA lives out the passage in 1 Corinthians 12:26. "And whether one member suffer, all the members suffer with it; or one member be honoured, all the members rejoice with it." AA knows that there are people who cannot carry life's burdens by themselves and that, as such needy persons try to carry their emotional baggage from the past, they need another *handle* on their baggage so that others can help them to carry it.

Second, we should recognize that there are some individuals who need to be forced to carry their own baggage and to assume responsibility for themselves. Paul writes about them in the same passage from Galatians 6 to which I alluded earlier. "For every man shall bear his own burden" (Galatians 6:5). Here Paul is referring to those individuals who must be helped toward independence. Otherwise, they will never develop into the kinds of persons that God intends for them to be. Every parent knows the need to push children to self-sufficiency and away from overdependency. Not to do so is to nurture children into being emotionally crippled adults.

I know of a teenage girl who was in a serious automobile accident while out on a date. Her boyfriend, with whom she was intensely involved, died in the crash, and she needed to be in a wheelchair for more than six months. When the time came for her to get up and walk, she couldn't. There were no physical reasons hindering her walking, but there were a host of psychological reasons. Nothing seemed to help her. She received the best professional counseling available, but to no avail. For months beyond what was necessary, this girl remained in her wheelchair.

One day, when no one was around, her father took her out in their backyard, lifted her out of her wheelchair, and propped her up against a tree. Then, standing some ten feet away, he ordered her to walk into his arms. His daughter cried out, "I can't! I can't!" to which her father answered, "You're going to have to, because I'm not going to help you to get around anymore."

The situation must have been agonizing for both of them. On the one hand, there was the crying, pleading daughter, wondering how her father could be so cruel. On the other hand, there was that agonized father, struggling against every nerve and sinew within him that wanted to rush to help his pleading child. But the father held fast, and after what must have seemed like an eternity, his daughter, haltingly at first, took the painful steps to her father's waiting arms.

Some people may need to be carried for a while, because they are overcome with grief from some personal loss or have undergone a traumatizing experience. But there comes a point in our loving of such people when we must realize that to keep on carrying them is to risk rendering them permanently, neurotically dependent. They need to be forced toward self-sufficiency. There are times when we must realize that if we go on answering life's questions and solving life's problems for someone else, then we are creating a crippling dependency that will prevent that person from reaching his or her own goals.

Sören Kierkegaard once described a boy trying to do his math homework without looking at the answers to the problems that were printed in the back of the book. Kierkegaard pointed out that the boy would have been able to get a good grade on his homework by using what was in the back of the book, but would never have learned how to do the math problems himself if he had kept on depending on somebody else's answers. Sometimes we have to force those we care about to work through their problems on their own. In such circumstances, it's not that we don't want to help. Quite the opposite! It is just that, if we do offer to help, we deny them the maturation that can come only as they struggle on their own to solve the problems of their lives.

Finally, we all need to be aware that there are limitations on what any of us can do. Christ recognized that His disciples could get so caught up in the rat race that they needed simply to stop and get away from it all. He recognized that in the hard work of serving others there was a need for His followers to go off someplace where they could catch their breath (Mark 6:31–32). All of us know of ministers who don't set limits on what they expect of themselves in their service to people in need. They lack the ability to stop when they reach the limits of their physical and psychological endurance. These are the ministers who burn out.

A friend of mine who used to be in ministry became a painful example of what any of us can do to ourselves if we do not draw lines and leave time and space for ourselves. He is a prime example of someone who, perhaps out of guilt, could not say no to anyone who turned to him for help, regardless of how tired he was or how little time he had left for his own spiritual and physical renewal.

One evening, when he was completely exhausted, he got a call to come to the home of a couple in the church who were in the midst of an extremely difficult argument. It was late at night, and he should either have put off the call or had someone go in his place. As it turned out, by the time he got to the couple's house, the husband had packed his things and left. The young pastor found only a totally distraught wife who, upon his arrival, collapsed sobbing into his arms. In the context of what she had just been through, she was in need of being hugged, but in his total exhaustion, that pastor lacked the will power to resist what followed the hugging. That night, the Evil One rang up another victory, and the kingdom of God suffered a great loss. A good pastor had his ministry destroyed, and a troubled wife was pushed over the edge to spiritual disaster.

There are only so many people any of us are able to help, and there is only so much time that any of us can give to meet the needs of others. There are times when we just have to be honest enough to admit that we can't help anybody carry his or her baggage, because we ourselves are at a time in life when we can't handle any additions to the load we are already carrying. Sometimes we may have to admit that we cannot handle even our own emotional baggage, let alone try to help someone else to carry theirs.

I always try to remind people that when the Bible calls upon us to do the good that God requires, Scripture does so only within the bounds of reasonable limits: "And let us not be weary in well doing: for in due season we shall reap, if we faint not. As we have therefore opportunity, let us do good unto all men, especially unto them who are of the household of faith" (Galatians 6:9–10). Even when we ourselves are able to handle the demands that are placed on us, we must realize that sometimes those who are in our immediate family may not be able to handle our overcommitment to others. How often has a child grown up bitter because a mother or father was so consumed in ministry to others that there was no quality time left for the child? How many wives or husbands have ended up bitter because of neglect at the hands of a partner who had time for everybody else but them?

What makes matters worse is that these victims of neglect often experience guilt on top of their bitterness, because they are made to feel that their claims for time are selfish or that they interfere with *God's work*. It is more than some family members can handle when they feel that they must compete with God in their cravings to have their own needs met by a loved one who deems helping everybody else a greater priority.

If you're not willing to give time to your immediate family, you shouldn't get married and have kids in the first place. That's exactly what Paul tries to tell us in 1 Corinthians 7:32–35:

> But I would have you without carefulness. He that is unmarried careth for the things that belong to the Lord, how he may please the Lord: But he that is married careth for the things that are of the world, how he may please his wife. There is difference also between a wife and a virgin. The unmarried woman careth for the things of the Lord, that she may be holy both in body and in spirit: but she that is married careth for the things of the world, how she may please her husband. And this I speak for your own profit; not that I may cast a snare upon you, but for that which is comely, and that ye may attend upon the Lord without distraction.

In trying to figure out when enough is enough in helping other people, I want to emphasize again how important it is for you to be in a support group of some close friends with whom you meet at least once a week. I have such a group, and at the weekly get-togethers of the three of us, we check up on one another to see if each is maintaining a healthy balance in life between doing too much and doing too little. We prod each other to do good works, but we also remind each other when service to others is being pushed too far.

There are times when each of us has to be there for another in a time of need. But all of us have to make sure that we do not end up so burned out that we are no good to those in our own families and not even any good to ourselves. Living a balanced life is hard to do. It is hard just to figure out what a balanced life looks like. That's why membership in a church and in a support group that meets regularly is so important. God calls us into relationships in which we can help each other to figure out what a balanced life of service looks like and in which we can keep each other from being manipulated into doing so-called Christian *things* that we ought not to do. In the Body of Christ, we need each other to keep us from being exploited and exhausted in service to other people, as strange as that may sound.

Concluding Words to the Wise—

Which *Should* Be Sufficient

I t's one thing for the world to reject Jesus because the people in secular society consider the gospel to be ridiculous. It is quite another thing for the world to reject the gospel because Christians are an embarrassment to God. The Bible warns us against conducting ourselves so that people end up rejecting Jesus, not because of who *He* is but because of stupid things *we* do and say. Hopefully, this book will help us to recognize and stop doing those things that embarrass God and turn people away from following Jesus.

However, even as I try to address those concerns in this book, I do so with just a little ambivalence. I am well aware that some of the great saints of the Church have been people whom the world viewed as embarrassments. St. Francis of Assisi has to be the prime example of this. That Medieval saint readily referred to himself as a jester in the court of the King of kings, and his followers had no problem calling themselves "Fools for Christ."

I recall being at a gathering of sophisticated scholars at the faculty club of an Ivy League university where we were engaged in *heavy* talk about religion. As I tried to impress my cynical audience (whom Frederick Schleiermacher would have called "Culture Despisers") with the reasonableness of Christianity, I made a joke of a man who I felt rightfully deserved their derision. I let them know that I didn't think much of that guy who holds up the sign with the Bible reference on it at televised football games, and that to me, this man's attempt to do evangelism was ridiculous and embarrassing. I remember saying, "You can't dismiss us evangelicals by equating us all with that ridiculous guy who holds up signs with Bible verses on them, just when it's time to kick the extra point. That guy's idea of an effective witness for the gospel is to hold up a verse like John 1:12. He thinks people are going to become Christians by seeing his sign on TV."

When I finished my mocking statement, one of the scholars sitting at the table pulled his pipe out of his mouth and said, "Interesting that you should mention that. Two years ago I was watching the Super Bowl, and just before halftime, the Dallas Cowboys scored a touchdown. As the Cowboys got set to kick the extra point, the man to whom you just referred held up a sign citing that exact same verse—John 1:12. During the halftime break, I got our old family Bible off the shelf and turned to that verse. Lying between the pages were some notes about that very verse that had been written by my mother a long time ago. I read over her notes and was reminded of many things I had once believed about Jesus Christ that had been left behind in my intellectual journey. I reflected on those things and there and then, during the halftime of the Super Bowl, I gave my life to Christ."

Score one point for a "fool for Christ." Strike one down on me for my readiness to put down a brother in Christ who was trying in his own way to preach the gospel. You never know what's going to touch people's lives. The moment you are sure that you know what are the acceptable and the unacceptable ways to share Jesus with the world, you can count on being brought down by something that humbles you and shows you how wrong you are.

Such was the case some years ago when my wife and I had a stopover in Honolulu on our way home from a preaching mission in Australia. We had just enough time to take a walk along Waikiki Beach. On our walk we came upon a middle-aged man with long hair and bare feet, holding an open Bible in one hand, and pointing at passersby with the other. Every so often, he would let fly with a long list of "Woe unto yous." Undoubtedly you've seen the crazy-looking type of person I'm talking about. You find them on the street corners of most major cities. As we strolled out of range of this wild man's ranting and raving, I said to my wife, "It's guys like him who disgrace the gospel! There ought to be some way of stopping people like that. It's stuff like he's doing that turns people off to Christianity!"

An hour or so later Peggy and I were walking back down the beach to catch the bus that would return us to the airport. We passed the same *crazy* man. But he wasn't preaching anymore. Instead, he was praying with two rather dignified-looking men who were dressed in business suits, each with a briefcase. He had his arms around their shoulders, and we heard enough of the prayer to know that those two men were inviting Jesus into their lives.

I walked the rest of the way to the bus stop in silence as I asked myself, "Well Campolo? How many people did you lead to Christ today?" What was worse, on the way to the airport I remembered a man who had wandered around downtown Philadelphia wearing a sandwich board which read on one side, "I am a Fool for Christ!" and on the other side, "Who are you a Fool for?" I remember snickering when I saw him coming toward me, and how, at the time, I didn't think at all seriously about the second message on the back of his sign.

In our attempt to be accepted by those who seem to be more sophisticated than we are, we sometimes allow ourselves to become despisers of sincere people who use what we consider to be low-class techniques for evangelism. We must never lose sight of the fact that God uses all kinds of *ways* to touch the hearts of all kinds of *people*. Paul once wrote this:

> Some indeed preach Christ even of envy and strife; and some also of good will: The one preach Christ of contention, not sincerely, supposing to add affliction to my bonds: But the other of love, knowing that I am set for the defence of the gospel. What then? notwithstanding, every way, whether in pretence, or in truth, Christ is preached; and I therein do rejoice, yea, and will rejoice. (Philippians 1:15–18)

One of the most touching stories I know was told to me by a pastor friend from Atlanta, Georgia. He relates how, one Wednesday evening at a prayer meeting at his church, a man gave testimony as to how he had become a Christian while in Sydney, Australia.

The man said, "I was at the street corner in Kings Cross when I felt a tug on my sleeve. I turned and found myself face to face with a street bum. Before I could say anything, the man simply asked me, 'Mister, if you were to die tonight, where would you spend eternity?' That question troubled me over the next three weeks," the man continued. "I had to find an answer, and I ended up giving my life to Christ."

My minister friend went on to tell me that, three years later, another man came to one of his Wednesday night prayer meetings and gave almost an identical testimony. He, too, had been at Kings Cross in Sydney, when a derelict had pulled on his sleeve and then asked him if he were to die that night, where would he spend eternity. This second man too explained that the question so haunted him that he eventually sought and found an answer in Jesus.

It wasn't too long after that when my pastor friend himself had to be in Sydney for a church conference. On one of his nights off, he decided to go to Kings Cross and see if he could find the man who had been mentioned at his prayer meeting by two different people. He was standing on a corner in Kings Cross when he felt someone tug on his jacket. He turned, and before the poor old man could ask him anything, he said, "I know what you're going to ask me! You're going to ask me if I were to die tonight where would I spend eternity?"

The man was stunned. "How did you know that?" he inquired. My pastor friend told him the whole story. As he finished, the man started to cry. "Mister," he said, ten years ago I gave my life to Jesus, and I wanted to do something for Him. But a man like me can't do much of anything, so I decided I would just hang out on this corner and ask people that simple question. I've been doing that for years, mister, but tonight is the first time I ever knew it did anybody any good."

All of this leads me to a simple conclusion: Let each of us judge ourselves, making sure that, insofar as possible, we live out our convictions with as much consistency, honesty, and intelligence as possible. And let none of us be condescending or judgmental toward those who are trying to do the same, even when they seem a bit foolish in our eyes. Let each of us be as wise as serpents as we judge ourselves, and as gentle as doves when it comes to judging others. Once more, what some of us might deem foolish or embarrassing may, in reality, be profoundly effective. It's one thing to be an embarrassment *to* God as we follow Jesus; it's something else entirely to be an embarrassment *for* God. Let us pray for the courage to be willing to be embarrassed for God.

CHAPTER 2

1. If you or your church would be interested in supporting a school as I have described, write to me for information at EAPE/ Campolo Ministries, P.O. Box 7238, St. Davids, PA 19087.
2. If you are interested in investing in Opportunities International, write to P.O. Box 3695, Oakbrook, IL 60522.
3. Robert Southey, *The Life of Wesley: And the Rise and Progress of Methodism* (London: Longman, Brown, Green and Longman, 1846), Vol. 2, 369–70.
4. Rupert F. Davies, *The Works of John Wesley* (Nashville: Abingdon Press, 1989), Vol. 9, 530.

CHAPTER 3

1. Should you want to help support this work by placing an order, write to Camden Printworks, 1012 N. 25th Street, Camden, NJ 08105. They will gladly send you samples. Perhaps your church, club, or company could place an order with them.

CHAPTER 5

1. Tony Campolo, *Carpe Diem* (Dallas: Word Publishing, 1994) 131–2.

CHAPTER 9

1. Stephen P. Covey, *Seven Habits of Highly Effective People* (New York: Simon and Schuster, 1989).

CHAPTER 13

1. Erich Fromm, *The Art of Loving* (San Francisco: HarperCollins, 1989) 9.

CHAPTER 14

1. Tony Campolo, *A Reasonable Faith* (Dallas: Word Publishing, 1983)111–19.

CHAPTER 20

1. Maribel Morgan, *The Total Woman* (Grand Rapids, Mich.: Revell, 1973).

CHAPTER 21

1. Robert Bellah, *Habits of the Heart: Individualism and Commitment in American Life* (Los Angeles: University of California Press, 1985).
2. Martin Luther, *Table Talk* (Frankfurt, Germany, 1566).
3. *Book of Common Prayer* (London: Church of England, 1559).